ESL Teacher's Activities Kit

Illustrated by
Eileen Gerne Ciavarella

Elizabeth Claire

PRENTICE HALL
Paramus, New Jersey 07652

Library of Congress Cataloging-in-Publication Data

Claire, Elizabeth.
    ESL teacher's activities kit.
    Includes index.
    ISBN 0-13-283979-2
    1. English language—Study and teaching—Foreign
speakers.   2. Activity programs in education.   I. Title.
PE1128.A2C515   1987   87-7271
428'.007—dc20   CIP

Printed in the United States of America

20   19   18   17   16   15   14

ISBN 0-13-283979-2

PE
1128
.A2
c515
1988

ATTENTION: CORPORATIONS AND SCHOOLS

Prentice Hall books are available at quantity discounts with bulk purchase for educational, business, or sales promotional use. For information, please write to: Prentice Hall Career & Personal Development Special Sales, 240 Frisch Court, Paramus, New Jersey 07652. Please supply: title of book, ISBN number, quantity, how the book will be used, date needed.

PRENTICE HALL
Career & Personal Development
Paramus, NJ 07652
A Simon & Schuster Company

On the World Wide Web at http://www.phdirect.com

Prentice-Hall International (UK) Limited, *London*
Prentice-Hall of Australia Pty. Limited, *Sydney*
Prentice-Hall Canada Inc., *Toronto*
Prentice-Hall Hispanoamericana, S.A., *Mexico*
Prentice-Hall of India Private Limited, *New Delhi*
Prentice-Hall of Japan, Inc., *Tokyo*
Simon & Schuster Asia Pte. Ltd., *Singapore*
Editora Prentice-Hall do Brasil, Ltda., *Rio de Janeiro*

Dedication

Six-year-old Anna did not speak a word of English. She was nervous on her first day of school and not at all prepared for the strangeness of finding no one there who spoke her language. Anna spent the first few days desperately trying to blend in with the other children. With each change of activity in the classroom, she feared she would do something wrong that would cause attention to focus on her. Each morning she entered the building terrified, and she waited in agony for the end of the day to come.

On the fourth day, early in the afternoon, a loud ringing of bells sent all the children marching outside. Anna, who had never experienced a fire drill before, thought it must be three o'clock. She set off in the direction of her house, puzzled that her mother was not waiting for her at the corner. Not knowing the way home, she wandered, lost for hours, unable to ask directions or communicate with anyone on the street. At last, a passerby saw her crying and took her to the police station, but she was unable to answer the police officer's questions or tell where she lived. She stayed there in tearful misery until her distraught mother finally arrived.

It was 1916.

Years later, Anna's children demanded to hear the story again and again. To them, it was gripping, it was horrifying, but it had a happy ending. The days of agony were over when Anna learned English and could communicate with her classmates and the people around her.

Anna's story is not unique—the first months of a new language and a new environment can hold either terror or challenge to children, depending on the provisions made for the newcomers by parents, school, and the community.

This book is dedicated to all children learning English as a second language, to the teachers who reach out to them, and especially to Anna, my mother.

About the Author

Elizabeth Claire graduated magna cum laude from the City College of New York, winning the Downer Medal of Excellence for Hispanic Studies and earning a Phi Beta Kappa key. She won an Experienced Teacher Fellowship Award to attend New York University, where she received a Master's Degree in Teaching English as a Second Language.

Ms. Claire has 20 years of experience teaching ESL at all levels to students of all ages from a multitude of language backgrounds. For the past ten years, she has been an ESL specialist with the Fort Lee, New Jersey, Public Schools.

Ms. Claire's other books include *HI! English for Children* (New York: Minerva Books, Ltd., 1985) and *A Foreign Student's Introduction to American Humor* (Rochelle Park, New Jersey: Eardley Publications, 1984).

Acknowledgements

This book could not have been written without the contributions of many others, and I would like to gratefully acknowledge their help and encouragement.

First, to Evelyn Fazio, whose vision is responsible for this book, and who counseled its progress and breathed life into it, as well as inspiring the energy and commitment necessary for writing it.

To International TESOL for providing a space for professional sharing and advancement, and to the many leaders and researchers in the field of teaching English as a Second Language whose writings, courses, seminars, workshops, and lectures have forged a new way of looking at language teaching. The philosophy of this book owes particular debts to Stephen D. Kraschen, Frank Smith, James Ascher, Betty Siegel, Carole Urzua, and Earl Stevick.

To David Van Orden for his patient editing of early drafts of the manuscript, and encouragement, support, and assistance with details too numerous to mention.

To the ESL/Bilingual staff at Fort Lee Schools for reading sections of the manuscript, testing activities in their classrooms, and providing a background of support: Jean Luppino, Sharon Amato, Claudia Poveromo, Judy Wheeler, Seong Sook Ahn, Lucy Chai, Honey Wada, Judith Hishikawa, Mayra Mateos, and Joan Costantino.

To my colleagues at School #2 in Fort Lee, New Jersey: Arlene Dukette, Leslie Greenberg, Claire Bufano, Cara Horowitz, Jill Ritch, Rita Frazer, Rose Natale, Janet LaRusso, Chris Theodoropolis, and Marilyn Shinall, who shared ideas and activities that worked in their classrooms or acted as consultants in specific areas.

To Marge Baffa, principal of School #2, and Dr. Alan W. Sugarman, superintendent of Fort Lee Public Schools, for their faith in me, their support and encouragement, and for engineering a district and a school that truly cares about the education of all of its children.

To Kyoko Nakajima, Mitsuko Fujii, Susan Simms, Barbara Wheeler, Marc Rosen, Bruce Larsen, Frank Koenemund, and many others for their assistance and encouragement.

I would like to acknowledge as well *The Forum* and the *Six-Day-Advanced Course*, designed by Werner Erhard, for enhancing my ability to keep going when the going got tough.

About This Kit

ESL Teacher's Activities Kit is for all teachers who want to be more effective in helping children learn a second language. Most of the activities are designed to provide natural language experiences, allowing the same developmental learning processes the student used when acquiring a first language. Other activities provide practice and reinforcement of specific skills in highly motivating games.

The 11 chapters in this Kit contain more than 160 activities, grouped according to the type of activity, which can be selected in the sequence that best fits your own students' needs. The Kit includes:

- Total physical response activities
- Action games, including games with songs
- Seat games and chalkboard activities
- Speaking games and guessing games
- Cooking and handicrafts
- Picture flashcards and tape recorder activities
- An English Bee
- Self-esteem and social contacts

Chapter One, "Helpful Hints Before You Begin," is meant to be read as a whole, either prior to setting up your program or to get suggestions to modify, enrich, and complete a program already underway.

In "Helpful Hints Before You Begin," you will find:

1. Suggestions for getting started in communicating with the English-limited child.
2. Tips to help you set up, supply, and manage the ESL classroom, with many suggestions for increased efficiency in organization, record keeping, and storage and retrieval of materials.

A special feature of *ESL Teacher's Activities Kit* is the "Language Needs Checklist" for creating a curriculum that responds to the unique needs, backgrounds, and abilities of your students. It is cross-referenced to make it easy to locate those activities that enhance learning of specific topics, vocabulary areas, grammatical structures, or communication skills.

While the Kit was field-tested mainly with kindergarten through sixth-grade children who were learning English in an English-speaking environment, these activities have also been used successfully with older ESL students and may be adapted and translated for use in *any* second-language teaching situation:

- High school and adult education classes in either ESL or foreign languages will welcome the effectiveness and fun on these pages. Teachers of older students will discover a multitude of devices for increasing motivation, participation, and retention of language learned.
- Mainstream classroom teachers who have just one or a small group of limited-English speakers can select from a wealth of whole-class teaching ideas that include the ESL learners.
- Tutors and volunteers who teach individual pupils will need no other source for ideas and lessons that are effective and fun.
- Special education, remedial programs, and speech therapy teachers will find the emphasis on natural language development particularly useful.

Elizabeth Claire

Table of Contents

5.   Seat Games and Chalkboard Activities • 99

6.   Speaking and Guessing Games • 139

1

Helpful Hints
Before You Begin

We all learned to understand and speak our first language by hearing and using it in natural situations, with people who cared for and about us.

This is the most effective and interesting way to learn a *second* language as well. The experts now advise language teachers to spend most of the classroom time on activities that foster *natural* acquisition, rather than on formal vocabulary and structure explanations and drills.

Using the *ESL Teacher's Activities Kit* will simplify your preparation for hundreds of activities. The detailed, step-by-step instructions remove any apprehension many teachers may feel when they leave the safety of the rigid language goals of textbook teaching. Once you have become accustomed to the rewards and pleasures gained from teaching through activities, you will wonder how second-language teaching ever got to be anything else. Your own ideas for activities and their management will flow, and your students' language-learning rates will soar!

Here are a few reminders about first-language learning that should influence your approach in the second-language classroom.

A. Listening is the first skill, upon which all others are based.

Babies listen to their first language for a long time before attempting to produce it. Family members and others patiently repeat single words while the baby is focusing on real objects, people, or activities. The parents talk about the child's daily routine and surroundings repeatedly. They sing, chant, and play rhythmic language games such as Patty Cake and This Little Pig Went to Market. The child's early efforts at speaking are greeted with excitement, while mistakes are not only overlooked but enjoyed and imitated.

Features of parents' or others' speech when talking to babies and toddlers include:

1. Slower, more clearly pronounced delivery.

1

2. Shorter and syntactically similar phrases and sentences.
3. Higher pitch and wider range of pitch, with exaggerated intonation.
4. Clear and simple meaning.
5. Lots of repetition.
6. High proportion of imperative and interrogative sentences with a low proportion of declaratives.
7. Referral to the child himself, current activity, already known objects and concepts, or previous utterances and activities.
8. Responses and comments based on the meanings in the child's speech, rather than on pronunciation or grammar.

B. It is the content, not the form, that is of interest to the child.

A toddler does not learn to say, "Cookie, please," in her native language because she is practicing the request form. "Cookie, please" (or more likely, "Coocoo, peeze") is learned because the child wants a cookie. The *need* is the motivation for the language.

In class, you might motivate a drawing lesson and deliberately neglect to pass out the crayons, creating the need for the request form. ("May I have some crayons, please?") You can accept "Crayons, please" as effective and adequate communication from those who cannot manage a larger mouthful, but the natural motivation for learning the structure derives from the students' needs in the circumstances you create.

C. Children learn with their whole beings.

Children learn the names of their clothes as they are dressing, of food as they are eating or shopping, of toys as they are playing, of actions as they or others around them are doing them. They learn vast quantities of words and concepts while being enchanted with stories read to them as they sit on their mothers' laps.

Whole-child involvement means that you arrange for the child's participation in the lesson with as many senses as possible. Seeing pictures of children performing actions and repeating, "The boy is running," "The girl is hopping" is not at all as effective as when students do the actions themselves in response to commands (and demonstrations) from the teacher.

Manipulating real objects, following directions, going on trips, working on arts and crafts, cleaning up, singing, cooking, eating, and learning to play games are all opportunities to use language with whole-being involvement.

D. Love, self-esteem, and confidence drive the desire to learn.

Patient repetition, cheers of approval for all progress, and building of self-esteem are part of the language-growth process. Provide the frequent praise, reinforcement, and acknowledgement of effort that help to lower anxiety and eliminate self-consciousness about potential mistakes.

COMMUNICATING ACROSS THE LANGUAGE GAP

Here are some do's and don'ts for teachers with beginning students:

Do use English as the language of instruction.

Don't fill up the airwaves with incomprehensible language. There is little point in speaking when meaning cannot be attached to your words. Speeches, lectures, explanations, and directions with no clues to meaning can cause students to tune out.

Don't cheat the children by reverting to their native language to give explanations and directions. It takes away the motivation for the effort to understand. ("If I wait long enough, I'll hear it in my own language, so why make the effort to understand?") Instead, plan to include giving directions as part of the English lesson.

Do speak slowly, in short sentences and discrete phrases.

Do act out meaning or use props, objects, pictures, or gestures to make meaning clear. Pause after each short sentence or phrase so meaning can become associated with a distinct set of sounds.

Do give clear demonstrations of the responses you require, or allow able children to demonstrate before calling on others.

Don't put an individual on the spot to produce language or responses when he is unlikely to be able to produce. Anxiety increases "mental static" and lowers the language-learning capacity. If no student is able to follow an instruction, take action yourself to get the action produced. For example, when you want a child to go to the chalkboard, say, "(Name), go to the chalkboard." If there is no response, go to the child, take his hand, and lead him to the chalkboard. And praise him! Then say the same thing to another child to check others' comprehension and take the pressure off the first student.

Do give examples of the response you require, even to the point of what you might think of as absurdity. If you wish a child to point to a picture, point first yourself. If there is no appropriate response, take the child's hand in yours, fold back the thumb and three fingers while extending the index finger, and point it for her while saying, "Point to the picture." And praise her!

Do repeat cheerfully and patiently and continue to associate clues for meaning with your words, as long as it is needed.

Do check students' comprehension frequently by:

1. Giving directions to follow.
2. Asking questions to which students need only answer yes or no, select from either/or alternatives, or give a one-word answer.

(For example, Can the little bird fly? Who is he looking for, his mother or his father? Who does he meet next?)

Do use pictures, props, and objects. See "Shoe Box English," Chapter Two, for more suggestions on this.

Do encourage the use of bilingual dictionaries. Students should have them in their possession at all times. If students do not have the skills to use them, teach at least the fundamentals of alphabetical order. Since you may not be able to read or speak the language in the bilingual dictionaries—or you have a variety of languages represented in your class—you might enlist same-language parents, school volunteers, or older children in teaching them how to use them.

Do look up hard-to-demonstrate words in the students' bilingual dictionary yourself and point to it, allowing the child to read the native-language definition. This is especially for students who are not able to use their dictionaries themselves.

Do encourage children to act out or draw a picture of their intended meanings when they want to communicate with you and don't have the needed vocabulary. If the drawing will take some time, continue the lesson and come back to the child when the drawing is finished.

Do keep picture files and a large picture dictionary to utilize pictures for communication.

Do learn to make quick sketches. Practice figures using as few strokes as possible to convey the meanings. Illustrate your talks on the chalkboard. Here are some examples:

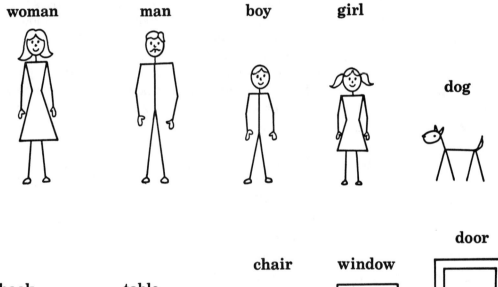

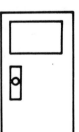

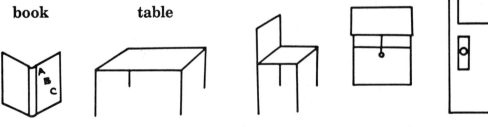

run   walk   sit   eat

happy   sad   angry   thinking   sleeping

dreaming   hungry   thirsty   sick

DISCIPLINE ACROSS THE LANGUAGE GAP

Children want to know what the rules are and what is expected of them and others. Most LE (limited-English) children have come from countries where classes were large, teachers were strict, and punishments (often corporal) clearly followed infractions of the rules or students' failures to produce results.

New arrivals in American schools are bound to notice that the reins are looser than those they are accustomed to, and they may regard with dismay the seeming (and sometimes real) lack of respect for teachers that American students show. Some children might, however, mistake loose reins for no reins at all, and will not feel safe until they know what the limits are.

Cultural differences will undoubtedly generate a good deal of misinterpretation on both sides. Japanese students are shocked to see American teachers sitting or leaning on a desk, the sacred place of learning! Many foreign children wonder what kind of women are these who wear pants and not dresses, or who wear makeup, which will prevent their ever going to heaven. Most wonder why American teachers don't require students to stand when they speak. And why is it that American teachers say, "Look at me when I am talking to you," when it is more respectful to look down?

It is natural that testing will go on to determine just what behaviors are acceptable. The pressures of the changes the child is facing can also result in restlessness, attention seeking, clowning, stealing, scapegoating, fighting, and other hostile behavior.

This combination of factors, added to the language barrier, makes discipline in an ESL class a real art. Learning English through activities may appear chaotic to students accustomed to sitting straight up in their seats, speaking only when called on, and learning through lecture, drills, and rote memorization. Students must get a sense of an underlying safety in the room and that you are in fact the source of control and direction. While LE children in general are often the sweetest, most respectful, most easily handled students in the school, you must be capable of firmness and reliable enforcement of the rules.

What rules are applicable to LE students? How do you communicate those rules when you have a dozen or two children who speak a dozen different languages and not a word of English?

Children are in school to learn and grow and contribute to the learning and growth of others. Most school rules of "shalts" and "shalt nots" stem from this fundamental rule.

There are times when you will want absolute silence and attention from your students. They will need to raise their hands to speak and listen when others speak. They need to know how to proceed in the halls, to keep their chairs under their desks when not seated, and to refrain from touching, hitting, pushing, or laughing at others. In the Total Physical Response Activities 1, 3, 4, and 5, the English necessary to convey these and other expected behaviors can be taught the very first days, in an activity that is both fun for the students and a confirmation of the ESL classroom as a safe place to be.

Acknowledge and compliment students for desired behavior; build self-esteem and class pride. Give students practice in controlling their impulses. (After learning "Don't talk," try an exercise with the entire class including yourself being quiet for one, two, or three minutes, watching the clock. "Thank you! That's wonderful!") Practice walking around the room on tiptoe or in the halls in total silence. (They don't always have to do it that way, but they will be pleased to discover that they can.) Teach the words "Stop," and "Wait." It is better to demonstrate and practice the rules as a lesson, rather than impose punishments when rules are broken. After you have taught "No talking," couple it with a nonverbal signal such as raising your fingers to your mouth, ringing a small bell at your desk, or turning off the lights. Teach students to immediately put down pencils, look up at you, and be completely silent.

Correction of misbehavior should be done with understanding and firmness. Observe a child who has been punished or reprimanded for a sign of improvement so you can reward the desired behavior and encourage the child in rejoining the group.

If a student misbehaves and disrupts a class activity, give one warning. ("Please stop that.") Indicate, if necessary, what it is to be stopped, and what the appropriate behavior is. If misbehavior continues, an angry voice is often enough punishment for younger children. If not, the child can lose the privilege of participating in the activity ("Go to your chair and sit down") until some time has gone by. The activities are fun; removal from them is often sufficient to warn others that cooperation is essential.

ORGANIZING AND MANAGING THE ESL CLASSROOM

Teaching ESL through activities requires convenient storage and easy retrieval of materials, objects, pictures, toys, games, conversation pieces, and other props. Ideally, you should have a room large enough for an audio center, a quiet work center, and an activity center. But even if you are a traveling teacher or teach in a broom closet, somewhere you should have a desk, closet, bookshelves, and a filing cabinet at your disposal.

Furniture Arrangement

If you keep your filing cabinet to the right or left of your desk, you will be able to reach at least the bottom three drawers without moving from your chair. Behind the chair, a low bookshelf will offer storage for everyday supplies, teacher's manuals, your texts, reference books, and "to-dos," keeping them in easy reach and helping you keep your desk-top work area free. The desk (and any lines of children that may form to see you when you are sitting at it) should not obstruct the other students' lines of vision to the chalkboard.

With small classes (one to eight students), try working at a large round table. Larger classes do well in a U-shaped formation or a horseshoe. Very large classes might work in groupings of four, six, or a double horseshoe. Try different arrangements to see what suits you and your students.

If you have any input into the ordering of furniture, there are cabinets, bookcases, and closets available on wheels, which make rearranging your room a breeze.

Students can get a motivational boost by mid-year (and so will you) from changing the furniture around.

Supplies, Teaching Aids, and Furniture

The following Checklist of Supplies, Teaching Aids, and Furniture is useful for a kindergarten to grade six pullout program.

CHECKLIST OF SUPPLIES, TEACHING AIDS, AND FURNITURE
FOR THE ESL CLASSROOM

_____ drawing paper

_____ composition paper, lined, ⅜ inch (grades 2 and up)

_____ composition paper, primary (kindergarten and grade 1)

_____ duplicating paper 8½ × 11; 8½ × 14

_____ yellow practice paper (lined)

_____ construction paper, 12 × 18

_____ #2 pencils, primary size pencils

_____ red pencils

_____ pencil erasers

_____ chalkboard erasers

_____ chalk

_____ colored chalk

_____ crayons, large (for kindergarten and first grade)

_____ crayons, small

_____ colored markers

_____ paste and glue

_____ scissors, blunt

_____ scissors, sharp

_____ paper clips, small

_____ paper clips, large

_____ string

_____ transparent tape

_____ masking tape

_____ Funtak®

_____ shoe boxes

_____ magazines to browse through and cut

_____ small objects such as toys, animals, plastic fruits, doll house furniture, buttons, feathers, stones, coins

_____ arts and crafts items: scraps of cloth, felt, Styrofoam, yarn, thread, spools, aluminum foil, dried beans, macaroni, paints, etc.

_____ picture files: commercial and teacher made

_____ dictionaries

_____ picture dictionaries

_____ wall maps and charts

_____ textbooks

_____ readers

_____ phonics books

_____ workbooks

_____ spelling books

_____ handwriting: print and cursive workbooks

_____ storybooks to read to the class

_____ books for students to read for pleasure

_____ chart paper, oaktag charts

_____ chart hanger

_____ paper towels, napkins

_____ manuscript and cursive alphabet charts

_____ small desk copies of alphabet

_____ puppets

_____ toys

_____ games

_____ letter-match games

_____ concentration games

_____ board games, dice

_____ large clock with movable hands, plus small individual ones

_____ teaching calendar

_____ facsimilies of American coins and bills

_____ folders

_____ desk organizers

_____ desk calendar

_____ desk, chair

_____ student desks and chairs

_____ filing cabinet

_____ closets

_____ bookcases

_____ tape recorder

_____ Language Master

_____ head phones

_____ filmstrip viewer

_____ TV, VCR

_____ computer

_____ software

Bulletin Board Displays

Some suggestions for bulletin boards include: scenes of students' native country and customs, the four seasons, manners, health, writing mechanics, holidays, safety, hygiene, nutrition, school rules, and so on.

Classroom Decor

Whether you teach in a full-size room or a converted stairwell, you'll want to take advantage of the learning possibilities available on the walls. Alphabets, calendars, color charts, and maps can be permanently displayed with a change at least monthly of seasonal pictures, information, student work, and projects. The incidental learning that occurs from just being in an interesting, language-stimulating environment can enhance your teaching considerably.

Ask the custodian for the best way to fasten string or ribbon from the lights or ceiling. At the end of each ribbon (cut curling ribbon to the length that would make it reachable by you on tiptoe after it's suspended from the ceiling), tie a paper clip. You can slip student-made decorations in and out of the clip as you change the decor with the seasons.

Seasonal Needs

Newly arrived students need timely lessons on holiday customs and seasonal events. Plan any of the following as the theme or focus of activities or lessons. Check your current calendar for the exact dates:

September
Labor Day (first Monday)
Citizenship Day
Autumnal Equinox (September 20 or 21)
Rosh Hashana—Jewish New Year (varies)
Yom Kippur—Jewish Day of Atonement (10 days after the New Year)

October
Puerto Rican Discovery Day
Columbus Day (October 12, now celebrated the second Monday)
Canadian Thanksgiving
United Nations' Day (October 24)
Halloween (October 31)

November
Election Day (first Tuesday following the first Monday)
Veterans' Day (November 11)
Thanksgiving Day (fourth Thursday)

December

Winter Solstice (December 20 or 21)

Christmas (December 25)

Hanukkah (varies)

January

New Year's Day (January 1)

Three Kings' Day (January 6)

Martin Luther King, Jr.'s, Birthday (January 15, now celebrated the third Monday)

Chinese New Year

February

Abraham Lincoln's Birthday (February 12, now celebrated third Monday with George Washington's Birthday as President's Day)

St. Valentine's Day (February 14)

George Washington's Birthday (February 22, now celebrated third Monday with Abraham Lincoln's Birthday as President's Day)

March

Fat Tuesday (Mardi Gras)

Ash Wednesday

St. Patrick's Day (March 17)

Spring Equinox (March 20 or 21)

National Women's History Week

March/April

Boys' (Children's) Day—Japan, Korea

Passover

Good Friday (first Friday after the first full moon after the Spring Equinox)

Easter (first Sunday after Good Friday)

May

May Day (May 1)

Girl's Day—Japan, Korea

Mother's Day (second Sunday in May)

Armed Forces' Day (May 16)

Victoria Day—Canada (May 18)

Memorial Day (May 31, now observed the last Monday)

June

Flag Day (June 14)

Father's Day (third Sunday)
Summer Solstice (June 20 or 21)

July
Canada Day (July 1)
Independence Day (July 4)

August
Ponce de Leon Day—Puerto Rico
Civic Holiday—Canada (first Monday)

This list of events can be expanded so that each week (or even each day) can have a special cultural or historical theme. You can also add your students' birthdays and ethnic holidays according to your student population.

Keeping Student Records

As students register for school, a copy of the intake form (see the sample shown on page 13) may be filled out by the parent, secretary, or school aide. You can then staple the form to the outside of the student's folder.

Inside the folder, keep a copy of the report card from the sending school; ESL entrance pretests and posttests; writing sample on entry; year-end writing sample; parent conference notes; and year-end report card.

If you have a large number of students, file the folders alphabetically, within each grade level. Use large colored dividers to divide grades. Behind the files of current students, place a divider for a section for those students who have exited, moved, or otherwise left your program. These may be filed alphabetically without regard to grade.

Keeping Track of Handouts to Students

Write a code number and/or letters on each duplicating master, in the bottom right corner, so every copy will contain the code number. Label each file folder with a corresponding number and any necessary additional information. This code should enable you or your students to file and retrieve the handouts with a minimum of confusion. Create the code according to your needs.

If you are generally going to follow a text series, your code may include the initials of the text and page that the handout corresponds with. File in numerical order. Example: You have created a handout of a blank calendar that students will fill in with the days of the current month (to supplement on page 61 in *HI, English for Children,* by Elizabeth Claire). Label the master "Hi-61" before you print any copies. On the folder write "Hi-61 CALENDAR." Store the master and the extra copies in the file folder.

If you have an activity-centered curriculum, your code might assign a number to each type of activity (1 = game, 2 = song, 3 = craft, 4 = magic, etc.)

INTAKE FORM

| Name | Sex | Language spoken | Entry date |

| Address | | Previous School | Grade |

| Telephone number | | | Birthdate |

Names and grades of siblings

TEST SCORES AND COMMENTS

K	1	2	3
4	5	6	7

and a second number to the handout in the order it was created. (Example: 1–game–4. Label the folder "1–game–4 BINGO.") File numerically by first number, then within the category by the second number.

If your curriculum is based on seasonal and holiday activities, the code could include month, holiday, and a number. (Examples: Oct–Columbus Day–3.) If you follow a grammar-based curriculum, creating your own materials, you can use the Needs Checklist and decide where in the list your handout fits. Give it the code number. File in numerical order.

Train students in the job of filing the loose handouts accumulated on your desk at the end of each day.

Keep an overall list of the handouts, by the sequence in which you will use them or by subject and level, with the code numbers noted. Post this on a wall near the filing cabinet.

Student Organization

Help students organize, too. Each day for the first few weeks, and randomly thereafter, grade students on their preparedness. (While teaching the structures "Do you have a _____?")

Students need to bring to ESL classes two pencils, an eraser, a bilingual dictionary, the textbook or workbooks, notebook, homework, a folder for handouts and returned papers, eyes, ears, mouth, and brain. (I give ten points for each item remembered, starting them off with 40 points.) Demonstrate that only ESL work is to be kept in the ESL notebook. You can also demonstrate the covering of textbooks.

Homework

Assign homework daily. Students should write a uniform heading on each paper handed in to you, including name, date, subject, and title of the homework, page number from text, and so on. Check it painstakingly the first few weeks to set a high standard. Return any papers for do-overs. Check off homework handed in. Train a monitor to take over this record-keeping function. Let students know that after a certain number of zeros in homework, the "ax falls." Students should keep pocket folders for returned papers (to accumulate to study for tests, etc.). Let them know when they may clean out these folders and no longer need carry the papers.

Assign the job of collecting homework. The papers from each class can be held with a clip until you are ready to process them.

A basket or area on your desk should be set aside for student work that needs your correction, processing, or handling.

If you have more than one class, here is a way to keep sets of papers neatly organized and off your desk:

Create a sturdy "envelope" for each class by stapling the sides of file folders together. Clearly label these (example: 10:30 class) and tack them open-side up onto a bulletin board. Place papers to be returned in the appropriate envelopes. Monitors can distribute these papers at the time you deem appropriate. If you are overwhelmed with papers to collect, correct, and distribute, adopt a more efficient correction-of-homework policy. Students correct their own or others' work; you note that it was done without collecting it. *Discreetly* file other routine-type homework in the wastebasket (that is, "deep six" it!).

Handouts to students who are absent may be labeled with the students' names and placed in the class folder for distribution the next day.

Organizing and Simplifying Paperwork

Many state-funded programs do not begin for the students "until the paper work is done," and the census taking, pretesting, record keeping, and paper work seem endless. Question the need for all paper work. Or at least question the deadline to see if some of it might be postponed to later in the season when you can ask for released time from classes to accomplish this necessary but tedious chore that steals from essential class-time instruction.

Test results can be far from valid, particularly on the speaking sections of the tests with younger children if the testing occurs before teacher–student rapport has been established. Try to postpone this testing until students have met with you several times.

Consider delegating some of the paper work to volunteers. Once you have a list of new students, a committee of parent volunteers can create folders for them, address the home notification letter, fill out parts of data needed for the first report cards, alphabetize student names by grade, write in dates and times for the first parent conferences and address a second envelope home, label tests with students' names and test dates, plus any other paper work that does not require your personal hand. (Official scores of pretests and posttests should be done only by you, but assistants may do much of the other work. Check all volunteer work.)

Storage

Store reusable bulletin board decorations in ten separate large flat paper bags, one for each month. Mark the bottom of the bag with the month. Pile the bags from September to June. As you take down the September bulletin board items, store them in their bag and place the bag at the bottom of the pile. October is now at the top of the pile.

Store small objects to be used as props in labeled shoe boxes. See Shoe Box English, in Chapter Two.

Permanent lessons: On large oaktag chart paper, keep those written lessons that will be used again and again over the years. (The pledge to the flag; words to "America" or other frequently sung songs, poems, illustrations, etc.)

Student Jobs

From the beginning, responsibility for the program's functioning, the room's neatness, and decor should be shared with the students. Teach the steps in the performance of the jobs in English to the entire class. Assign jobs on a rotating basis, monthly or weekly, in pairs (for development of social skills).

These jobs may include:

cleaning chalkboards

taking attendance

collecting homework

distributing and collecting paper, crayons, scissors, books, milk, straws, napkins, lunch, etc.

keeping closets, shelves, and bookcases neat and tidy

keeping various areas of the room neat

opening and closing windows, and pulling shades

going on errands
watering plants
feeding animals
turning on/off lights

LANGUAGE NEEDS CHECKLIST

When you teach English through activities, the focus of the lesson is on the *object of the activity,* not on English. You will be using natural (albeit simple) *whole* language—whatever is needed—for explaining and participating in the game, craft, trick, or other project. This will provide *listening* practice through a wide range of structures and vocabulary and *speaking* practice at *whatever level the students can perform,* whether it be single words, short phrases, simple sentences, or complex discourse.

The advantages of this approach are that in heterogeneous classes, not only are the more advanced students not bored, they contribute a great deal of modeling of English for the beginning students. Since the focus is on the action or project, cooperation replaces competition in learning the language.

In what order should you select activities? This will depend a great deal on the age, abilities, and needs of your class, as well as the season of the year, facilities, and equipment at your disposal.

The level of English needed by students who would benefit most from the activities is stated for each activity. This is a rough guide. With experience you will be able to increase or decrease the challenge of the lessons for your classes.

Activities for Beginning Students

Activities designated as *Beginner* are suitable for those students who understand very little or no English. Beginning students have limited passive and active vocabulary, and very limited control of structures. Beginning students may understand a smattering of speech in common situations and speak in one-word sentences, but they are usually frustrated by an inability to communicate.

For completely new beginners:

1. Use ten to fifteen minutes of Total Physical Response activities on a daily basis to quickly build listening skills and a large passive vocabulary bank.

2. Build an active base of words and sentence patterns for immediate spoken use, using "Shoe Box" English lessons.

3. Read short, simple stories several times a week for enjoyment, exposure to extensive vocabulary, structures, and the rhythm of English.

4. Learn a simple song.

5. Read and copy words and sentences students are familiar with through previous presentations.

6. Learn the order and formation of letters of the alphabet, with sound/ symbol correspondences, using words they are familiar with.

As you build a sense of comfortable repetition and structure in your lessons and students know what you expect of them, begin to add the other activities, projects, and games.

Activities for Intermediate Students

Activities designated as *Intermediate* are suitable for students who understand some English and have a large passive vocabulary but limited active vocabulary with limited control of structures. Intermediate students speak on many topics but hesitate frequently due to limited vocabulary. Misunderstandings arise owing to errors in word choice, grammar, pronunciation, and idioms.

Activities for Advanced Students

The activities designated as *Advanced* are suitable for those students who understand a good deal of spoken English, with a large receptive and active vocabulary. They may be able to express most feelings fluently but not necessarily grammatically, with hesitations to search for appropriate words. Advanced students may have large gaps in vocabulary and have not yet mastered more complex sentence structures.

Cross-Referencing

You may use these lists as a guide or a checklist for your course syllabus. We did not intend nor is it efficient to provide activities that specifically cover each point of grammar, reading, and writing development. The activities in this book will naturally include whole language, with a wide range of syntactical forms. Children learning a second language through activities and plenty of comprehensible listening will acquire most structures without specific instruction in the details of the underlying grammar rules. The activities that *do* concentrate on or reinforce specific language areas are cross-referenced here for your convenience. If you are teaching colors, for example, you can see that activity #62 (Bluebird, Bluebird), #98 (Matching Games), #27 (Colors), and #46 (I See) can be used to introduce, reinforce, or extend vocabulary and concepts for colors. But they also have a value in and of themselves as games, with the whole language used in the explanation of the games and talking about them.

A Final Word

While some things must precede others (the student should know how to count before being asked to tell time or tell the value of coins, for example), there is no reason to work for mastery of one grammatical principle before exposing students to the next. Given exposure to whole language, the brain will demonstrate its own hierarchy of structures. Students' ease in acquiring various structures will differ depending upon the degree of similarity to the structures in their native language.

LANGUAGE NEEDS CHECKLIST

Needs Area	Activity Number/Level		
	Beginner	**Intermediate**	**Advanced**
SURVIVAL NEEDS & VOCABULARY AREAS			
_____ 1. Greetings and farewells	70, 158		
_____ 2. Question and answers about name, age, country, grade, teacher, school, telephone, address		163	
_____ 3. School materials	1, 2, 3, 6, 12, 13, 16, 98, 159B		
_____ 4. School places	49, 90, 144, 145	145	
_____ 5. Request forms	25		
_____ 6. Colors	13, 14, 15, 18, 19, 27, 46, 62, 98, 101, 154		
_____ 7. Numbers	19, 28, 48, 69, 98, 101, 125	51, 53, 73	
_____ 8. Alphabet: recognition, formation (capital/lower case), order, script	92, 101		
_____ 9. Following classroom instructions	1–20, 47, 68, 93		
_____ 10. Parts of the body	1, 2, 47, 63, 64, 70, 98, 101	105	
_____ 11. Left/right	63	64	
_____ 12. Aches and pains			
_____ 13. Health and hygiene	159A		
_____ 14. Seeing a doctor/dentist			
_____ 15. Verbs	1–23, 68	35, 36, 37, 67, 91, 98, 101	

LANGUAGE NEEDS CHECKLIST (continued)

Needs Area	Activity Number/Level		
	Beginner	**Intermediate**	**Advanced**
_____ 16. Telling time	98, 125		
_____ 17. Calendar: days, date, months, birthdays	98, 101		
_____ 18. Weather, temperature, seasons	80	75	
_____ 19. Taking written tests			
_____ 20. Family members and relationships	70		
_____ 21. People in school	144		
_____ 22. Counting money (coins and bills)	101, 159D		
_____ 23. Asking prices and making change		150	152
_____ 24. Food	24, 98, 99A, 101, 110	111–116	117
_____ 25. Nutritional information			110–117
_____ 26. Buying, bringing, eating lunch	22		
_____ 27. Setting the table		159E	
_____ 28. Table manners	109, 112	109–117	152
_____ 29. Likes and dislikes	24, 109		116
_____ 30. Clothing	21, 47, 98, 101, 154		
_____ 31. Shopping for clothing: sizes, fabrics, parts			
_____ 32. Emotions and states of being	98		
_____ 33. Animals	24, 65, 98, 101	88, 91	151, 155
_____ 34. Rules and vocabulary for common games		46–68, 166	
_____ 35. School subjects, homework directions, understanding grades, report cards			

LANGUAGE NEEDS CHECKLIST (continued)

Needs Area	Beginner	Intermediate	Advanced
_____ 36. Houses, rooms of the house	98, 101, 154	159C	
_____ 37. Furniture	101	159C	
_____ 38. Manners for visiting			
_____ 39. Safety and school safety		147	
_____ 40. Fire safety		149	
_____ 41. Saying no to strangers/abuses			
_____ 42. Drug abuse prevention			
_____ 43. Community workers and occupations	67, 101, 154	144–152	
_____ 44. Community places		144–153	
_____ 45. Reading a map		142	
_____ 46. Giving and following directions	1–23, 30, 47, 48, 49, 93	84, 118, 109–140	117
_____ 47. Manners and expected conversation for other occasions (birthdays, achievements, funerals, graduations, conferences)			
_____ 48. Measurements		110–117	
_____ 49. Using the telephone	127	124, 129	

LINGUISTIC FORMS

Needs Area	Beginner	Intermediate	Advanced
_____ 1. Verbs (command forms)	1–23, 30, 47	109–130	
_____ 2. Verbs (negative commands)	4, 5		
_____ 3. Nouns (singular)	24		
_____ 4. Nouns (with conjunction *and*)	26		
_____ 5. Nouns (plural)	28, 90		
_____ 6. Numbers	28, 69, 98, 101	73	

LANGUAGE NEEDS CHECKLIST (continued)

Needs Area	Activity Number/Level		
	Beginner	**Intermediate**	**Advanced**
____ 7. Sentence pattern: VERB + (noun marker) + NOUN	1–23, 30, 47		
____ 8. Prepositions (to, in, on, under)	3, 9, 12, 14, 15		
____ 9. Subject pronouns	103	104–105	
____ 10. Adjectives (colors)	13, 14, 15, 18, 19, 27, 29, 46, 62		116
____ 11. Be (is, am, are) and BE + NOT	31, 61, 70, 103	89	
____ 12. Contractions			
____ 13. A, an, some	99A,	99B	
____ 14. Have	32, 99A		
____ 15. Don't have	32		
____ 16. Object pronouns			
____ 17. Possessive pronouns			
____ 18. Question words (who, what, where)	79, 160	160	160
____ 19. Possessive forms		109	
____ 20. This/these; that/those			
____ 21. Prepositions (over, behind, near, next to)		30	
____ 22. There is/there are		106	
____ 23. Subject + (BE) + VERB + ing	35, 89	104	
____ 24. Subject + (BE) + VERB + ing + NOUN	35	104	107
____ 25. Subject + (BE) + VERB + prepositional phrase	35		
____ 26. Question words (why, how)			
____ 27. Simple present tense (affirmative)	99	105	

LANGUAGE NEEDS CHECKLIST (continued)

Needs Area	Activity Number/Level		
	Beginner	**Intermediate**	**Advanced**
____ 28. Simple present tense (negative, question)	99	105	108
____ 29. Was, were			108
____ 30. Past continuous (was + VERB + ing) and future with *will*		107	
____ 31. Future with *going to*		109	
____ 32. Other prepositions	35		
____ 33. Simple past (regular)	50	35	
____ 34. Simple past (question, negative forms)		91	108
____ 35. Simple past (irregular)		83, 91	108
____ 36. Comparison of adjectives		34, 124	
____ 37. Empty IT subject (It's raining.)		75	
____ 38. VERB + to + VERB			
____ 39. Adverbs (frequency)			
____ 40. Adverbs (manner)			
____ 41. Adverbs (time and place)			
____ 42. Comparison of adverbs			
____ 43. Short answers			108
____ 44. Tag questions			
____ 45. Countable/noncountable nouns			109–118
____ 46. Many, much			
____ 47. A. an, the			109
____ 48. Idioms			
____ 49. Perfect tense			
____ 50. Past perfect tense			
____ 51. Habitual past (used to + VERB)			109

Needs Area	Activity Number/Level		
	Beginner	**Intermediate**	**Advanced**
____ 52. VERB + gerund			
____ 53. Compound sentences			
____ 54. Modal auxiliaries			37
____ 55. If clauses (present, future, past, real, unreal)			
____ 56. Passive sentences			
____ 57. Noun clauses			
____ 58. Relative clauses			
____ 59. Adverbial clauses			
____ 60. Sentence variety			
____ 61. Sequence of tenses			
____ 62. Either/or; neither/nor			
____ 63. Two-word verbs			
____ 64. Elliptical sentences			
____ 65. Direct and indirect speech			
____ 66. Transitionals (however, therefore, meanwhile, etc.)			

FUNCTIONS

Students may have adequate vocabulary and command of English grammar but not yet be able to fit in with the natives. Students need to be aware of the particular ways in which Americans go about expressing different functions, since the idioms used, the set phrases and the cultural expectations, and the degree of politeness are also foreign to the newcomer. The following is a partial list; you can readily add to it from your students' experiences.

	Beginner	Intermediate	Advanced
____ 1. Requesting information			
____ 2. Requesting help, a service, or object	25, 48		
____ 3. Showing appreciation	25		
____ 4. Agreeing		179	

LANGUAGE NEEDS CHECKLIST (continued)

Needs Area	Beginner	Intermediate	Advanced
_____ 5. Disagreeing		167	
_____ 6. Persuading		167	
_____ 7. Clarifying meaning			
_____ 8. Beginning a conversation		167	
_____ 9. Interrupting a conversation			
_____ 10. Ending a conversation		167	
_____ 11. Giving orders			
_____ 12. Acknowledging responsibility		167	
_____ 13. Making excuses		167	
_____ 14. Apologizing		167	
_____ 15. Paying compliments			
_____ 16. Expressing pleasure and displeasure		167	
_____ 17. Describing			
_____ 18. Complaining		167	
_____ 19. Criticizing		167	
_____ 20. Initiating friendship	166		
_____ 21. Inviting; accepting and refusing invitations		167	
_____ 22. Offering assistance	166	167	
_____ 23. Expressing sympathy		167	
_____ 24. Expressing love, approval, similarity	166	167	
_____ 25. Expressing dislike, disapproval, anger		167	
_____ 26. Insulting			
_____ 27. Defending against insult			

LANGUAGE NEEDS CHECKLIST (continued)

Needs Area	Beginner	Intermediate	Advanced
WRITING			
____ 1. Letters (upper and lower case)	8, 9		
____ 2. Script			
____ 3. Words	9, 10, 96	96	
____ 4. Spelling	98, 101, 156	154	
____ 5. Spelling rules			
____ 6. Short sentences			
____ 7. Word order			
____ 8. Periods, question marks			
____ 9. Proper nouns, capitals			
____ 10. Commas, quotation marks			
____ 11. Other punctuation			
____ 12. Descriptive paragraph			
____ 13. "How to" paragraph	129	46–58	
____ 14. Friendly letter			
____ 15. Story			
____ 16. Book report			
____ 17. Opinion		165	
____ 18. News article		165	
____ 19. Business letter			
READING			
____ 1. Recognizing letters	92		
____ 2. Beginning sounds	38, 97		
____ 3. Ending sounds			
____ 4. Rhyming words	61, 63, 64, 66, 68	71–74	77, 83–85

LANGUAGE NEEDS CHECKLIST (continued)

Needs Area	Activity Number/Level		
	Beginner	Intermediate	Advanced
_____ 5. Short vowels	70, 80	75, 76	
_____ 6. Long vowels, diphthongs			
_____ 7. Digraphs			
_____ 8. Blends			
_____ 9. Sight words	39,	94, 154	
_____ 10. Silent letters			
_____ 11. Homographs and homonyms		98, 116	
_____ 12. Root words			
_____ 13. Syllables			
_____ 14. Prefixes and suffixes			
_____ 15. Phrase grouping			
_____ 16. Sentences			
_____ 17. Context clues			
_____ 18. Synonyms and antonyms	101	101	101
_____ 19. Stories			
_____ 20. Details			
_____ 21. Main idea			
_____ 22. Characters			
_____ 23. Setting			
_____ 24. Conflict			
_____ 25. Inference			
_____ 26. Purposes of reading			
_____ 27. Study skills			
_____ 28. Skimming			
_____ 29. Outlining			
_____ 30. Identification/enjoyment			

LANGUAGE NEEDS CHECKLIST (continued)

Needs Area	Activity Number/Level		
	Beginner	Intermediate	Advanced
____ 31. Plot			
____ 32. Theme			
____ 33. Style			
PRONUNCIATION			
____ 1. Individual sounds			
____ 2. Sound clusters			
____ 3. Accent		102	
____ 4. Intonation		102	
____ 5. Rhythm and fluency		102	102

2

Getting Started

Listening and understanding might sometimes be referred to as passive skills, but the mental and physical performances are anything but passive when these activities get going!

WHOLE-BODY INVOLVEMENT
WITH TOTAL PHYSICAL RESPONSE ACTIVITIES

Total Physical Response activities (TPR) greatly multiply the amount of language input that can be handled by beginning students. TPR activities tie comprehension with performance in nonthreatening, low-anxiety, whole-body responses. Speech is not required. Students build self-confidence along with a wide-ranging passive vocabulary base.

We recommend that you spend five to ten or more minutes on listening and responding activities at the beginning or end of every beginner's class.

Students become ready to talk sooner when they are under no pressure to do so. Much more material may be taught for "passive" recognition than when production is required.

TPR activities help the student adjust to the school. You can prepare students to understand the behavior required and the instructions they will hear in mainstream classrooms, in the halls, on fire drills, on trips, at assembly programs. Discipline with LE students works when the language basis for appropriate behavior has been set up in a pleasant learning situation.

Grades: Kindergarten to adult

English level: New beginners (and up)

Objectives: To develop listening skills, vocabulary, learn command forms of verbs and English Verb + object, and Verb + prepositional phrases word order; to have fun and physical exercise

Presentation:

1. Gather materials indicated for each drill.

2. Give the instruction to the entire class, modeling the performance expected.

3. Repeat, varying the order of instructions, and continue to model the performance.

4. Repeat the instructions a third time, without modeling, allowing students to copy other students. Praise the students generously.

5. Select small groups of students to go through the actions while the remainder of the class watches.

6. Call on individual volunteers to act out the instructions. The idea is to keep the anxiety low with a "no failure" activity, yet still challenge the students with a swift pace and variety of modes, with humorous inclusions of impossible or silly tasks.

7. On the second day, review the first set of commands, allowing abler students to model the actions, giving lavish praise for performance. Introduce new directions while you model the actions.

8. Each day review segments from previous lessons, combining them with new material, keeping a rapid pace.

9. Add whatever is appropriate to extend vocabulary in areas needed in your classroom and school.

10. Reading lessons may be based on the drills. Make enough copies for your class. Read each command and signal for the class to repeat after you. Call on volunteers to read individual sentences. Allow abler students to give all the commands as others act them out.

11. Create your own TPR drills to introduce or reinforce any new topic—adjectives, comparisons, clauses, compound sentences. "Go to the tallest boy." "Bring me the book with the most pages." "Point to the girl who is wearing a pink vest."

TPR 1: Stand/sit/raise/close/open + eyes/mouth/hands/book

Materials needed: Book of any kind for each student

Stand up.
Sit down.
Stand up.
Sit down.
Raise your hand.
Put your hand down.
Stand up.
Raise your hand.
Put your hand down.
Sit down.

(Model each action as you give the command until most students participate without hesitation.)

(Repeat and review commands after you add new ones. Then repeat the new ones, recombining them before adding more. Keep students feeling successful.)

Raise two hands.
Put one hand down.
Put the other hand down.
Open your book.
Close your book.
Open your hands.
Close your hands.
Close your eyes.
Open your eyes.
Stand up.
Raise your hand.
Put your hand down.
Raise your book.
Put your book down.
Open your book.
Open your mouth.
Close your mouth.
Close your book.
Sit down.
Open your mouth.
Close your mouth.
Shhh. (*whisper*) Be quiet.
That's very, very good.
Wonderful!

(Put a finger to your lips; hold
students quiet for 30 seconds.)
(Applaud their accomplishment.)

TPR 2: Touch/put + ears/pencil/chair/table/crayons/boy/girl

Materials needed: Students' desks (tables), chairs, pencils, crayons, erasers

Touch your eyes.
Touch your nose.
Touch your mouth.
Close your eyes.
Open your mouth.
Open your eyes.
Close your mouth.
Touch your ears.
Touch your hands.
Raise your hands.
Put your hands down.
Touch your book.

Raise your book.
Put your book down.
Touch your pencil.
Touch your chair.
Touch the table.
Raise the table.   *(Include for humor, not necessary for performance.)*
Touch the crayons.
Touch a girl.
Touch a boy.
Raise your eyes.   *(Roll eyes up—also for humorous effect, rather than serious.)*
Raise your nose.   *(Repeat above.)*

TPR 3: Around the room

Materials needed: Chairs, desks, classroom objects. (Omit items not in your room. Add items that are in your room.)

Stand up.
Put your chair under your desk.
Go to the door.
Touch the door.
Open the door.
Close the door.
Go to the chalkboard.
Go to the window.
Open the window.
Close the window.
Go to the sink.
Touch the sink.
Go to the teacher.
Go to the teacher's desk.
Touch the teacher's desk
Raise the teacher's desk.
Go to the map.
Touch the map.
Go to the flag.
Touch the flag.
Go to the calendar.
Girls go to the door.
Boys go to the window.
Girls go to the map.

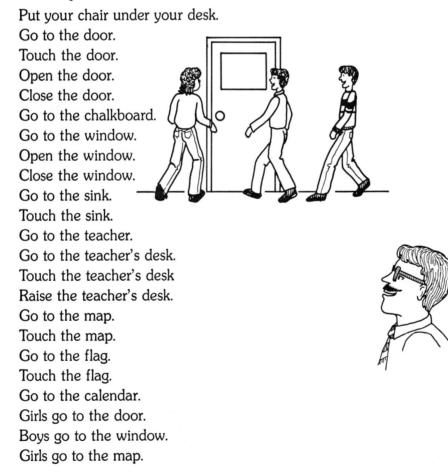

Boys go to the chalkboard.
Girls go to the boys.
Everybody go to your chair and sit down.

TPR 4: Verb commands + negative commands with "stop"

Materials needed: None

Walk.

(Model this by walking in place, unless your class is small and the students can walk around the room.)

Stop walking.
Run.   *(In place.)*
Stop running.
Walk.
Jump.   *(In place.)*
Stop jumping.
Push.   *(Model gently pushing a student or an imaginary door.)*

Stop pushing.
Hit.   *(Model hitting the chair or desk.)*
Stop hitting.
Talk.   *(Model speaking: Hello, what's your name? How are you? etc.)*

Stop talking.
Write.   *(Use a pencil or mime with fingers holding imaginary pencil.)*

Stop writing.
Walk to the door.   *(Small group.)*
Push the door.   *(Individual.)*
Run to the chalkboard.   *(Individual.)*
Write on the chalkboard.   *(Hand chalk to an individual.)*
Jump to the teacher's desk.
Hit the teacher's desk.
Stop hitting the teacher's desk.
Talk to the boys.
Talk to the girls.
Stop talking.
Jump to your chair.
Push your chair.
Stop pushing your chair.
Sit down in your chair.

TPR 5: Verb commands + negative commands with "don't"

Materials needed: None

Walk.
Don't walk.
Run.
Don't run.
Jump.
Don't jump.
Hit.
Don't hit.
Push.
Don't push.
Laugh.
Don't laugh.
Laugh.
Stop laughing.

(Let students understand that there are two different negative commands with the same meaning. They will hear both in their mainstream classes and around the school and in the playground.)

Don't run to the door; walk to the door.
Don't walk to the flag; jump to the flag.
Don't push your chair; hit your chair.

TPR 6: Verbs of motion + places

Materials needed: None

Walk tiptoe.
Walk tiptoe to the teacher's desk.
Walk tiptoe to the map.
Hop.
Hop to the chalkboard.
Hop to the door.
Fly.   *(flap arms)*
Fly to the closet.
Fly to the teacher's desk.
Skip.
Skip to the window.
Skip to the closet.
Walk slowly.

Walk slowly to the wastebasket.
Walk slowly to the door.
Crawl to your chair and sit down.
Dance.
Dance to the chalkboard.
Dance to the teacher's desk.
Walk slowly to the light switch.
Turn off the lights.
Turn on the lights.
Walk quickly to your desk and sit down.

TPR 7: More verbs of motion + places

Materials needed: None

Go to the door.
Don't run.
Walk slowly.
Open the door.
Close the door.
Jump to the window.
Touch the window.
Run to the closet.
Open the closet.
Close the closet.
Walk tiptoe to the teacher's desk.
Touch the teacher's desk.
Girls fly to the chalkboard.
Touch the chalkboard.
Girls walk tiptoe to your chairs and sit down.
Boys, hop to your chairs and sit down.

(You can repeat these and any TPR actions, addressing different groups in your class. Examples: (Fourth) graders, children from (Columbia), (third) grade (boys), hop to the calendar.

TPR 8: Write/erase + name/numbers/letters/words

Materials needed: Chalkboard and/or writing paper. (Some students follow instructions at the chalkboard while others write on their papers or watch.)

Go to the chalkboard. *(or take out a sheet of paper)*
Write your name.
Write your last name.
Write numbers 1, 2, 3, 4, 5.
Write A B C D E.
Write b-o-o-k. What is it?
Write p-e-n. What is it?
Erase your name. *(model or mime the action)*
Erase book. Erase number three.
Erase C D E.
Erase pen.
Erase everything.
Hop to your chair and raise your hand.
Put your hand down and sit down.

TPR 9: Draw/cross out + line/circle

Materials needed: Chalkboard or writing paper

Go to the chalkboard. *(or take out a piece of paper)*
Write 1, 2, 3, 4, 5, 6, 7, 8, 9, 10.
Write A B C D E F G H I J.
Draw a line under number 4.
Draw a line under 6, 7, 8.
Draw a line under 9, 10.
Draw a line under e f g.
Draw a line under I J.
Draw a circle around 1, 2.
Draw a circle around A B.
Draw a circle around F.
Cross out number 1.
Cross out numbers 3 and 4.
Cross out A B C.
Erase 1, 2, 3, 4.
Erase E F G.
Erase everything.

TPR 10: Copy + word (number) times

Materials needed: Chalkboard or writing paper

Go to the chalkboard.   *(or take out a piece of paper)*
Write *boy.*
Copy the word *boy* two times.
Write *girl.*
Copy the word *girl* three times.
Write *book.*
Copy the word *book* two times.
Write *go.*
Copy the word *go* five times.
Write *pen.*
Copy the word *pen* four times.

TPR 11: Go/turn on/fill/drink/spill/take/sharpen/get

Materials needed: Sink, paper cups, pencil sharpener, pencils, student lunchboxes or bags. (This drill is best done by one student at a time as you demonstrate for that student, with class observing.)

Go to the sink.
Turn on the water.
Fill the cup.
Drink some water.
Turn off the water.
Spill the rest of the water in the sink.
Go back to your seat.   *(chair)*
Take your pencil.
Go to the pencil sharpener.
Sharpen your pencil.
Go back to your seat.
Go to the closet.
Get your lunchbox.
Go back to your seat.

TPR 12: Point to/look at + objects/map/countries/calendar

Materials needed: None

Point to the chalkboard.
Point to the door.
Point to the window.
Point to the flag.
Point to the calendar.

Point to the alphabet.
Point to the piano.
Look up.
Look down.
Look at the chalkboard.
Look at the window.
Look at the bulletin board.
Look at me.
Look at your book.
Look in your desk.
Look in your pocket.
Look at the picture.
(*Student name*), stand up. Jump to the map.
Point to the United States.
Point to (*student's country*).
Hop to your chair and sit down.
(*Student name*), stand up.
Walk to the calendar.
Point to today.
Run to your chair and sit down.

TPR 13: Bring + (color) object and object

Materials needed: Pencils (1 yellow), 4 books (1 green), paper, erasers, crayons (1 red). (Place the materials around the room as needed by the instructions you will give. Individual students perform as others watch.)

Go to the (*teacher's desk, bookcase, table*).
Bring me a pencil, please. Thank you.
Go to the table. Bring me a book, please. Thank you.
Go to the (*desk*). Bring me an eraser, please. Thank you.
Go to the (*desk*). Bring me two books, please. Thank you.
Go to the (*desk*). Bring me a red crayon, please. Thank you.
Go to the (*desk*). Bring me a yellow pencil and a green book, please. Thank you.
Go to the (*desk*). Bring me two sheets of paper and an eraser, please. Thank you very much!

TPR 14: Take/put + on/next to

Materials needed: Book, pencils, pens, crayons (two purple), colored paper, erasers. (If students are sitting around a common table, the items may be placed on the table. Otherwise, you might circulate around the students at their desks, with items on a large tray or a shallow cardboard box. Direct your commands to individual students as other students observe.)

Take the book.
Take the pencils.
Take the pens.
Take the purple crayons.
Take the orange paper.
Take the erasers.
Put everything on the table.
Put the orange paper here.
Put the book on the paper.
Put the pens on the book.
Put the pencils on the book.
Put the crayons next to the pencils.
Put one eraser next to the crayons and one eraser next to the book.

TPR 15: Take/put + (color) object (or it/them) + on/next to/under

Materials needed: Pencils, crayons, markers, and paper of various colors

Take a pencil and put it on the table.
Take a black crayon and put it next to the pencil.
Take the orange crayon and put it next to the black crayon.
Take the red crayon and the green crayon and put them next to the orange crayon.
Take two brown papers and put them under the book.
Put the yellow paper under the brown paper.
Put the green paper under the yellow paper.

TPR 16: Take out/raise/put/point to/put away + textbook names

Materials needed: Student subject area textbooks

Take everything off your desk.
Take out your spelling book. Put it on your desk.
Take out your math book.
Take out your social studies book.
Take out your notebook.
Raise your notebook.
Put your notebook down.

Point to your math book.
Point to your spelling book.
Take out a piece of paper.
Take out your science book.
Take out your phonics book.
Take out your reading book.
Open your math book.
Close your math book.
Put your spelling book away.
Put your reading book away.
Put your science book away.
Put all your books away.

TPR 17: Open/close + textbook names and pages

Materials needed: Student textbooks

Take out all your books.
Open your spelling book to page five.
Turn the page.
Close your book.
Open your math book to page
   twenty-five.
Turn the page.
Close your book.
Open your phonics book to page ten.
Turn to page twenty.
Turn to page thirty.
Close your book.

Open your science book to page
   thirty-one.
Turn to page forty-one.
Turn to page fifty-one.
Close your book.
Put your math book on your spelling book.
   (or whatever books, papers, notebooks, pencil cases they have)
Put your phonics book on your math
   book.
Put your reading book on your pho-
   nics book.
Put all your books away.

TPR 18: Take out/open/point to/pick up/write with/draw with + (color) crayons

Materials needed: Box of crayons for each student, writing paper

Take out your crayons.   *(or, Go to the _____ and get a box of crayons.)*
Open the box.
Raise the green crayon.
Put it down.
Raise the brown crayon.
Put it down.
Raise the red crayon.
Put it down.
(etc.)
Pick up the blue crayon.
Write your first name with the blue crayon.
Put the blue crayon back in the box.
Pick up the orange crayon.
Write your last name with the orange crayon.
Put the orange crayon back in the box.
Pick up the purple crayon.
Draw a line under your name with the purple crayon.
Put the purple crayon back in the box.
Pick up the red and the green crayons.
Put them back.
Pick up the orange and the yellow crayons.
Put them back.
Cover the box.
Hand in your paper.
Hand in your crayons.
Put the crayons away.

TPR 19: Color/draw + first/second/third/fourth

Materials needed: Crayons, pencils, and paper. (Demonstrate on a large sheet of chart paper at the front of the room.)

Take out your pencil and paper.
Write your name on the paper with the pencil.
Draw ten small circles with your pencil.

Open your box of crayons.
Color two circles red.
Color three circles black.
Color one circle green.
Color four circles purple.
Draw four more small circles.
Color the first circle red.
Color the second circle blue.
Color the third circle orange.
Color the fourth circle yellow.
Put the crayons in the box.
Put the cover on the box.
Hand in the crayons.
Hand in your paper.

TPR 20: Hand out and collect

Materials needed: 8 crayons, a number of pencils, papers, scissors, erasers, books. (Do this exercise with individuals.)

(*Name*), please hand out the pencils.
(*Name*), please hand out the crayons.
Please hand out the paper.
Please hand out the scissors.
Please hand out the books.
Please collect the pencils.
Put them on the teacher's desk. (*or wherever it is that pencils belong in your room*).
    Thank you.
Please collect the papers.
Put them on the (*teacher's desk*). Thank you.
Please collect the scissors.
Put them in the (*closet*). Thank you.
Please collect the erasers.
Please collect the books.
Put them in (*the bookcase*). Thank you very much.

You can create Total Physical Response activities for any vocabulary area, content area, or holiday activity. Props may be used or actions may be mimed, as long as the students are aware of the underlying content.

TPR activities are best written out in advance, so you can execute them swiftly.

TPR 21: Getting dressed

Materials needed: None. (This can be mimed.)

> Put on your socks.
> Put on your shoes.
> Tie your shoes.
> Put on your shirt and your pants.
> Button your shirt.
> Zip your pants.
> Put on your belt.
> Buckle your belt.
> Put on your sweater.
> Put on your hat.
> Put on your coat.
> Button your coat.
> Put on your gloves.
> Take off your hat.
> Unbutton your coat.
> Take off your coat.
> Take off your gloves.
> Take off your sweater.

TPR 22: Lunch time

Materials needed: Lunchbox, wrapped sandwich, milk container, straw. (Students mime the action as you demonstrate with the props. Point out an area of the room that will be where the students go to get their lunchboxes and another area that will be the "lunchroom." Or let their own desks be the "lunchroom.")

> Look at the clock. It's time for lunch.
> Stand up.
> Get your lunchbox.
> Line up.
> Go to the lunchroom.
> Sit down.
> Open your lunchbox.
> Take out a sandwich.
> Unwrap the sandwich.
> Take a bite of the sandwich. Mmmm it's good.
> Open your milk container.

Put in the straw.
Drink some milk.
Eat the rest of your sandwich.
Drink the rest of the milk.
Wipe your face with your napkin.
Close your lunchbox.
Stand up.
Clean up the table.
Take the garbage to the garbage can.

TPR 23: "Snow Wonder"

Materials needed: Snow. (Go outdoors on the first snowy day or mime without props.)

Look out the window.
It's snowing!

(Mime snow with hands gently falling, fingers waving.)

You are very happy.
Put on your boots.
Put on your coat and hat.
Put on your gloves.
Go outside.
Pick up some snow.
Feel it.
It's cold and wet.
Make a snowball.
Throw the snowball.
Don't throw it at a person.
Let's make a snowman or a snow woman.
Make another snowball.
Roll it in the snow.
Roll it and roll it and roll it until it is very, very big.
This is the snowman's feet.
Now make another snowball.
Roll it and roll it and roll it.
Put the second snowball on top of the first snowball.
This is the snowman's chest.
Make one more snowball.
Roll it in the snow.

Put the third snowball on top of the chest.
This is the snowman's head.
Make the snowman's eyes, nose, and mouth.
Put a hat on his (*her*) head.

SHOE BOX ENGLISH

The number of lesson activities that can flow out of a shoe box full of small items is endless. The dozen activities suggested here should serve as a jumping off place for your own lesson creations. Expand and modify the lessons as your students' needs suggest and according to the actual items in your shoe box.

Assemble a collection of small items. (This is the perfect place to channel your pack-rat tendencies.) Items should be nonbreakable and useful in developing vocabulary. Here are some of the things in my own constantly growing collection, which generally come from my house, the classroom, donations from other teachers, the children themselves, and garage sales:

small dolls	junk jewelry	stone	plastic flowers
doll's tea set	ribbon, box	pencils	tree
doll garments	feathers	chalk	watch
toy animals	piece of fur	crayons	rubber band
music box	sandpaper	eraser	mini houses
furniture	jar	plastic fruit	small box
toy cars	play money	keys	nuts

After you have been collecting objects for a while, sort them according to your needs into a number of shoe boxes. If you sort according to beginning letter, whenever you need a prop for a lesson or a story that you are reading, you can find the alligator in shoe box *A*, a dinosaur in box *D,* and a turtle in box *T.*

You also have a handy set of items that begin with whatever letter you are teaching in your phonics lessons to beginning readers. In your *H* shoe box, for example, you may have a horse, hat, house, hen, hundred-dollar play-money bill, small doll with long hair, heel from a shoe, and handkerchief.

In addition to boxes of items stored by letter, you might have an adjective box—small (tiny), medium, and large dogs; red, green, purple, and black cars; rock (hard); fur (soft); sandpaper (rough); satin (smooth); wide and narrow ribbon; long and short string; clean and dirty paper; old and new toy cars; beautiful and ugly masks; turtle and rabbit (fast and slow); whole and broken items; hippopotamus (fat); tiger (dangerous); and plastic prune (wrinkled).

Other boxes hold items that belong together or that are used with a taped lesson (see Chapter Nine).

It won't take long to create a comprehensive collection if your students and fellow teachers donate items. ("I need some little things that begin with *w,*" I announced, and the next day I was inundated with a supply of watches, wires, whistles, tiny wheels, and a window from a doll house.) But even a single box of assorted items will perk up your students' interest in handling and communicating about the objects.

24. VOCABULARY DEVELOPMENT

Objective: To develop vocabulary

Presentation: Students sit around a table. Clear the table except for the items you are teaching. Say the names of the items several times for passive recognition. At first, limit the number of items taught to three or even two, as you gauge your students' abilities. Add items at a rate that will add interest and challenge but not overload or confuse.

    a. No language response necessary:

        Point to the spoon.
        Point to the dog.
        Where is the ring?

    b. Yes or no response needed.

        Is this a ring? *(yes)*
        Is this a spoon? *(no)*

    c. After passive recognition, practice the vocabulary for active use:

        Is this a pen or a paper? *(a pen)*
        What's this? *(a spoon)*
        What's this? *(a dog)*

(*Note:* Language lessons will be more successful when there is plenty of opportunity for listening comprehension prior to speaking. Lessons for beginners should involve students in physical responses to commands or giving one-word answers. Act out the meaning of your commands as you give them, and repeat as often as necessary. Praise students for nonverbal responses as well as for one-word responses or complete sentences. You can request complete sentences later, when they can more easily handle the complexity of sounds, word order, and structure.)

25. REQUEST FORMS

Objective: To comprehend and respond to requests; to make requests

Presentation:

    1. After teaching the names of several items placed in front of the student, hold out your hand and say, "May I have the spoon please?"

    If necessary, pick up the student's hand and fold his fingers around the spoon, bringing his hand and the spoon to your outstretched other hand as you repeat the request. An effusive smile and "thank you" will complete the meaning.

    Repeat the same pattern, so each child has an opportunity to give you one thing or so that the group has at least ten occasions to hear the request form.

This is an opportunity for you to be aware of the potential for cultural differences in the simple act of handing items to a person. (Korean children are taught to hand things to an elder with both hands, for example, and Arabic children must use only the right hand. They will be aware and possibly offended when things are given to them with the left hand, as that hand is reserved for "dirty" work.) It is not just language forms they are learning but typical American body language as well. Most Americans are unaware of the right/left significances that other cultures place on simple actions. The students will note the differences between their new environment and their own culture in this behavior as well as in other areas. Consciously or unconsciously, they will be creating hypotheses to explain our behavior that may be far from the truth. (This American is rude, disrespectful, dirty, etc.)

2. Help students say the words, "May I have the (object)," in chorus, breaking the sentence down to individual words when necessary.

Teacher	*Student*
May	May
I	I
have	have
May I have	May I have
the pen	the pen
May I have the pen	May I have the pen
please?	please?
May I have the pen, please?	May I have the pen, please?

The pitch and melody of each word in the whole phrase is as important as the pronunciation of the words, so the final utterance should have the "polite request form melody." (Da da da da DA da?) (Students can benefit in getting the melody practice without the distraction of difficult sounds to remember and produce.)

Hold up one of the items that is now familiar. A student must say, "May I have a _____ please?" Give it to him or her, wait for a thank you, and say, "You're welcome."

26. AND

Where are the pen and the pencil?
Point to the dog and the cat.
Take the car, the dog, and the cat.
May I have the pencil, the pen, and the dog, please?
(etc.)

27. COLORS

Where is the blue car?
Point to the black cat.
Take the yellow pencil and the red pen.
May I have the green car and the red truck, please?
(etc.)

28. NUMBERS AND PLURAL FORMS

Count the marbles: One, two, three, four marbles.
May I have three marbles, please?
May I have two red pencils and four blue crayons?
(etc.)

29. ADJECTIVES

Where is the big spoon?
May I have the small cup, please?
May I have the clean paper (*the old car, the new car, the long pencil, the short pencil, the dirty paper*), please?
Which animal has long ears? Which animal has a short tail?
(etc.)

30. COMMAND FORMS AND PREPOSITIONS OF PLACE

Take the doll, the green crayon, and the red car.
Put the doll on the table.
Put the crayon in the desk. Put the car under the table.
Put everything in the box.
Give the red cup to Juan.
Place the shovel against the fence.

31. IS/ARE; IT/THEY

The truck is red.
Is the car red?   *(yes/no)*
The dog is big. Is the cat big?   *(yes/no)*
Where is the crayon? *(It's)* in the box.
The yellow pencils are long.

Are the red pencils long?   (*No, they aren't/Yes, they are.*)
Where are the cups?   (*They are under the table.*)

32.   HAVE/HAS

Distribute one or more items to each child and to yourself. Teach *have* and *don't have* on one day. Reinforce before teaching *has* and *doesn't have*. These will take longer. Come back to the third person singular form on other occasions.

I have a spoon.
What do you have?
I have a dog and a cat.
Do you have a doll?
No, I don't.
Juanita has a doll.
Andy has a truck.
Does Carlos have a truck?
No, he doesn't have a truck, he has an engine.
(*etc.*)

33.   A/AN

Continue work on *have* and *has*. Add objects beginning with vowels (alligator, elephant, orange, apple, umbrella, old car, ugly mask, etc.).

34.   COMPARISONS

The pencil is longer than the pen.
The truck is bigger than the car.
The truck is the biggest thing in the box.
The green ring is more beautiful than the red ring.
Which is more expensive, the ring or the ribbon?
What is smaller, the ring or the flag?
What is the smallest thing in the box?
What is the most beautiful thing in the box?
(*etc.*)

35.   VERB TENSE PRACTICE

I am (*not*) holding a penny.
What are your holding?

Where is the rabbit sitting?
What am I doing to the truck?
You *(are pushing) (pushed)* the truck.
Jenni *(is counting) (counted)* the money.
Paul *(is taking) (took)* the money.
I *(see) (saw)* the *(lion)*.
You put the *(flower)* on the book.
(etc.)

36.   VERB TENSE COMPARISONS

The green car is going to drive past the house.
The green car is driving past the house now.
The green car drove past the house.
The red car didn't drive past the house.
(etc.)

37.   MODALS

Set up situations with the objects. Example: place the house next to the edge
of the table:

What will happen if I drive the car past the house?
It will fall off the table.
Should the car drive past the house?
No, it shouldn't.
What would happen if the car drove past the house?
It would fall off the table.
(etc.)

38.   PHONICS

What things begin with the sound /b/?   *(box, ball, basket, etc.)*
Find something that rhymes with *up.*   *(cup; star, car, etc.)*
What is the beginning sound of *marble?*   *(m), crayon? (c), chair? (ch)*
Find something that begins with the same sound as *dinosaur.*   *(dog)*
How many things can you find that begin with the sound /t/?
Put all the things that begin with the same sounds together.

39. SIGHT READING

After you have taught the names of (ten) objects, write each word on a 3 × 5 index card. Place the cards around the table. Distribute the objects and let the students place the correct object next to each word card.

40. MEMORY DEVELOPMENT

Place ten (or more) objects on a tray in front of the class. Let the students study the tray for thirty seconds. Then have them close their eyes as you remove one or two objects. Have them open their eyes and tell what's missing.

41. SENSORY DEVELOPMENT

Place an item in a paper bag without letting students know what it is. Students feel the item and guess what it is.

42. CATEGORIES

Distribute items and have the students sort them into subgroups such as: all the animals, all the furniture, all the toys, transportation items, red things, blue things, things that begin with the letter *m,* etc.

43. LISTENING COMPREHENSION

Guessing game:

I am thinking of one of these objects. It is long and yellow. You can write with it.
  (pencil)

This is small and round. It is like a very little ball. It is hard. It is made of glass.
  (marble)

This is something that goes fast. It has wings. It can fly. *(airplane)*

44. CREATIVE SENTENCES

Select two or three items at a time at random. Students must make up sentences linking the items.

(*Chair, rabbit*) The rabbit sat on the chair. The chair fell on the rabbit. The rabbit made a chair. The rabbit saw the chair. Etc.

(*Car, flag,*) I put a flag on the car.

45.   CREATIVE STORYTELLING

Select two or three "character" items (animals, people, monsters) and some setting items (house, tree, money, apple). Students create a story. You might demonstrate the possibilities yourself first to give an example, then pick out other characters for them to try their imaginations on. Students may work in a large group or small groups or individually. This may be done as a written exercise as well.

*   *   *   *   *

Other Uses for Shoe Box Items

Teach vocabulary for a storytelling session.

For special prizes, moving away, birthdays, and so on, the items are available as souvenirs. Select some replaceable items and allow the student to pick one as a gift to remember your class by.

When students want to draw certain items and need a model, the shoe box may have it.

Action Games

46. I SEE

Grades: K and up

English level: Beginner

Objectives: To reinforce classroom vocabulary; to increase listening skills

Materials needed: None

Presentation: Move the furniture to the side of the room if feasible, or at least ensure that chairs are under desks and aisles are clear. Divide students into teams. Each team lines up behind their team leader. Decide whether a run or a fast walk is appropriate for your group.

When you say, "I see a (table, map, clock, or any classroom object)," the first student in line on each team goes to that object. The first one to reach it scores a point for that team. Each player goes to the end of her team's line.

Students may help teammates by pointing or naming objects but not by translations into native language.

You can add balancing skill as an ingredient of the fun by requiring that the student whose turn it is must balance a chalkboard eraser on his head as he goes to the object. If the eraser falls off, the student must replace it before continuing.

You can vary the clues according to the language ability of the class.

Examples:

I see something *(red).*

I see something *(new, old, beautiful expensive, dangerous, useful, dirty, long, tall, hard, soft, electric, small, big, funny, etc.).*

I see something that you can sit on.

I see something that has two hands and numbers and tells us the time.

I see something you can write with.

I see something we made yesterday.

I see something that belongs to _____.

I see something you can eat.

I see something that tells the date.

I see something made out of *(wood, paper, metal, cloth, glass, plastic, etc.).*

I see something that helps us learn English.

I see something that tells us the meaning of words.

I see something that we can play with.

47. SIMON SAYS

Grades: K and up

English level: Beginners and up

Objectives: To motivate and practice careful listening; to reinforce command forms of verbs, parts of the body, objects in the classroom

Materials needed: None

Presentation: Draw a sketch of a king on the chalkboard.

> This is Simon. He is a king. He is very big and strong. You must do what Simon says.

Draw a word balloon from Simon's mouth and write "Touch your nose" in the word balloon.

> Simon Says, "Touch your nose." You must touch your nose.   *(demonstrate)*

Erase "Touch your nose" from the word balloon, leaving it empty. Point to the word balloon as you say and demonstrate each of these statements:

Simon says, "Touch your ears."
Simon says, "Touch your neck."
Simon says, "Touch your shoulders."
Simon says, "Touch your mouth."

"Now listen carefully. If Simon doesn't say it, don't do it."

Touch your back.
No, don't do it. Simon didn't say it.
Simon says, "Touch your back."
Good, now you can touch your back. Touch your legs.
No, don't do it. Simon didn't say, "Touch your legs."
Simon says, "Touch your legs." Good. Now you can touch your legs because Simon said, "Touch your legs."

Continue in this manner until several children have caught on. Then when some children make an error, point to them and say *"Out!"* After several practice rounds say, "Now if you are *out,* you will have to sit down."

Simon Says may be used to reinforce understanding of words for body parts, verbal directions, and classroom objects. Example: "Simon says, (clap your hands, jump, hop on one foot, pick up the orange crayon, put the book on the floor, etc.)."

Allow students to take turns being Simon. On special days, you can change Simon Says to Columbus Says, George Washington Says, Martin Luther King Says, or if it is a child's birthday, that child's name may be substituted for Simon.

As students become adept at doing only those things that Simon says, increase the difficulty by giving one command while modeling a misleading cue. (Example: Say, "Pick up the orange crayon," while you model picking up a green crayon. Of course you have to emphasize that only the spoken command counts, and then only when "Simon" says it.)

48. GIANT STEPS, ESL Style

Grades: K and up

English level: Beginners

Objective: To practice requests for permission

Materials needed: None

Play: One person is the "Teacher" and must be addressed as (Miss or Mr.) (last name). Others in turn request permission to advance, using the request forms, "Miss _____, may I come to school?" The teacher says, "You may take (1, 2, or 3 giant, baby, umbrella steps, hops, or jumps) or combinations of these. (A giant step is the longest step one can take. A baby step is the length of one's shoe. An umbrella step is made by whirling around as one advances two steps.)

The student must politely ask, "May I?" The teacher says "Yes, you may," or "No, you may not." If the student advances without saying, "May I?" the teacher instructs him to go back to the start. If a student moves without asking permission or moves more than the given number of steps, he must go back to the start.

49.   ALL AROUND THE SCHOOL

Grades: 1 and up

English level: Beginner

Objectives: To reinforce names of places in the school; to practice polite request forms. (This activity is a follow up of a tour of the school building.)

Preparation: On 8 × 12 oaktag or construction paper, write the words *gym, office, nurse, bathroom, library, ESL class, lunchroom, computer room, lost and found, auditorium,* or any other special rooms in your school.

Using masking tape or Funtak®, post the signs around the room.

Presentation: Send students, one or two at a time, to the various areas designated by the signs. "(Name), go to the office (etc.)."

Students then raise their hands in turn and request permission to go somewhere else. They must say the entire phrase correctly. You may write it on the chalkboard for the first few rounds until it is familiar enough for most to say correctly.

(*Miss*)_____, may I go to the _____, please?

If the request is correct, say, "Yes, you may." If incorrect, "No, you may not," and call on another student. Play continues until most students have had two or three chances to move about the room. Allow students to take turns being the teacher. Review the following day.

50.   I SAW THE CAT

(This is the ESL version of Huckle Buckle Beanstalk.)

Grades: K to 6

English level: Low intermediate

Objectives: To practice observation skills; to practice past tense and verb + object word order

Materials needed: Small toy cat or other animal. (Change the name of the game to fit the animal you have.)

Presentation: Show a small plastic cat or other object to the students and explain that they will close their eyes while you hide it somewhere in the classroom where they will be able to see it if they look carefully. They will get a chance to walk around the room, and when they see the object, they are not to touch it or take it but go to their chair and sit down. After they are seated, they say, "I saw the (cat) and the (cat) saw me." When the last person has seen it, the first person gets up, gets the object, and has a turn to hide it.

Sample Conversation:

> This is a (*cat*). What is it? *(a cat)*
>
> I am going to hide the (*cat*). *(walk around the room to demonstrate hide)* But not in a drawer. Not in a closet. You can see it. Can you see it? *(yes)*
>
> Then you will walk around the room. Look for the (*cat*).
>
> When you see the (*cat*), don't take it. Will you take it? *(demonstrate take)* *(no)*
>
> Don't touch it. *(demonstrate touch)* Will you touch it? *(no)*
>
> Go to your desk. Sit down. Then say, "I saw the (*cat*)." Repeat, "I saw the (*cat*) ."
>
> (*Student*), can you say that? (*I saw the [cat].*)
>
> Good, who else can say that?

Individuals say it, with help if necessary. Class repeats.

> Now close your eyes. Don't look. Don't peek. I am going to hide the (*cat*).

Go around the room, hide the object, making false trips to different areas of the room to conceal the sound clues to the hiding place.

> Okay, open your eyes. Stand up. Put your chair under your desk. Look for the (*cat*).

When everyone has found the (*cat*) and taken his/her seat, the first person to have done so gets the (*cat*) and says to the class:

> Close your eyes. Don't peek. I am going to hide the (*cat*).

When the (*cat*) has been hidden, the student says:

> Open your eyes. Stand up. Look for the (*cat*) now.

Continue play until several students have had a chance to hide the (cat).

51. MILK MASH (ESL Bowling)

Grades: K to 6

English level: Beginners

Materials needed: 10 empty 1-quart milk cartons; a six-inch ball

Preparation: Wash out the milk cartons; tape or staple the tops closed

Objectives: To learn the rules and actions for a simple game and the English needed to talk about the activity; to learn the English needed to express enthusiasm and disappointment and to keep score

Preparation: Set up the milk cartons as in the diagram. (Mark these spots with a chalked *X* or masking tape, to simplify setting up by students.) Mark a line on the floor to show students where to stand (*A*).

Presentation: Act out each sentence as you explain the game to the students

> We are going to play Milk Mash. Here are the milk cartons. How many cartons are there? *(ten)*
>
> One, two, three, four, five, six, seven, eight, nine, ten. The cartons are standing. You will take turns. Stand here. Roll the ball at the cartons. You want to knock them down. *(Name)* will roll the ball back. You will have two chances. Roll the ball again. Count the cartons you have knocked down. That is your score. The cartons are down. Stand the cartons up for the next person.
>
> We will take turns. *(Name)* is first.

Elicit responses to determine comprehension:

> Where are the milk cartons? *(here, there, or students point)*
> What is this? *(ball)*
> I am rolling the_____. *(ball)*
> How many cartons did I knock down? *(number)*
> Do I roll the ball again? *(yes)*
> How many milk cartons did I knock down all together? *(number)*
> What is my score? *(same number)*
> Do I roll the ball again? *(no)*

What do I do now?   *(stand the cartons up)*
Who is next?   *(name)*

As students take turns playing, provide a running commentary on their actions. Students listen but need not repeat unless they choose to.

Example:

Carlos has the ball. He is rolling the ball. The ball knocked down four cartons. Maya got the ball. She rolled it back to Carlos. He goes again. He is rolling the ball. He missed.

What's his score?   *(four)*
Does he go again?   *(no)*

After several turns with several commentaries, ask questions:

Whose turn is it?   *(student names turn)*
What is *(she)* doing?   *(rolling the ball)*
How many cartons did *(she)* knock down?   *(number)*
What's *(her)* score?   *(number)*
(etc.)

After several rounds during which the English is presented, you may select teams to compete. If necessary, create two bowling alleys and four teams to speed up turntaking. Choose a student to be the scorekeeper. Select a more advanced student to act as the "sports announcer," commenting, as you did, on the actions. In the heat of the game, students forget they are to practice English, since they may have very little English to use. Hold the balls to stop the game and have them repeat some of the English they might use.

Whose turn is it?
It's my turn.
It's your turn.
It's (name's) turn.
Stand behind the line.
Don't step on the line.
Roll the ball.
Knock down the cartons.
How many did you knock down?
I *(he, she)* knocked down _____ cartons.
Keep score.
What's the score?
You go again.
Don't step on the line.

Don't bounce the ball.
Get the ball.
Hurry up.
Hurray!
No good.

For readers, these may be written on the chalkboard. Or you may keep them permanently on oaktag chart paper, to take out whenever your class "goes bowling."

Follow up: This pattern can apply to all the games. Adjust the questions accordingly.

What did we do yesterday? *(We played Milk Mash.)*

What did we need? *(We needed ten milk cartons and a ball.) (Sketch game diagram on the chalkboard.)*

Did we throw the ball *(demonstrate, miming)* or roll the ball? *(demonstrate)* We rolled the ball.

Where did we stand, in front of the line *(draw on board)* or behind the line? *(behind the line)*

Writing/Reading: Write the title *Milk Mash* on the chalkboard. Ask questions to elicit sentences about the activity. Example:

Yesterday, we played Milk Mash. First we set up the cartons. Then we stood behind the line. We rolled the ball and knocked down the cartons. We had two teams. _____ team won. The score was _____ to _____.

Students read the paragraph several times, individually and in unison. Clarify any meanings. They may then copy the sentences.

Younger children may draw a picture of playing Milk Mash. Have them identify the milk cartons, the ball, the person, and the line to stand behind.

52. DUCK, DUCK, GOOSE

Grades: K to 3

English level: Beginner and up

Objectives: To learn an American game and the English needed to play and talk about the game

Materials needed: (optional) Toy duck and goose or pictures of them

Presentation: The children form a circle and squat down like ducks (or may sit with legs folded)

Hold hands. *(demonstrate)*
Form a circle.

Sit down. You are the ducks.   *(show toy duck or picture, or quack like a duck)*
(Student), you will be "it." Walk around the outside of the circle.   *(demonstrate)*
Touch each person lightly on the head and say, "duck."   *(demonstrate)*
Duck, duck, duck, duck, duck.   *(touch five or six children this way)*
Choose one person and say, "Goose!" when you touch that person's head.
   (demonstrate)

When "it" says "Goose," the goose must get up (have the child stand up) and run after "it" (demonstrate). The goose tries to tag "it" before she gets all the way around the circle to the space where the goose was sitting. If "it" gets to the empty space without being tagged, she sits down, and the goose becomes "it."

If the goose tags "it" before she gets to sit down, "it" must sit in the center of the circle, and stays there until another player is tagged and takes her place.

Sample conversation:

Walk around the circle.
Touch each person on the head.
Say, "Duck." Say, "Goose."
Goose, get up! Quickly!
Run! Run around the circle.
Catch him! *(her)* Tag him! *(her)*
Sit down in the empty place.
Now you are "it."
Sit in the center of the circle. Sit here.

During the game, make a running commentary on the children's actions.
Examples:

Maya is "it." She is walking around the circle. She said "Goose." Nero is chasing her. Oh, he didn't catch her. Maya sat in Nero's place. Now Nero is "it."
Berta is chasing Nero. She caught him! Now Nero has to sit in the center of the circle.

Follow up: Create a language experience chart:

We played Duck, Duck, Goose.
We sat in a circle.
(Name) was "it."
(Name) touched each person on the head.
When she said, "Goose," *(Name #2)* had to chase her.
We had fun. I like being "it."

Invite American students to come to the ESL class to explain the games. Write up the rules or follow up on oaktag charts.

53.   ESL HOPSCOTCH

Grades: 1 to 6

English level: Intermediate

Objectives: To learn the local American version of an almost universal game; to share international versions of Hopscotch; to practice structures and vocabulary connected with the game's rules

Materials needed: Masking tape; small objects to use for stones (gum erasers or wads of paper will do)

Preparation: Learn the local version of Hopscotch from the local children. Mark off the playing squares on the floor with masking tape. If playing outdoors, use chalk.

Play: The students take turns. The first player stands behind the line and drops his stone into square #1. He then walks or hops into each square in turn, with one foot only in each square, without stepping on the lines. All students count out the numbers as the player steps in the squares. On reaching #8, the player turns around, comes back, and picks up the stone before stepping in the square that had the stone. If successful, the player continues his turn, drops the stone into square #2, and repeats the action. A player is *out* if:

> he or she misses the square the stone was tossed to
>
> ...steps on a line
>
> ...puts both feet into the same square
>
> ...forgets to pick up the stone before stepping in the square to which the
>   stone was thrown

To equalize play between students of different coordination abilities, you might vary the rules: Older children must hop on one foot, while younger children can walk.

Sample structures:

> Take turns.
> It's (*your, my, his, her*) turn.
> Whose turn is it?
> I'm next.
> You're (*I'm*) on number (*four*).
> Throw the stone.
> You (*I, he, she*) missed.
> Hop.
> Walk.
> Turn around.

Pick up the stone.

Don't step on the lines.

You stepped on the line.

You're out.

Make a running commentary on the actions the students are performing. Example:

It's Maya's turn. She's throwing the stone. Whoops, she missed. She's out. Now it's Pita's turn. He threw the stone. It's good. It's in the square. Pita is hopping. Don't step on the lines, Pita. Oh, oh, he forgot to pick up the stone.

Follow up: Children may draw diagrams of the Hopscotch patterns used in their countries. Discuss who plays Hopscotch (age groups, girls only, boys only, or both sexes).

Writing/Reading: Write "How to Play Hopscotch." Elicit rules and procedures from the students. Connect vocabulary with pictures and the written words:

First, draw squares for Hopscotch.

Stand behind the line.

Throw your stone into square #1.

Step or hop in each square from 2 to 10.

Turn around and come back and pick up your stone.

Don't step on the lines. (Etc.)

54. ESL HIDE-AND-SEEK

Grades: 2 to 6

English level: Intermediate

Objectives: To learn the local jargon and local rules for a universal game

Materials needed: None

Preparation: Check the local children's variations on Hide-and-Seek so you will be presenting useful and accurate language forms for your students. Examine your room for potential hiding places (for example, behind teacher's desk, in a closet). Clear these areas to make them suitable, so you can direct hiders to them quickly (before they decide to hide in the paint cabinet and knock over all the paint bottles).

Play:

We're going to play Hide-and-Seek. *(demonstrate hide by hiding)*

Seek means "Look."

Let the door be "home base." Send one student out of the room to be "it." This student must count to 100. Select one or more other students to "hide" within the classroom. Since this is a demonstration rather than a complete participation game (not enough hiding places and the noise level must be kept within bounds) students should go through this in "slow motion" (that is, walking). When "it" reaches 100, she comes into the room to look for the hiding students. When she finds someone, there is a walking race back to the base. If a hider can come back to the base before being tapped, he is home free.

Presentation:

We're going to play Hide-and-Seek.

You're "it."

Close your eyes and count to one hundred.

I (*we, you, they*) am/are going to hide.

When you get to one hundred come in. Look for the people hiding. If you see someone, touch the base and say, "Tap, tap on_____ (*person's name*)."

(*Hider*), try to get back to the base first and say, "Home free!"

Other structures:

Ninety-eight, ninety-nine, one hundred...anyone around my base is "it"!

Allee allee in free!

Come out, come out, wherever you are!

Carry on a running commentary as the students go through the actions of the games.

Example:

Cheng is "it." He's going out into the hall. He will count to one hundred. Joon and Lee are going to hide. Joon is hiding in the yellow closet. Shh. Lee is hiding behind the teacher's desk. Hurry up, Lee. Now, everyone else just watch. Don't look at Joon or Lee. Here comes Cheng. Did you count to one hundred, Cheng? What is Cheng doing now? (*He's looking for Joon and Lee*) What are you doing Cheng? (*I'm looking for [seeking] Joon and Lee*) There goes Lee. He got to the base. He's home free. Now Cheng has to find Joon. Oh, he found him. Cheng ran back to the base. He tapped Joon. Now Joon is "it."

Follow up: Discuss whether Hide-and-Seek is played in their native country. Who plays? What are good hiding places? What are the variations of rules in their country?

Ask questions for students to give information for the purpose of writing a paragraph about Hide-and-Seek.

Examples:

What did we play yesterday? (*Hide-and-Seek*)

Who was "it" first? (*Cheng*)

Where did Cheng go? (*out into the hall*)

What did he do?   *(count to 100)*

Who hid in the closet?   *(Joon)*

Where did Lee hide?   *(behind the teacher's desk)*

Did Cheng find Lee?   *(no)*

What did Lee do?   *(he ran to the base)*

What did he say?   *(home free)*

Did Cheng find Joon?   *(yes)*

What did he do?   *(he tapped on the base)*

What did he say?   *(tap, tap on Joon)*

Write a paragraph about Hide-and-Seek for students to read, discuss, and copy. Write sentences about whatever occurred in your classroom while playing the game.

Example:

> Yesterday we played Hide-and-Seek. First Cheng was "it." He went out of the room and counted to one hundred. Joon and Lee hid. Joon hid in the closet and Lee hid behind the teacher's desk. Cheng didn't find Lee. Lee ran to the base and got in home free. Cheng found Joon and tapped. "One-two-three on Joon." Then Joon was "it."

55.   ESL TAG

Grades: K to 6

English level: Beginner

Objective: To learn the English required for playing a universal game

Materials needed: None

Play: One student is "it" and chases others. Whoever she tags is then "it" and must chase the others. One spot may be designated as a base, where the runners can rest. For indoor play, students must balance a book or chalkboard eraser on their head.

Language practiced:

You're "it."

Run.

Chase him, chase her.

Ha, ha, you can't catch me.

Times!

The eraser fell.

Pick it up.

Put it on your head.

56.   FREEZE TAG

Grades: K to 6

English level: Beginner

Objective: To learn English necessary to play a simple game

Materials needed: None

Play: One student is "it" and chases the others. When tagged, the person must freeze in the position he was in when tagged. "It" then proceeds to run after each of the other people, trying to freeze all of them. If any of them touch a "frozen" playmate, that releases that person from the freeze and he is free to run again. If "it" freezes all the other players, a new "it" is chosen, usually the first person caught.

Language practiced:

> You're "it."
> Freeze.
> Unfreeze her.
> You moved.

Writing/Reading: We played Freeze Tag. First, Fredi was "it." She tagged Joon. Joon was frozen. He could not move. Then Fredi tagged Lee. Lee was frozen. Osvaldo touched Joon and unfroze him.

57.   PRISONER'S BASE (outdoors)

Grades: K to 8

English level: Beginner

Objective: To learn the English necessary to talk about and play a game

Materials needed: None

Play: The group is divided into two teams: Prison Guards and Free. One area is designated as a prison. The prison guards chase the other players, and as they tag them, they put them "in jail," where the prisoners must stay unless tagged by a free player. If the prison guards manage to catch all of the other players, the imprisoned players then become the prison guards.

Language practiced:

> Run!
> I got you.
> You're in prison.
> Stay here.
> Come save me!
> You're free!

58. ESL RED LIGHT

English level: Beginner

Objectives: To learn the rules for a game and the English needed to talk about it

Materials needed: Books or chalkboard erasers

Play: One student is the "traffic cop," who guards the base. The other students balance a book or eraser on their heads. They begin at the opposite end of the classroom, away from the traffic cop. The traffic cop says, "Green light," turns around, and counts to ten. While her back is turned, the others must take very tiny baby steps (outdoors, run as fast as they can), hoping to tag the traffic cop before she turns around. If the eraser falls, the student must replace it before continuing. When the traffic cop sees anyone moving, even a small step, she tells him to go back to the starting line. If an eraser falls at this time, the student must go back too. When the traffic cop is satisfied that all players are completely motionless, she says "green light" again and turns around to count. The first person to reach and tag the traffic cop will become the next traffic cop.

Language practiced:

> Count to ten.
> Red light, green light.
> Take tiny steps.
> You moved.
> I didn't move.
> Yes, I saw you.
> Go back.
> Balance the (*eraser*).
> It fell.
> You can't hold it with your hands.

Writing/Reading: We played Red Light. First, Carla was the traffic cop. She said, "Green light." She turned around and closed her eyes and counted to ten. We walked quickly, with tiny steps. Carla said "red light" and turned around. We all stopped. Carla saw Gilad moving. She told Gilad to go back to the start. Then Carla said "green light" again. We walked again. Jee Yong tagged Carla. Then Jee Yong was the traffic cop.

59. ESL PAPER BASEBALL

Grades: 2 and up

English level: Intermediate

Materials needed: Illustration of baseball diamond; paper bat; paper ball; markers for home plate, pitcher's mound, first, second, and third bases

Preparation: Make a paper bat by rolling an 18 x 24 sheet of construction paper into an elongated cone and securing it with masking tape. (Alternatively, use two tubes from paper towel rolls. Make a four-inch cut in one and insert the other. Fasten in place with masking tape.)

Make a paper ball by crumpling up a sheet or two of paper into the shape of a ball. Wrap this ball with masking tape to keep its shape.

Make copies of the baseball diamond for each student.

Presentation: Distribute the baseball diamond handout. Draw a large diamond on the chalkboard. Teach the names of the bases and the players.

Map out a baseball diamond in the classroom, posting the names of the bases on the wall as well as having bases on the floor. (See the illustration.)

Have a student start at home plate and walk around the bases: Go to first base. Go to second base. Go to third base. Go home.

Assign students to the different positions.

You are the pitcher. Who are you?   (*I'm the pitcher.*)

Throw the ball to one player and call out directions for throwing the ball to different players in turn:

Throw the ball to the catcher. Throw the ball to the first baseman. Throw the ball to the center fielder.   (*etc.*)

Choose students to be pitcher, batter, and catcher. Have the other students sit down. Do the following demonstration in mime without the bat or the ball. Give the directions and demonstrate the action required if necessary.

To batter:

You're up. Stand here at home plate.

To pitcher:

Throw the ball.

To batter:

Swing! (*batter swings; demonstrate if necessary*) Strike one.

To catcher:

Catch the ball. Throw the ball back to the pitcher.
Pitch.
Swing! Strike two.
Catch and throw the ball back.
Pitch.
Swing! Strike three, you're out.
Catch and throw the ball back.
Select a new batter.
Pitch.
It's too high. Don't swing. Ball one.

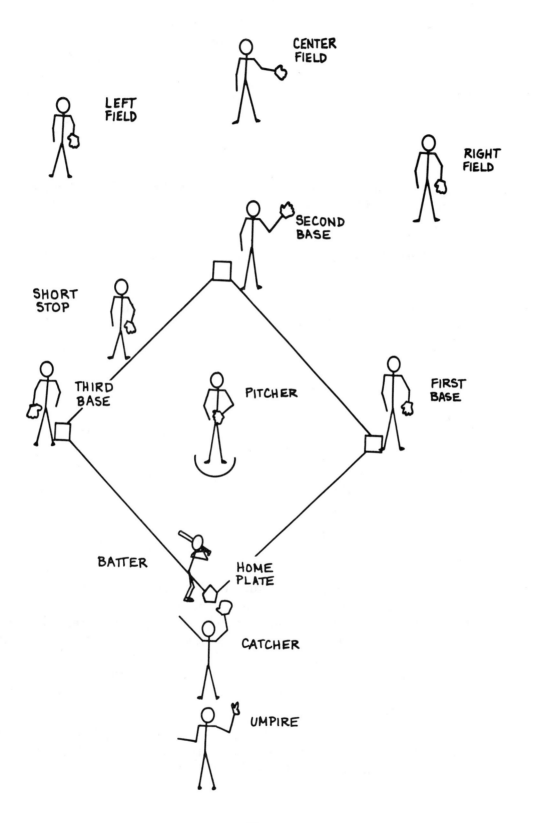

CENTER
FIELD

LEFT
FIELD

RIGHT
FIELD

SECOND
BASE

SHORT
STOP

FIRST
BASE

THIRD
BASE

PITCHER

BATTER

HOME
PLATE

CATCHER

UMPIRE

Continue the miming action, demonstrating the meanings of: Ball two, too low. Ball three, outside. Ball four, inside. Walk to first base.

A third batter can swing and hit a fly ball, which you mime catching. *Out.* Two outs.

A fourth batter:

Swing! Foul ball. Don't run. Strike one. Swing! A hit. Run to first base! You're safe! It's a single!

A fifth batter:

Swing! A hit! Run to first base! Now go to second base. (*Name*), run to second base, now third base. You're safe! It's a double!

A sixth batter:

Swing! A hit! Run to first base! Catch the ball. Throw it to first base. You're out.

A seventh batter:

Swing! A hit! It's a home run! (*Name*), run home! One run! (*Name*), run to third base and run home! Two runs! (*Batter*), run all around the bases. Three runs!

As each is mentioned, write the vocabulary on the chalkboard:

swing	fair ball
strike	foul ball
out	fly
ball	hit
too high	single
too low	double
inside	triple
outside	home run
walk	score

Before being ready to play the game in slow motion in your classroom, you may want to "train" some students as umpires. Have the pitcher throw the ball and show where the strike zone is located: over the base and between the batter's shoulders and knees. Help the umpire trainee to determine the calls until accurate enough for the game.

You are now ready to play the game in slow motion in your classroom. Divide class into two teams and select the umpire. Keep a running commentary on the actions of the students.

Yoshi is up. Jung is pitching the ball. Yoshi swung. He missed. The umpire called a strike. Wow, he hit the ball. It's a single. He's running to first base. Mariko got the ball. She threw it to first base. Too late. Yoshi is safe   *(etc.)*

Yumi is up. Here comes the pitch. Foul ball! Strike one! *(etc.)*

When ready, you might take the class outside for the actual playing of the game with paper ball and paper bat. (This is to restrict the area needed for the game, so that all instructions and commentary may be heard. The paper equipment also slows the action and eliminates danger.)

60. WHO GOES FIRST?

Grades: K and up

English level: High beginner and up

Objective: To learn the local playground customs for determining the first players in a game

Preparation: Find out what current jingles are used if the rhymes following are not used in your area.

Presentation: Whenever you want to select a single student or team, point to each student as you say each word (or breath group, as marked on the right).

Eeny meeny, miny, mo,	EÉNy MEÉNy MÍNy MÓ
Catch a tiger by the toe.	CÁTCHa TÍger BÝthe TÓE
When he hollers, let him go,	WHÉNee HÓLLers LÉTim GÓ
Eeny, meeny, miny, mo.	EÉNy MEÉNy MÍNy MÓ.

The person whom you point to as you say "MO" is selected, or that person's team goes first.

After hearing you choose persons in this way, students will clamor to learn the rhyme.

Illustrate *catch, tiger, toe, holler, let go.*

Allow students to listen several times and then repeat it line by line after you.

Write it on the chalkboard if students can read.

Alternative choosing rhyme: This method of selecting a first player takes a little longer, but students find it an enjoyable activity in itself:

One potato, two potato,
Three potato, four,
Five potato, six potato,
Seven potato *more.*

The children stand in a circle around the caller. They hold their hands made into fists in front of them. The caller, also with both hands in fists, uses his right hand to lightly tap each child's fists in order around the circle. (In order to tap his own right fist, he raises it to his mouth.) Fists that are tapped at the word *more* are put behind the player's back. The choosing continues until only one person has a fist inside the circle. That person is "it."

Action Games With Songs and Chants

61. TALL AND SMALL

Grades: K, 1

English level: Beginner

Objective: To learn a simple game and the English needed to talk about it

Presentation: Students stand in a line. The child at one end of the line is the leader for the students' actions in answer to the question at the end of the song.

I'm very, very tall.   *(raise hands above heads, stand on tiptoes)*

I'm very, very small.   *(squat down)*

Sometimes tall,   *(up again)*

Sometimes small,   *(squat again)*

Guess what I am now.   *(The leader stands or squats as he chooses. The others follow.)*

After students know what to do, one child is "it" and stands in front of the line, with her eyes closed, back to the others. The student must guess how the others are: tall or small. If she guesses correctly, she becomes the leader, and the child at the other end of the line becomes "it."

Follow up: Draw something tall and something small (tree/flower; skyscraper/doghouse; man/baby; or things suggested by the children).

62. BLUEBIRD, BLUEBIRD

Grades: K, 1, and 2

English level: Beginner and up

Objectives: To play a game; to reinforce color words; to follow directions; to learn the preposition *through*

Materials needed: Sheets of various-colored construction paper; words and music to "Bluebird"

Play: Students form a circle, holding hands, arms raised. One child is the Bluebird and carries a piece of blue construction paper as he weaves in and out of the circle under the "windows" formed by the raised hands. On the words, "Oh, Johnny, I am tired," the Bluebird stops in front of a child who becomes the next bird. Give this child a red paper to hold and the children sing, "Redbird, redbird," (etc.). Continue with Yellowbird, Greenbird, Blackbird, etc.

Follow up: Draw pictures of birds, coloring each a different color. Label the colors.

BLUEBIRD

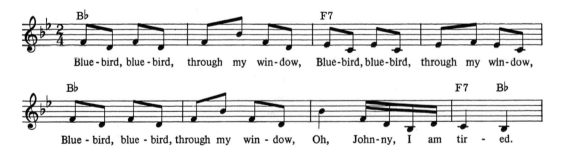

Blue-bird, blue-bird, through my win-dow, Blue-bird, blue-bird, through my win-dow,

Blue-bird, blue-bird, through my win-dow, Oh, John-ny, I am tir - ed.

63. LOOBY LOO

Grades: K to 3

English level: Beginner and up

Objectives: To learn an American game and the English needed to talk about the activity; to practice right–left discrimination

Materials needed: Stickers, gummed stars, or washable marker

Presentation: Place a sticker or gummed star (or draw a star with a washable marker) on the back of your right hand and say, "This is my right hand."

Place one on each student's right hand as you say, "This is your right hand."

Have students perform various actions with their right hands. Examples:

Raise your right hand.
Touch your nose with your right hand.
Touch your head with your right hand.
Shake hands with your right hand.

Gently slap your right hip with the right hand:

This is my right hip.

Repeat with right leg, right foot, right side.

The left hand is the hand with *no* sticker.

Then teach the left hip, left side, left leg, left foot.
Children form a circle and join hands.

Here we go Looby Loo, *(walk slowly to center of the circle, raising hands high)*
Here we go Looby Light, *(walk backward, making circle large, lowering hands)*
Here we go Looby Loo, *(in again)*
All on a Saturday night. *(out again)*
I put my right hand in,
I put my right hand out,
I give my right hand a shake, shake, shake,
And turn myself about.
Chorus: Here we go Looby Loo, *(etc.)*
I put my left hand in, *(etc.)*
Chorus.
(Continue with right foot, left foot, right hip, left hip, head, whole self.)

Follow up: Write *right* and *left* on the chalkboard.

Left begins with the letter *L*. Put your hands out in front of you with your fingers up and your thumb down. Which hand forms the letter *L*? This is your left hand.

Have students trace both right and left hands on paper. (Partners may be needed to trace the writing hand of the children who cannot coordinate the nonwriting hand to do this.) Label the hands "right" and "left."

Add vocabulary such as *thumb, wrist, index finger, ring finger, pinkie, fingernails, knuckles,* as appropriate to your class, and have students label them.

64. HOKEY POKEY

Grades: 2 to adult

English level: Beginner and up

Objectives: To learn an American group "dance"; to learn right–left discrimination. This activity is similar in objective and language practiced to "Looby Loo" but has a faster melody and is more appealing to older students.

Materials needed: Stickers (optional)

Presentation: Students form a circle. Say the sentences slowly as you demonstrate the actions and students imitate you. Go through as many stanzas as necessary to help them hear the language. Encourage them to join in saying the sentences as they do the activity. Then begin from the beginning with the music.

HOKEY POKEY

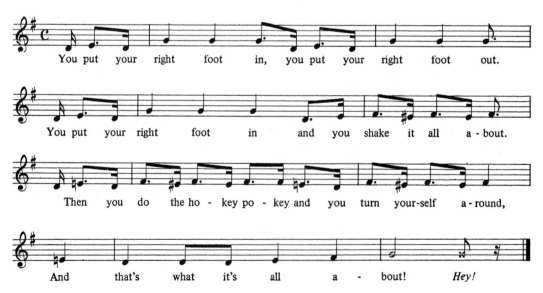

You put your right foot in, you put your right foot out.

You put your right foot in and you shake it all a-bout.

Then you do the ho-key po-key and you turn your-self a-round,

And that's what it's all a-bout! *Hey!*

1. You put your right hand in,
   You put your right hand out,
   You put your right hand in,
   And you shake it all about.
   Then you do the hokey pokey,   *(elbows bent, point index fingers up, rotate hips)*
   And you turn yourself around.
   And that's what it's all about.   *Hey!   (clap hands)*
2. You put your left hand in,   *(etc.)*
3. You put your right foot in,   *(etc.)*

(Continue with the left foot, right hip, left hip, head, and whole self.)

Follow up: See follow up for "Looby Loo."

65. ESL FARMER IN THE DELL

Grades: K to 3

English level: Beginner to intermediate

Objectives: To learn an American game and song; to learn family and farm vocabulary

Materials needed: Pictures to illustrate the words *farm, dell* (valley), *farmer, wife, child, nurse, dog, cat, rat, cheese*—or make quick sketches on the chalkboard

Presentation: We are going to play The Farmer in the Dell. Present vocabulary through the sketches or pictures. If using pictures, post them or line them in the chalk tray.

Stand up. Everybody hold hands. Form a circle.

Select one student to be the farmer in the center of the circle. Say, "(Jo) is the farmer in the dell."

THE FARMER IN THE DELL

The   farm - er   in   the   dell, _____ The   farm - er   in   the dell,

Hi - ho,   the der - ri - o,   The farm - er in   the dell.

Sing the first verse:

The farmer in the dell, the farmer in the dell,

Hi-ho, the derrio,

The farmer in the dell.

The children may sing along with you or not, as they are able. The outer circle of children join hands and circle around clockwise, turning and going counterclockwise when they come to "Hi-ho, the derrio." Or the children may stand in place and clap hands as you sing.

Continue by saying, "Now, (Jo), you must take a wife."

Sing verse 2:

The farmer takes a wife,   *(etc.)*

(Both farmer and wife stay in the circle.)

Point to each of the pictures made or posted on the board in turn to show who has to choose what as the verses continue:

#3: The wife takes the child,   *(etc.)*

#4: The child takes the nurse,   *(etc.)*

#5: The nurse takes the dog,   *(etc.)*

#6: The dog takes the cat,   *(etc.)*

#7: The cat takes the rat,   *(etc.)*

#8: The rat takes the cheese,   *(etc.)*

All eight players are in the center of the circle at this point. Then they leave in the same order: Each steps, in turn, out of the center and rejoins the circle, as you sing the verses. Children clap hands in rhythm.

The farmer leaves the wife,

The farmer leaves the wife,

Hi-ho, the derrio,

The farmer leaves the wife.

The wife leaves the child,   *(etc.)*

The child leaves the nurse,   *(etc.)*

The nurse leaves the dog,   *(etc.)*
The dog leaves the cat,   *(etc.)*
The cat leaves the rat,   *(etc.)*
The rat leaves the cheese,   *(etc.)*
The cheese stands alone.   *(etc.)*

Follow up:

Talk about the sequence of events using the cues from the chalkboard.

Write the vocabulary words. Write one sentence for each item.

Practice the past tense forms—The farmer took a wife; the rat left the cheese; the cheese stood alone; etc.

66.   A-HUNTING WE WILL GO

Grades: K to 3

English level: Beginner to intermediate

Objectives: To learn an American game and the English needed to talk about it

Materials needed: Box and pictures or sketches of a fox and a hunter

Presentation: Illustrate and teach the words *fox* and *box*. Demonstrate *catch a fox, put him in a box,* and *let him go.*
  Children form a circle and join hands. One child is chosen to be the fox. The fox walks around the outside of the circle in one direction while the children circle in the other direction, holding hands.

Sing:

A-hunting we will go,
A-hunting we will go.
We'll catch a fox
And put him in a box,
And then we'll let him go.

On the words, "We'll catch a fox," the two children nearest the fox lift their arms and bring them down on the other side of the fox, bringing him into the circle. The circle slowly tightens to trap the fox in a "box." On "let him go," the children raise their arms and allow the fox to get out of the circle. The fox chooses a student to be a new fox. They switch places, and the game continues.

Sample conversation:

Join hands.
Make a circle.
Go this way.

Raise your arms.
Catch the fox.
Make the circle smaller now.
Come closer.
Make a box.
The fox is in the box.
Now let the fox go.
Choose another fox.

Follow up: Practice the past tense in talking about the activity:

We went hunting. Yung Jo was the fox. We caught the fox. The fox was in the circle. We made the circle smaller. We put him in a box. Then we let him go.

67. DID YOU EVER SEE A LASSIE? (LADDIE)

Grades: K to 3

English level: Beginner and up

Objectives: To learn an American game and the English needed to talk about it; to reinforce animal or occupation vocabulary

Materials needed: None

Play: Children join hands and form a circle. One child is the lassie or laddie in the center. The children circle around as you sing until the words, "this way and that." Then the child in the center performs some action, such as dancing, marching, swaying, hopping, reaching and bending, or whatever, and the others must imitate the action. The lassie chooses a new lassie or laddie and the game continues.

Did you ever see a lassie, a lassie, a lassie?
Did you ever see a lassie go this way and that?
Go this way and that way, go this way and that way,
Did you ever see a lassie go this way and that?

The game may be played with the child in the center choosing some occupation, animal, or object and acting out some activity that pertains to this choice. Examples: hammering for a carpenter, jumping for a frog, swaying for a tree. They may use vocabulary they already know or you might teach them names of appropriate occupations or animals. In this case, the child may say what she is (carpenter, tree, cat, frog, rabbit, driver, farmer, dentist, doctor, teacher, dancer, police officer, etc.) and the children sing the verse:

Did you ever see a (carpenter), a (carpenter), a (carpenter)?
Did you ever see a (carpenter), go this way and that?
Go this way and that way, go this way and that way,
Did you ever see a (carpenter), go this way and that?

Follow up: Draw a picture of an animal or worker in action. Tell or write a sentence about the picture. Examples: A carpenter builds houses. A dancer dances. A frog jumps.

68. ESL MULBERRY BUSH

Grades: K to 3

English level: Beginner and up

Objectives: To reinforce vocabulary and structures needed to talk about everyday activities

Play: Students form a circle. The leader—you at first but in subsequent playings of the game, choose a student to be a leader. At the end of each verse, a new leader is chosen to decide the activity for the next verse.

MULBERRY BUSH

This is the way we wash our face
Wash our face,
Wash our face.
This is the way we wash our face,
So early in the morning.

Continue with

This is the way we:
    wash our hands, *(etc.)*
    brush our teeth, *(etc.)*
    comb our hair, *(etc.)*
    eat our breakfast, *(etc.)*
    dress ourselves, *(etc.)*
    walk to school, *(etc.)*
    write our words, *(etc.)*

read a book, *(etc.)*
play on the swings, *(etc.)*

Or choose any other verses you or the students want to create.

FINGER GAMES AND HAND-CLAPPING GAMES

Coordinating finger actions with rhythmic language delights all children. Present the following familiar American games with the necessary objects, pictures, or actions to make the language comprehensible as well as enjoyable.

69. TEN LITTLE INDIANS

You can rename this Ten Little Children, Puppies, Kittens, Witches, Turkeys, Snowmen, Bunnies, etc., to correspond with whatever seasonal or situational vocabulary you have been working with.

Grades: Preschool to 3

English level: Beginner

Objectives: To learn a common American counting song; to reinforce numbers 1–10

Materials needed: None

Presentation:

One little, two little,
Three little *(Indians)*;
Four little, five little,
Six little *(Indians)*;
Seven little, eight little,
Nine little *(Indians)*;
Ten little *(Indian boys)*.*

(Hold hands, fists closed, in front of you, with palms facing out. Raise fingers one at a time as you count.)

(Fold down fingers as you count down.)

Ten little, nine little,
Eight little *(Indians)*;
Seven little, six little,
Five little *(Indians)*;
Four little, three little,
Two little *(Indians)*;
One little *(Indian boy)*.

*Puppy dogs, kitty cats, happy children, Halloween witches, Thanksgiving turkeys, winter snowmen, Easter bunnies, etc.

Options: Instead of counting out on fingers, children may form a circle and walk around the circle as you or a leader counts children into the center of the circle.

Follow up: Children make a "booklet" of numbers. Cut 8½ × 11 paper in half and fold the halves. Children write one number on each page and draw a corresponding number of items that they know the names for: flowers, trees, girls, boys, pencils, pennies, balls, cats, houses, hats, cars, etc.

70. WHERE IS THUMBKIN?

Grades: Preschool to 3

English level: Low beginner and up

Objectives: To learn an enjoyable rhythmic language activity; to practice conversational structures: "Where is _____?" "How are you?" "Very well, thank you" (etc.)

Materials needed: None

Preparation: None necessary

Presentation: Children sit in a circle with their hands behind their backs.

Where is Thumbkin?
Where is Thumbkin?
Here I am.   *(Bring one hand in front of you, with the thumb raised, the other fingers closed.)*

Here I am.   *(Bring the other hand in front, with the thumb raised.)*

How are you today, sir?   *(The thumb on one hand "speaks," bowing to the other thumb.)*

Very well, I thank you.   *(The other thumb "answers," bowing.)*

Run away.   *(One hand returns behind the back.)*
Run away.   *(The other hand returns behind the back.)*

Where is Pointer?
(etc.)   *(Repeat the entire exercise with the index finger.)*

Where is Tall Man?   *(Repeat with middle finger.)*
(etc.)

Where is Ring Man?   *(Repeat with ring finger.)*
(etc.)

Where is Pinkie?   *(Repeat with little finger.)*
(etc.)

Where is Hand?
(etc.)

The same rhyme and actions may be used with different vocabulary. For example, "Where is Father (Mother, Sister, Brother, Baby, Family)?"

Follow up: See follow up for "Looby Loo."

WHERE IS THUMBKIN?

71. TWO LITTLE BLACKBIRDS

This "magic trick" will intrigue children. When they have seen it often enough to figure it out, they will delight in practicing the language so they can play the trick on their friends.

Grades: Preschool to 6

English level: Low intermediate

Objectives: To learn a "magic" trick in a rhythmic game; to practice an easy rhyme; to practice pronunciation of the /l/ sound, both alone and in blends, and the /j/ sound

Materials needed: Black paper, glue, tape or paste, pictures of a hill and a bird

Preparation: Cut two tiny pieces of the black paper and glue them to the nails of each of your index fingers. Cut enough small pieces to have two each plus extras for each of your students. Place these in an envelope.

Present the vocabulary through pictures of a hill and a bird.

The children should be sitting opposite you at a table. Make fists except for the index finger. Place your hands off the edge of the table with the "blackbirds" (index fingers) resting on the table.

Two little blackbirds	*(Lightly bounce your index fingers on the edge of the table.)*
Sitting on a hill—	
One name Jack,	*(The right finger bounces on the table.)*
And one named Jill.	*(The left finger bounces.)*

Fly away, Jack.

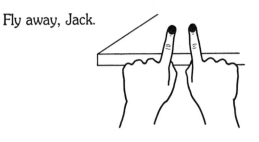

(Raise your hand up rapidly above your head as you do this; tuck your index finger down while raising your middle finger; bring your hand down quickly and place your middle finger on the table—it will seem that Jack has truly flown away and disappeared.)

Fly away, Jill.   *(Repeat with the other hand.)*

Come back, Jack.   *(Raise your hand and quickly switch fingers, bringing the blackbird back into view.)*

Come back, Jill.   *(Repeat above—the hand is truly quicker than the eye.)*

Repeat this until a number of children have caught on and discovered the trick. Then distribute the pieces of black paper and help students glue or tape the "blackbirds" to their index fingers. Practice several times over the next few days.

72. THE ITSY BITSY SPIDER

Grades: Preschool to 3

English level: Intermediate

Objectives: To learn a familiar American finger game; to practice pronunciation difficulties of /ts/ and /sp/, and /d/ past-tense endings.

Preparation: (optional) Look at pictures of spiders. Count their legs. Talk about what spiders eat, how they make their webs.

THE ITSY BITSY SPIDER

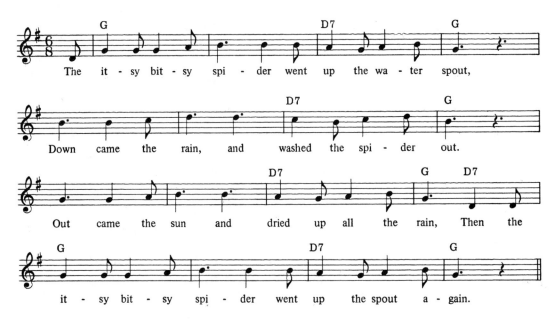

The itsy bitsy spider
Climbed up the water spout.

> (*Hold hands out in front of you, with your index fingers touching the thumbs of the opposite hands; "climb" by separating the bottom thumb and finger and bringing them together again above the other pair of fingers; repeat, alternating fingers.*)

Down came the rain

> (*Hands move down, with fingers spread to show rain.*)

And washed the spider out.

> (*Hands whisk away spider.*)

Out came the sun and

> (*Hands frame face, fingers show rays of sun.*)

Dried up all the rain.

> (*Big smile.*)

And the itsy bitsy spider
Walked up the spout again.

> (*Repeat first action.*)

Follow up: Draw a picture of a spider.

73. TEN LITTLE BLACKBIRDS

Grades: Preschool to 3

English level: Intermediate

Objectives: To learn a rhythmic language activity; to reinforce numbers, rhyming words; to learn the English needed to talk about the activity

Materials needed: Sketches of blackbirds, gate, sticks, sky

Preparation: Preview vocabulary with the pictures or illustrate it as it comes up in the rhyme

Ten little blackbirds,
Feeling mighty fine.
One flew away
And then there were nine.
Nine little blackbirds
On the garden gate.
One flew away
And then there were eight.
Eight little blackbirds looking up at heaven.
One flew away and then there were seven.
Seven little blackbirds picking up sticks.
One flew away and then there were six.
Six little blackbirds feeling quite alive.
One flew away and then there were five.
Five little blackbirds tapping at the door.
One flew away and then there were four.
Four little blackbirds happy as could be.

(continued next column)

(Tap side of the table with all ten fingers.)
(One finger curls under each time the number of blackbirds decreases.)

(continued)
One flew away and then there were three.
Three little blackbirds with nothing much to do.
One flew away and then there were two.
Two little blackbirds were having lots of fun.
One flew away and then there was one.
One little blackbird sitting all alone.
He flew away and then there were none!"

74. THIS IS THE CHURCH

Grades: Preschool to 6

English level: Low intermediate

Objectives: To enjoy a common American finger game and the English needed to talk about it

Materials needed: None

Preparation: None

This is the church,	*(Clasp hands with fingers "hiding" inside.)*
And this is the steeple.	*(Raise index fingers, forming a point.)*
Open the doors,	*(Move thumbs aside.)*
And see all the people.	*(Open hands slightly, wiggle the fingers.)*
Close the doors.	*(Return thumbs to closed position.)*
Where are the people?	*(Raise shoulders in puzzlement.)*
Open the doors.	*(Move thumbs aside.)*
There go the people.	*(Fingers "walk" away.)*

75. THE RAINY DAY SONG

Grades: Preschool to 6

English level: Low intermediate and up

Objectives: To cheer up a rainy day; to learn a common American song

Materials needed: None

It's raining, it's pouring.	*(Hands wave down to show rain.)*
The old man is snoring.	*(Hands under head as a pillow.)*
He bumped his head	*(Bump head in hand.)*
When he went to bed,	*(Hands under head; close eyes.)*
And he didn't get up the next morning.	*(Shake head "no.")*

76. I'M A LITTLE TEAPOT

Grades: K to 3

English level: Intermediate and up

Objectives: To learn a common song; to increase vocabulary

Materials needed: None

Presentation: Draw a teapot on the chalkboard. Teach the words *handle* and *spout*.

I'm a little teapot	*(Stand tall and proud.)*
Short and stout.	*(Pat head; pat hips.)*
Here is my handle;	*(Right hand on hip.)*

Here is my spout.	(Left hand forms spout.)
When I get all steamed up,	(Bounce in excitement.)
Then I shout.	
Just *tip* me over and	(Bend to the spout side.)
Pour me out.	
I'm a clever teapot	(Swell chest with pride.)
That is true.	
Just take a look at what I can do.	
I can change my handle	(Right hand becomes spout.)
And my spout.	(Left hand becomes handle.)
Just *tip* me over	(Bend over to the spout side.)
And pour me out!	

77. DO YOUR EARS HANG LOW?

Grades: 3 to 6

English level: Advanced

Objectives: To learn a silly song; to increase fluency and speed of speaking

Materials needed: None (optional: picture of a long-eared dog)

Presentation: Sing very slowly and deliberately. Each gesture should be carefully done.

Do your ears hang low?	(Hold hands at shoulders holding
Do they wobble to and fro?	imaginary floppy ears; flap hands.)
Can you tie them in a knot?	(Mime tying long ears.)
Can you tie 'em in a bow?	
Can you throw them over your	(Mime throwing ears over shoulder.)
shoulder	
Like a continental soldier?	(Salute.)
Do your ears hang low?	(Repeat first gesture.)

Sing the song again, at an increased pace. The third time should be very fast.

78. THE LITTLE BUS

Grades: K to 6

English level: Intermediate

Objectives: To learn a song; to increase vocabulary; to have fun acting out the song

Materials needed: None

Presentation: Students form a double line. One student at the front of the line is the driver. Several students will be the passengers waiting at a "station."

The wheels of the bus
  go round and round,
Round and round,
  round and round.
The wheels of the bus
  go round and round.
All on a rainy morning.
	(The driver mimes steering and leads the bus slowly around the room; the other students move their arms as wheels going around.)

The driver of the bus says,
  "Move on back,
Move on back, move on back."
The driver of the bus says,
  "Move on back."
All on a rainy morning.
	(The passengers "board the bus," and the driver waves his hand back; the other students wave their hands back too.)

The people on the bus
  go up and down,
Up and down, up and down.
The people on the bus
  go up and down.
All on a rainy morning.
	(Passengers bob up and down as the bus travels slowly.)

The horn on the bus says,
  "Beep, beep, beep,
Beep, beep, beep; beep, beep, beep."
The horn on the bus says,
  "Beep, beep, beep."
All on a rainy morning.
	(Students mime pressing horn.)

The windshield wipers go
  Swish swish swish,
Swish, swish, swish; swish, swish,
  swish.
The windshield wipers go
  Swish swish, swish.
All on a rainy morning.
	(Two hands imitating windshield wipers.)

79. WHO TOOK THE COOKIE?

Grades: Preschool to 2

English level: High beginner and up

Objectives: To learn a simple hand-clapping chant; to teach questions with *who*; to learn denials

Materials needed: None

Presentation: This is great after a milk and cookie snack. Teach the words *cookie, cookie jar.* Demonstrate *take, took.*

Group: Who took the cookie from the cookie jar?	*(Children clap in rhythm.)*
Leader: Bobbie took the cookie from the cookie jar.	*(Leader names a child.)*
Bobby: Who, me?	
Group: Yes, you.	
Bobby: Couldn't be.	*(Child denies it.)*
Group: Then who?	
Bobby: Dana took the cookie from the cookie jar.	*(Child names another child and chant continues.)*
Dana: Who me?	
(etc.)	

80. SUMMER IS HOT

Grades: K to 6

English level: Low intermediate and up

Objective: To enjoy a hand-clapping language game

Materials needed: None

Presentation: Say the rhyme as students listen:

Summer is hot.
Winter is cold.
I had a birthday,
And I'm (*nine*) years old.

Repeat the rhyme and add the hand movements, without partners.

Summer is hot.	*(Slap your lap, clap your hands, face palms front.)*
Winter is cold.	*(Repeat above.)*

I had a birthday,	*(Slap your lap, clap hands, right palm front.)*
And I'm *(nine)* years old.	*(Clap, left palm front, clap, both palms front.)*

(Practice this with students several times. Then show how it works with a partner.)

Summer is hot.	*(Hands slap lap, clap; slap other's hands.)*
Winter is cold.	*(Repeat.)*
I had a birthday,	*(Slap your lap, clap your hands, partners slap right hands.)*
And I'm *(nine)* years old.	*(Clap, slap left hands, clap, partners slap both hands.)*

81. PEASE PORRIDGE

This uses the same clapping pattern as the previous activity. Pease porridge = cereal.

Pease porridge hot.
Pease porridge cold.
Pease porridge in the pot
Nine days old.
Some like it hot.
Some like it cold.
Some like it in the pot
Nine days old.

82. ENGLISH HAS BEGUN

Grades: K to 3

English level: Beginner and up

Objective: To enjoy a hand-clapping language game

Materials needed: None

Presentation:

English has begun	*(Hands in lap, clap, lap.)*
When we're all done	*(Lap, clap, lap.)*
We'll say a little,	*(Lap, clap.)*

Play a little,   *(Lap, clap.)*
Have a little fun.   *(Lap, clap, lap.)*

83. MISS LUCY

Grades: 2 to 6

English level: Advanced

Objectives: To learn a hand-clapping or rope-jumping chant; to practice past-tense forms of verbs; to develop coordination

Materials needed: None or a jump rope

Presentation: Teach the following hand-slapping pattern before presenting the words to the activity:

1. Clap own hands
2. Slap right hands with partner
3. Clap own hands
4. Slap left hands with partner
5. Clap own hands
6. Slap both hands with partner
7. Clap own hands
8. Slap hands on lap

Then teach the words without the slapping. When the words are understood, you can say them as students slap hands with a partner. Repeat with:

Miss Lucy had a baby.
His name was Tiny Tim.
She put him in the bathtub
To see if he could swim.
He drank up all the water.
He ate up all the soap.
He tried to eat the bathtub,
But it wouldn't fit in his throat.
Miss Lucy called the doctor.
Miss Lucy called the nurse.
Miss Lucy called the lady
With the alligator purse.
"Mumps," said the doctor.
"Measles," said the nurse.

"Nothing," said the lady
With the alligator purse.
Miss Lucy thanked the doctor.
Miss Lucy thanked the nurse.
Miss Lucy hugged the lady
With the alligator purse.

JUMP ROPE GAMES

84. TEDDY BEAR

Grades: 1 and up

English level: Intermediate and up

Objectives: To learn American playground games and the English needed to talk about them; to learn command forms of verbs

Materials needed: Jump rope

Presentation: Two children turn the rope as a third jumps, performing the indicated actions:

Teddy Bear, Teddy Bear,
Turn around.
Teddy Bear, Teddy Bear,
Touch the ground.
Teddy Bear, Teddy Bear,
Show your shoe.
Teddy Bear, Teddy Bear,
That will do!
Teddy Bear, Teddy Bear,
Go upstairs
Teddy Bear, Teddy Bear,
Say your prayers.
Teddy Bear, Teddy Bear,
Switch off the light.
Teddy Bear, Teddy Bear,
Say good night! *(finish)*

85.   DOWN BY THE OCEAN

Grades: 1 and up

English level: Intermediate and up

Objectives: To learn American playground games and the English needed to talk about them; to learn the command forms of verbs

Materials needed: Jump rope

Presentation: Two children turn a rope as a third child jumps. At the question "How many spankings did he receive?" the turners begin to turn the rope very fast. Score is kept among the children as to the number achieved.

> Down by the ocean,
> Down by the sea,
> Johnnie broke a bottle and blamed it on me.
> I told Ma.
> Ma told Pa.
> Johnnie got a spanking.
> Ha, ha, ha.
> How many spankings did he recieve?
> One, two, three, four, etc.   *(jump fast, counting)*

BALL-BOUNCING GAMES

86. ABC BOUNCE

Grades: 2 and up

English level: Intermediate

Objectives: To learn a common ball-bouncing game; to increase vocabulary of American names, places (have a map available), objects

Materials needed: Good bouncing balls

Presentation: Teach the rhyme and elicit vocabulary that begins with the appropriate letters in each category. Then combine the rhyme with the bouncing of the ball. On the names of the person (husband or wife), place, and product sold, the child swings his or her leg over the ball. If the ball is missed, the turn is over. If the rhyme is completed, the player goes on to the next letter.

> *A,* my name is *Annie,*
>   and my husband's name is *Andy.*
> We come from *Alabama,*
>   and we sell *apples.*
> *B,* my name is _____,
>   and my husband's *(wife's)* name is _____.
> We come from _____,
>   and we sell_____s.
> *(etc.)*

87.   CATEGORIES BOUNCE

Grades: 2 to 6

English level: Intermediate

Objectives: To learn a game; to increase vocabulary in various categories

Materials needed: Ball for bouncing and chalk or tape to mark off squares

Preparation: Mark off and label squares as in the diagram (6, 8, or 10 squares) with the name of a category in it. Categories may be girls' names, boys' names, animals, toys, flowers, birds, countries, colors, cities, foods, cars, games, etc.

X→	GIRLS	BOYS	COLORS	COUNTRIES
	FLOWERS	FLAVORS	ANIMALS	STATES

Play: Player stands behind the line and rolls the ball into the first square. She steps into the square and stops the ball before it rolls out of the square. This square determines the category. She then bounces the ball and names one item in each square. Example: Girls' names: Jean, Mary, Beth, Christie, Jo Young, Mariko, Carmen, Yang-Li. If successful on the first category, the player continues to the second category, first rolling the ball into the second square, then walking to stop the ball before it leaves the square.

The difficulty of stopping the ball increases the farther along the player is. The player is *out* if the ball leaves the square before it is stopped or if she stops on a line, misses the ball, or cannot name an item in the required category.

SONGS

88.   OLD MACDONALD HAD A FARM

Grades: 1 and up

English level: Beginner and up

Objectives: To learn an American song; to reinforce animal vocabulary

Presentation: After learning animal vocabulary, this song is a lot of fun. You may sing it in unison or divide the students into two groups, the "here" group and the "there" group.

Old MacDonald had a farm,	*(Both groups sing.)*
Eee yi, eee yi, oh!	
And on this farm he had some cows,	
Eee yi, eee yi, oh!	
With a "moo, moo" here,	*(Only "here" group sings.)*
and a "moo, moo" there.	*(Only "there" group sings.)*
Here a "moo."	*("Here" group.)*
There a "moo."	*("There" group.)*
Everywhere a "moo, moo."	*(Both groups.)*
Old MacDonald had a farm,	
Eee yi, eee yi, oh!	

Repeat with:

dogs *(bow wow)*
chickens *(quack, quack)*
pigs *(oink, oink)*
cats *(meow, meow)*
turkeys *(gobble, gobble)*
sheep *(baa, baa)*
horses *(nay, nay)*
donkeys *(hee haw)*

89.   ARE YOU SLEEPING?

Grades: K and up

English level: High beginner and up

Objectives: To learn a common song; to learn to sing in a round (older children): to invent original words to the song to practice question forms

Presentation: Teach the words to the song, demonstrating and illustrating new vocabulary. On a subsequent day, divide class into two groups and sing as a round: Group one begins the song, and when the third line is reached, group two begins the song from the beginning while group one continues singing. Sing through twice.

Are you sleeping, are you sleeping,
Brother John, Brother John?
Morning bells are ringing.
Morning bells are ringing.
Ding, ding, dong,
Ding, ding, dong.

Follow up: When students are familiar with the song, demonstrate how intermediate and advanced students might make up their own words to the song. Students may work in pairs or groups and sing their creations to the class.

Examples:

Are you cooking,
Are you cooking,
Mother dear, Mother dear?
I am very hungry.
I am very hungry.
Yum, yum, yum,
Yum, yum, yum.

Are you thinking,
Are you thinking,
Boys and girls,
Boys and girls?
We will have a test soon.
We will have a test soon.
Oh, no, no!
Oh, no, no!

Seat Games and Chalkboard Activities

90. AT THE PLAYGROUND

Grades: 2 and up

English level: Beginner

Objectives: To learn the English and rules for a typical board game; to learn and practice names of objects found in a playground; to distinguish between singular and plural forms of nouns, using "a" with singular forms only

Materials needed: Playing "boards" for each student or group of students (students may play in groups of 2, 3, or 4); dice (enough for each group to have one die); marker (such as a coin, small eraser, tiny plastic animal or toy, etc.) for each student

Preparation: Photocopy the two pages of the game board; tape the two sheets together to make the complete game board

Presentation: Go over the words and directions in the game with the class so that the vocabulary is familiar. Have students work in pairs, moving seats if necessary.

Students shake the die. The one with the highest number goes first. Each then moves in turn the number shown on the die and follows any directions on the square he lands on.

All students in the group are to read the words in the squares as they land on them. Alternatively, they can make a sentence, "I see (trees, a water fountain, etc.)." The student who reaches OUT first wins. The group should play at least three times.

Circulate among the players to help with the reading, pronunciation, and understanding of the rules.

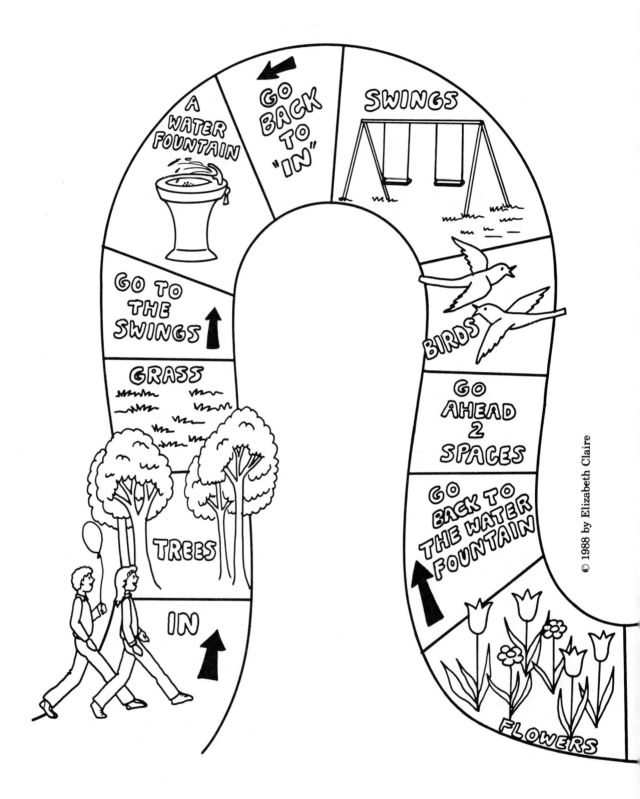

A SLIDE

GO BACK TO THE LAKE

A SEE SAW

A JUNGLE GYM

A BASEBALL FIELD

A LAKE

GO TO THE SLIDE

GO BACK 3 SPACES

2 PICNIC TABLES

2 BENCHES

GO TO THE SEE SAW

OUT

© 1988 by Elizabeth Claire

Sample conversation:

We are going to play a game.

The name of the game is At the Playground.

Here is the game.   *(tape a copy to the chalkboard)*

Look at the game.

What can you see in this game?   *(swings, seesaw, slide, grass, trees, children, benches, baseball field, picnic tables, lake, jungle gym, benches, water fountain, flowers)*

Let's read the words in the game.

Start here. This says IN.

We are going *into* the park.

Let's look at what we can see.

We see trees. We see grass.

Go to the swings.

When you land on "Go to the swings," where will you go?

Yes, here are the swings. Go here.

What's after "Go to the swings."   *(water fountain)*

After "water fountain" is "Go back to IN."

Where will you go if you land on "Go back to IN"?

Right, here.   *(show)*

What's next?   *(swings)*

Birds, go ahead two spaces.   *(demonstrate)*

Proceed in this manner until you reach the picnic area. The first person to reach OUT is the winner!

Choose a partner.

Move your seats.

You need only one game board.

Here are markers. Everyone will get one marker.

Put your marker on IN.

This is a die. I have many dice.

(Name), please give one die to each group.

Shake the die.

The number on top shows how many spaces to move.

(Name), shake the die. What number did you get?   *(number)*

Good. Now *(name)* will move her marker *(number)* spaces.   *(demonstrate on the game board you have taped up front)*

Where is she?   *(example: at a water fountain)*

Can you read this?

Everybody read the words together.

What does she have to do?

Make a sentence: "I see a water fountain."

(*Name*), shake your die. What number do you see?   *(example: five)*

(*demonstrate on the chalkboard*) Five. One, two, three, four, five. What is here? Go back to IN.

What does (*name*) have to do?   *(move her marker back to IN, etc.)*

When you finish the game, play again.

Follow up: Play the game succeeding days.

Play the game with other friends and family for homework.

Write sentences using the words in the squares. (Examples: I see trees. The trees are in the park, etc.)

91. LAST SUNDAY AT THE ZOO

Grades: 2 and up

English level: Low intermediate

Objectives: To learn the rules and vocabulary for playing a typical American children's board game; to review and reinforce the correct use of the past tense of regular and irregular verbs; to learn and practice names of animals; to practice reading

Materials needed: Dice or a spinner; markers (buttons or coins or tiny items from your shoe box collection)

Preparation: There are two separate playing boards for the game. The first board is the teaching and practicing board. The second is the challenge board. Make enough copies of the two pages for Board #1 and the two pages for Board #2 for each student. (Tape the two pages together to create a complete playing board.)

Presentations: Distribute Board #1 to the students. Beginning at START, read the sentences as the students listen and read along silently. Clarify all meanings through gestures or the pictures. Have individual students read the sentences.

To develop listening/reading recognition, read one sentence at random and have students tell the number of the sentence. Or read one sentence and students tell what happened next.

When students are familiar with the sentences, they may play the game in groups of two to five students.

Students take turns shaking the dice and moving their markers. As they land on a space, they must read the sentence and follow any directions on that space. Others may help. The first student to go home from the zoo wins.

Students may copy the sentences for reinforcement.

Play the game a number of times during class sessions, and assign the game for homework with friends or family.

BOARD 1

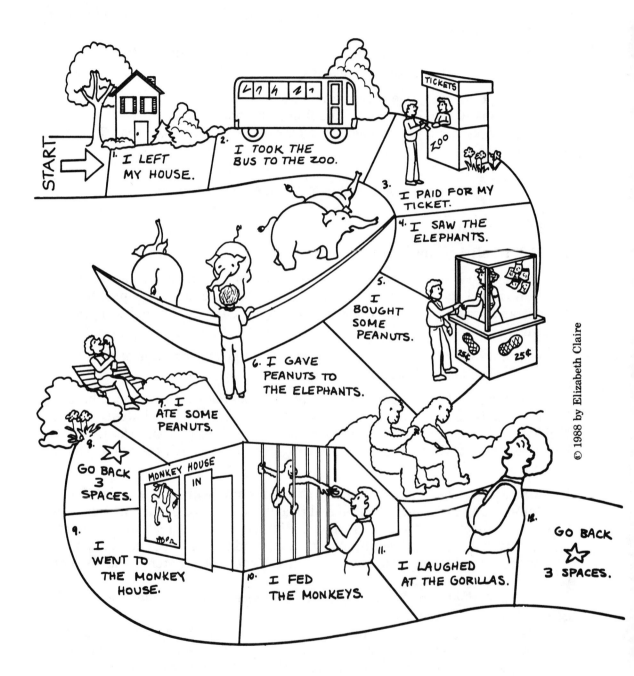

BOARD 1

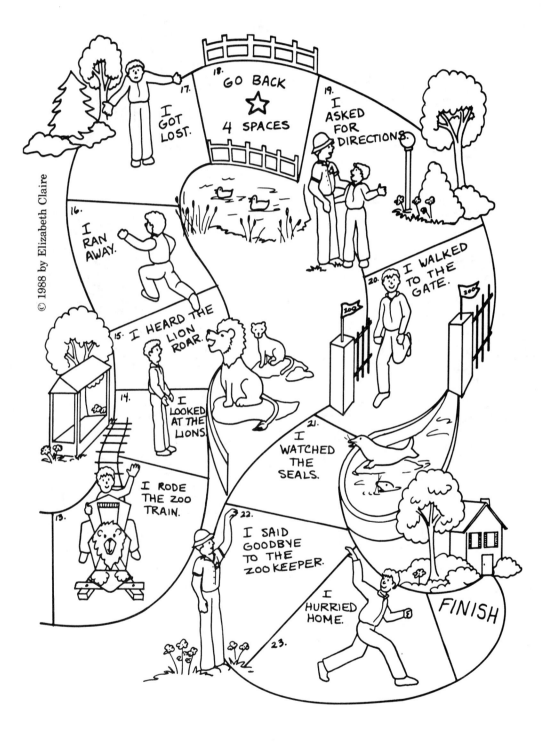

© 1988 by Elizabeth Claire

BOARD 2

START

1. LEAVE
2. TAKE A BUS
3. PAY
4. SEE
5. BUY
6. GIVE
7. EAT
8. GO BACK 3 SPACES
9. GO
10. FEED
11. LAUGH
12. GO AHEAD 4 SPACES.

TICKETS
ZOO
25¢ 25¢
MONKEY HOUSE
IN
ZOO

© 1988 by Elizabeth Claire

BOARD 2

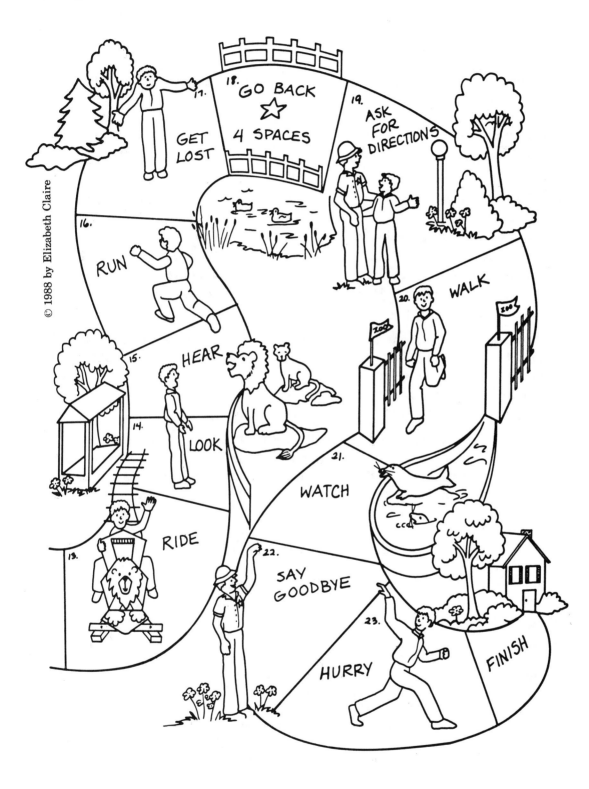

When you feel they are ready, distribute Board #2, which has only the basic form of the verbs. In this game, each student must construct the past tense sentence correctly. If the sentence is incorrect, the player must go back one space. One student may act as the referee by consulting the original board or the copied sentences.

Board #2 may also be used to practice other tenses: "Every Day at the Zoo." You may change from the first person to the third person singular, or other person; "Tomorrow at the Zoo," etc.

Examples:

Every day I leave my house. I take a bus to the zoo. I pay the cashier. I see the elephants.

Every day (*Billy*) leaves his house. He takes a bus. He pays the cashier. He sees the elephants.

Tomorrow I will leave my house. I'll take a bus. I'll pay the cashier.

Tomorrow, I'm going to leave my house. I'm going to take a bus.   *(etc.)*

When I was young, I used to leave my house. I used to take a bus.   *(etc.)*

Follow up: Write sentences for each square. Write two or three paragraphs about a trip to the zoo. Combine sentences. Add specific information and details to make the story interesting.

Example:

Last week, I went to the Fort Lee Zoo. I left my house early and took the Number 40 bus. When I got there, I paid the cashier two dollars to get in.

First I saw the elephants, so I bought some peanuts to give to them. Then I went to the monkey house and fed the monkeys. I laughed at the gorillas because they were so funny.

CHALKBOARD ACTIVITIES

92. LETTER DRILL

Grades: 1 and up

English level: Beginner

Objectives: To discriminate sounds and shapes of letters of the alphabet. This activity works both for practicing sound/symbol correspondences as well as practicing shaping the forms of the letters. It is useful for students whose native writing system does not employ the Latin alphabet, or who experience negative interference from a native alphabet that assigns different sounds to the letters, or whose native language does not have counterparts to certain English sounds. Examples: For Hispanics and many other groups—A, E, I, Y, B, V, C, S, Z, G, H, J; for many Asians—L, R, B, P, F, V.

Presentation: Send as many students as can fit at the board while the others write at their seats.

a	e	i	y	r

Draw a sample grid, as shown, with five columns. Choose letters on which students need aural recognition practice. A letter heads each column. Students copy this chart at the board or at their seats.

Dictate the letters at random. Students must write the letter in the correct column. Offer corrections as errors occur. Increase the speed as students become more accurate. The grid might look like this:

a	e	i	y	r
a	e	i	y	r
a	e	i	y	r
a	e		y	r
a			y	r
a			y	
			y	

Have students at the board erase their grid and write words as you dictate letters. Choose words already in the students' vocabulary. Examples: e-a-r, e-y-e, h-a-i-r, r-e-a-d, y-e-s, m-a-y-b-e, etc.

93. FOLLOW DIRECTIONS

Grades: 2 and up

English level: Beginner

Objectives: To practice and reinforce letter/sound correspondence; to practice spelling simple familiar words

Presentation: Send students to the board. Allow them to copy each other's work as in a Total Physical Response drill. Other students work at their seats. Check each performance immediately and circulate to check seated students' work. Spell out words for students who cannot spell them. When the board is filled, students erase the board and go to their seats while seated students take a turn at the board.

Write your name.

Write your last name.

Draw a line under your name.

Draw a line under your last name.

Write *book.*

Write *pen.*

Write *boy.*

Draw a line under *boy.*

Draw a line under *book.*

Draw a line under *pen.*

Continue, using simple familiar words (act out meaning if necessary). Add *over, on, next to,* and *draw a circle around.*

yes	no	go	man
woman	girl	chair	table
desk	flag	door	day
hi	hello	good	bad
is	am	I	you
me	my	name	paper
walk	run	sit	play

94. FIND IT FAST

Grades: 2 and up

English level: Beginner

Objective: To reinforce reading of familiar vocabulary words

Play: The chalkboard is divided into two sections. A list of fifteen to twenty words is written in the first section, and the same words in a different order are written in the second section. (Choose words you wish to review or reinforce.)

Divide the class into two teams. The first person in each team goes to the board, and you announce one of the words. The students must find the word and circle it. The first one to find the word earns a point for his team. Other students may help their teammates by directing them to "look up, look down, look under

_____, look in the left column, look in the right column, that's right!" *(etc.)* They may not use their native language during the game.

Presentation and sample conversation:

> We are going to play a game called Find It Fast.
> There are fifteen words here on the chalkboard.
> There are fifteen words here.
> These are the same words, but they are mixed up.
> We will have two teams.
> This side of the room will be on Team One.
> And this side of the room will be on Team Two.
> One person from each team will come up to the board.
> You have to find the word that I say.
> When you find it, draw a circle around it.
> The first person to draw a circle around the right word gets a point for his team.
> This game is to help you practice English.
> You can help your team if you use English.
> If you use your language, your team loses a point.
> Then the next person goes to the chalkboard.

Follow up: Copy one list of words.

95. THE DISAPPEARING ACT

Grades: 2 and up

English level: Beginner, intermediate, advanced

Objectives: To aid in memorizing grammar or spelling rules, word order, lines of poetry or dialog

Presentation: This is a useful technique whenever you have an item that you want students to memorize. Write the entire piece on the board. Read it to the class and have several students read it individually and the class read it in chorus.

Example:

> A noun is the name of a person, place, or thing.

Erase two words in the sentence and leave blanks in their place:

> A noun is the _____ of a person, place, or _____.

Ask a volunteer to read it and supply the missing words. Erase two more words.

> A noun _____ the _____ of a _____, place, or _____.

Continue until the class can "read" the sentence from the board even though it's no longer there!

96. HANGMAN

Grades: 2 and up

English level: Beginner and up

Objectives: To learn a common game and the English needed to talk about it; to practice vocabulary recognition, spelling, letter sounds, and word patterns

Materials needed: Chalkboard and chalk or paper and pencil

Play: The "hangman" chooses a secret word (this is best taken from the students' known vocabulary list). The hangman checks spelling with you or copies it from the book. She writes a dash for each letter in the word on the board. Students take turns guessing the missing letters. As a letter is guessed correctly, it is written in the proper dash. If a letter is guessed and it does not appear in the word, the hangman adds a part of the body to the person being hanged.

If the class guesses the word before the man is hanged, the class wins, and a new hangman is chosen. If the man is hanged before the word is guessed, the hangman wins and goes again.

Presentation and sample conversation: Draw a scaffold on the chalkboard. Then show the class the steps in hanging a man from the scaffold.

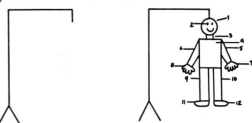

We are going to play a game called Hangman.

I am the hangman.

This is the hanging place.

I am hanging a man.

First I draw the man's head.

Then I draw his *eyes, nose,* and *mouth.*

(Let class supply the names of the things as you draw them.)

Next his *neck,* then his *body,* then one *arm,* the other *arm,* his *hand* and *fingers,* his other *hand* and *fingers,* one *leg,* the other *leg,* one *foot,* and the last *foot.* Now he's dead.

(Erase the board.)

I am thinking of a word.

It has ten letters, so I will write ten blanks. One, two, three (etc.).

Guess a letter in this word.

(Student guesses a letter; for example "d.")
(Write the letter on the appropriate dash.)

Good. There is a *d* in this word.

__ __ __ __ __ __ __ __ __ <u>d</u>

Guess another letter.	(Student guesses, perhaps an "n.")
No good. There is no *n* in this word.	*(Continue until word is guessed or man is*
So I will draw the head.	*hanged.)*

97. WHAT BEGINS WITH *B*?

Grades: 2 and up

English level: High beginner and up

Objectives: To reinforce vocabulary, spelling, concentration skills, cooperation between students

Materials needed: Paper and pencil

Preparation: None

Presentation: This is a great warm-up activity or it can be used to fill in several minutes between other subjects. If desired, students may work in pairs or groups of three, choosing one person to write the words the others tell.

"How many things in this room begin with the letter *b?*" (Students offer boy, book, bookcase, blouse, etc.)

"Now let's see how many words you can find that begin with *c* in three minutes. Write them down." (The winning team can line up first for lunch, erase the board, or have some other privilege.) Have students write the best they can, without asking you for spelling assistance.

At the end of the time, the group with the lowest number of items gives their list first. You can write the words on the chalkboard so all can check spelling.

In addition to "words that begin with _____" other categories may be "things that are (red, flavors, fruits, vegetables, birds)."

CARD GAMES

Card games are ideal for supplying the great amount of repetition needed to reinforce specific vocabulary and the structures of a new language. The game rules are simple; play is highly motivating and allows for peer tutoring.

To make cards that will last through many playings over the years:

1. Make three or four copies of the accompanying grid for each game.
2. Type or print the words in half of the squares. Make simple line drawings of the items to match the words in the other half of the squares.
3. Photocopy your master sheet onto sturdy oaktag sheets. You can make more than one set at a time this way. (Take them to a printer if your school copier cannot handle oaktag.)
4. Scribble with a marker on the backs of the oaktag, using a different-colored marker for each different set of cards. This way you can make

several separate games, and you or your students will quickly be able to sort the games if they happen to get mixed up.

5. Laminate the entire sheet or cover at least the picture/word side with clear self-stick vinyl.

6. Cut the sheet along the lines.

Keep all cards in any one game fastened with a rubber band. The color-coded scribbling on the back will help you quickly separate cards when games get mixed together.

Alternative: Make games on 3 × 5 cards. Cut them widthwise for word/picture matching games and lengthwise for question/answer matching games.

If your own artwork leaves something to be desired, give this project to a talented parent volunteer or older student.

98. MATCHING GAMES

Grades: 1 and up, depending on the individual game

English level: Beginner; intermediate

Objectives: To provide extensive reinforcement for vocabulary, spelling, and structures; to learn a common game and the English for playing it

Materials needed: 16 or more pairs of cards for each set, matching any of these pairs:

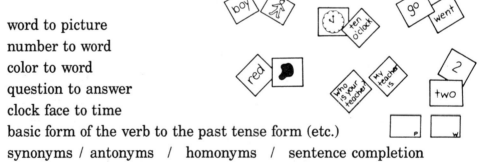

word to picture
number to word
color to word
question to answer
clock face to time
basic form of the verb to the past tense form (etc.)
synonyms / antonyms / homonyms / sentence completion

On the back of each card, you might write a code letter. Example: W = word, P = picture, Q = question, A = answer, C = color, N = number, B = basic form of the verb, PT = past tense form, etc.

Play: Present the word/picture matches to the group, having them pronounce the words as they look at the picture.

Game One—SCRAMBLE: For one or more players: Place all of the cards face up in front of the players. Mix the pairs thoroughly. At the word "go," students

pull out matching pairs and place them in front of them. When all the cards are in pairs, check to see that they are correctly matched. Students read the words from their pairs of cards. The student with the most pairs wins. If there is only one player, he plays against the clock, attempting to better his previous time.

Sample conversation:

> This game is called Scramble.
>
> Some cards have pictures, and some cards have words.
>
> These cards are in pairs. This word goes with this picture.   *(demonstrate several or all if the words are new)*
>
> First mix up all the cards.
>
> Put them on the table, face up.   *(demonstrate)*
>
> You have to find the picture and the word that go together.
>
> Look at the clock.
>
> See how fast you can find all the pairs.
>
> Find pairs. The one who has the most pairs wins.

Game Two—CONCENTRATION: Place the cards in rows in front of the players. Separate the cards into the two categories, using the letter codes on the back.

Student One picks up one card, turns it over in place, and says the name of the picture or reads the word. He then tries to find a matching card from the other group. He turns over another card, says the name or reads the word, and if it is a matching pair, keeps the two cards. He gets one extra turn. If the cards do not match, they are turned over in the same place they were found and the player to the left begins his turn.

The player who has the most pairs of cards at the end of the game wins.

The point of the game is to ensure that the least proficient student learns the names of all the vocabulary items and is able to read the words, so it is important that all participate by reading and saying the words as they are played.

Sample conversation:

> This game is called Concentration.
>
> The words have the letter *w* on the back.
>
> The pictures have the letter *p* on the back.
>
> Turn over one picture card.
>
> Say the name of the picture.
>
> Now you have to find the word that matches.
>
> Turn over a word card.
>
> Read the word.
>
> Do the cards match?

They don't match.
Turn the cards face down.
It's your turn.
Turn over a picture card.   *(etc.)*
They match!
You have a pair.
Keep the pair.
Each pair is one point.
You go one more time.
Count your pairs.
How many pairs do you have?
Who has the most pairs?
(Name) has the most pairs.
(Name) is the winner.
Can you read all yours pairs?
Play it again.
This time, *(name)* goes first.

Word lists:

1. <u>Things to wear</u>	2. <u>Things to wear</u>	3. <u>Fruits</u>	4. <u>Vegetables</u>
hat	belt	banana	beets
coat	jacket	apple	carrots
dress	mittens	pear	onions
shoes	boots	cherries	celery
socks	scarf	grapes	cabbage
shirt	slippers	pineapple	corn
skirt	pajamas	orange	potatoes
pants	bathrobe	lemon	peas
gloves	sneakers	peach	green beans
bag	jeans	watermelon	tomatoes
glasses	ring		lettuce
tie	necklace		
suit	watch		
sweater	stockings		
shorts	vest		
blouse	T-shirt		

5. Animals
   - bird
   - dog
   - cat
   - horse
   - cow
   - sheep
   - goat
   - snake
   - monkey
   - lion
   - tiger
   - elephant
   - skunk
   - deer
   - seal

6. Animals
   - turtle
   - rabbit
   - mouse
   - pig
   - parrot
   - donkey
   - giraffe
   - alligator
   - frog
   - chicken
   - duck
   - goose
   - raccoon
   - owl
   - squirrel

7. Classroom
   - teacher
   - door
   - window
   - chalkboard
   - book
   - pen
   - pencil
   - notebook
   - eraser
   - chair
   - desk
   - table
   - map
   - clock
   - crayons

8. Body
   - eye
   - nose
   - mouth
   - hair
   - hand
   - foot
   - neck
   - shoulder
   - arm
   - leg
   - foot
   - fingers
   - toes
   - knee
   - elbow
   - eyelash

9. Body
   - eyebrow
   - thumb
   - cheek
   - chin
   - waist
   - wrist
   - ear
   - mustache
   - beard
   - ankle
   - heel
   - back

10. Furniture
    - chair
    - table
    - sofa
    - picture
    - bed
    - dresser
    - toilet
    - sink
    - bathtub
    - shower
    - refrigerator
    - stove
    - closet
    - mirror
    - arm chair
    - rug

11. Transportation
    - car
    - bus
    - train
    - bicycle
    - sailboat
    - ship
    - motorcycle
    - jet
    - rocket
    - truck
    - van
    - helicopter
    - canoe
    - raft
    - rollerskates

12. Communication
    stereo
    radio
    telephone
    television
    letter
    tape recorder
    newspaper
    book
    record
    movie
    microphone

13. Colors
    red
    blue
    green
    purple
    orange
    yellow
    brown
    black
    gray
    pink

14. Numbers
    one
    two
    three
    fifty-five
    etc.

15. Times
    one o'clock
    two thirty
    three forty-
       five
    etc.

16. Verbs
    go/went
    come/came
    do/did
    have/has
    eat/ate
    get/got
    have/had
    lose/lost
    make/made
    read/read
    see/saw
    win/won
    bite/bit
    forget/forgot
    hide/hid
    hear/heard

17. Verbs
    break/broke
    speak/spoke
    drive/drove
    ride/rode
    choose/chose
    steal/stole
    tear/tore
    wake/work
    wear/wore
    tell/told
    sell/sold
    blow/blew
    draw/drew
    fly/flew
    grow/grew
    know/knew
    throw/threw

18. Verbs
    buy/bought
    bring/brought
    fight/fought
    think/thought
    catch/caught
    teach/taught
    keep/kept
    sleep/slept
    sweep/swept
    weep/wept
    feel/felt
    creep/crept
    fall/fell
    feed/fed
    meet/met
    leave/left
    hold/held

19. Verbs
    bend/bent
    build/built
    lend/lent
    spend/spent
    begin/began
    drink/drank
    ring/rang
    run/ran
    sing/sang
    sink/sank
    sit/sat
    stink/stank
    swim/swam
    shake/shook
    stand/stood
    take/took
    understand/
       understood

20. Verbs
    lay/laid
    lie/lay
    pay/paid
    say/said

    find/found
    grind/ground
    wind/wound
    beat/beat

    cut/cut
    hit/hit
    hurt/hurt
    beat/beat

    put/put
    set/set
    shut/shut
    burst/burst

21. <u>Questions/Answers</u>

What's your name?	My name is (Joe).
What's your last name?	My last name is (Lee).
Where are you from?	I'm from (Peru).
How are you?	I'm fine, thank you.
How old are you?	I'm (eleven) years old.
What day is today?	Today is (Friday).
What time is it?	It's (two) o'clock.
Where do you live?	I live at (321 Main Street).
Do you speak English?	Yes, I speak a little English.
What school do you got to?	I go to (Roosevelt) school.
When is your birthday?	My birthday is (May 6).
What is this?	This is a (hat).

22. <u>Complete the Sentences</u>

Today is_____	Thursday.
I see with_____	my eyes.
I hear with_____	my ears.
I smell with_____	my nose.
I taste with_____	my tongue.
I can cut with_____	scissors.
I can write with_____	a pencil.
I can speak_____	English.
I can ride_____	my bicycle.
Where is the_____	office?
What time_____	is it?
How are_____	you?
I like to_____	read.
There are seven days_____	in a week.
My teacher's name is_____	Mrs. Lee.
The grass is_____	green.
May I have an apple,_____	please?
Open the_____	window, please.

23. <u>Abbreviations</u>
    (See Bingo in this chapter.)

24. <u>Synonyms</u>
    (See Bingo in this chapter.)

25. <u>Antonyms</u>
    (See Bingo in this chapter.)

99A. GO GET IT

Grades: 2 and up

English level: Beginner and intermediate

Objectives: To learn the rules for a common game and the English for playing that game; to reinforce the following structures:

Do you have any _____s?

Yes, I have (two, three) _____s.

No, I don't have any _____s.

Materials needed: Either 3 × 5 cards cut in half widthwise or a photocopy on oaktag of the grid given at the beginning of this section

Preparation: Create twelve sets of four "books" (matching pictures). Write the word under the picture. Laminate the cards if desired, then cut.

Choose from these easy-to-picture sample words or items you want to practice:

penny	flag	book	dog
telephone	banana	hat	house
shoe	window	cat	basket
box	pen	ruler	cup
radio	spoon	nickel	dollar
flower	picture	fish	comb
sock	bed	chair	table
paper	tree	star	window
boat	car	ball	apple

To practice distinguishing when to use *a, an,* and *some,* create sets of cards with the following items:

Do you have a/an/some _____(s)?

Yes, I have a/an/some _____(s).

No, I don't have any _____s.

egg	airplane	ice cream cone	umbrella
elephant	eraser	orange	insect
alligator	igloo	ear	eye
old hat	ugly mask	American flag	empty glass
apple	grapes	cherries	strawberries
cookies	bananas	peanuts	raisins

To practice *a pair of,* create sets of cards with the following items:

Do you have a pair of _____?

Yes, I have a pair of _____.

No, I don't have a pair of _____.

a pair of pants	a pair of shoes
a pair of socks	a pair of mittens
a pair of boots	a pair of gloves
a pair of glasses	a pair of scissors
a pair of twins	a pair of dice
a pair of tights	a pair of curtains

Play: Two, three, or four students may play. Deal five cards per player unless there are only two players; in which case, seven cards each. The rest of the deck is placed face down in the center of the table.

The object of the game is to complete as many "books" (four matching cards) as possible.

The player to the dealer's left goes first. This player names another player and asks, "(Name), do you have any _____s?" The player asking *must* have at least one of the cards asked for.

If the other player has any of the requested cards, she hands them all over, saying, "Yes, I have a (two, three) _____(s)."

If she does not have any of that card, she answers, "Go get it." The asker must take the top card from the deck in the center of the table.

If the asker receives the card asked for, he goes again. He may ask another person for the same card or the same person for a different card.

If told to "go get it" and the card picked from the deck is the card asked for, he goes again. The turn ends when he is not successful in getting the card asked for. The next person to the left goes.

As soon as a player has all four cards of one object (a "book"), the book is laid down on the table in front of the player. The one who gets the most books wins the game.

If when laying down a book a player uses up all the cards in his hands, he may draw one card from the deck to continue being in the game. When the deck is used up, players with cards left in their hands continue in turn to ask others for cards until all books are complete.

Presentation and sample conversation: Gather students around a table. If all cannot sit, some stand behind the seated players.

We are going to play a card game.

This game is called Go Get It.

This is the deck.   *(show cards)*

There are four cards that match.   *(show four)*

Four cards with the same picture make one book.

In this deck we have (*pennies, cats, hats, flags—etc.*).   *(show cards)*

First we will practice the game.

(Deal each seated student and yourself five cards face up. For this practice round, these cards should be visible to everyone.)

Look at my cards. I have two houses. I want to get four houses.

(*Name—someone who has houses*), do you have any houses?   *(yes)*

Say, "I have a house," and give me the house.

Thank you. I go again.

(*Another name*), do you have any houses?

Yes, I have a house.

Thank you. Now I have four houses. This is a "book." I will put it on the table in front of me.

Look at my cards. I have a *shoe* and a *box*.

(*Name—someone who does not have a shoe*), do you have any shoes?   *(no)*

Say, "I don't have any shoes. Go get it!"

(*Name*) doesn't have any shoes. I have to take a card from the deck.   *(take the top card)*

Is this a shoe?

No, it isn't a shoe. My turn is finished.

Now (*player on left*) goes.

Let's all practice the question: "Do you have any_____s?"

(Have students repeat this about eight times, using a different card as a cue for the last word to be substituted in the question.)

Practice the answers:

No, I don't have any _____. (*eight examples*)

Yes, I have a _____. (*eight examples*)

Now we are ready to play.

Five people can play at this table. Everyone else will watch them play. Then you will play at that table.

(*Name*), shuffle the deck.

(*Name*) is shuffling the deck.

(*Name*), you can be the dealer.

Give each person one card at a time. Everyone gets five (*seven*) cards.

Look at your cards.   *Don't show anyone your cards.*

(*Name*) is dealing the cards. She is the dealer.

Count your cards. Does everyone have five cards?

Hold your cards carefully. Don't let anyone see your cards.

Don't look at someone else's cards.

(*Name*), you go first. Look at your cards.

Ask someone for the cards you want.

(*Name*), give him the card(s).

Set up the other groups of students and help each group get started playing. Circulate among the players, assisting with the correct structures and pronunciation as needed.

99B. GO GET IT

(Present continuous tense practice)
Grades: 2 to adult

English level: High beginner

Objectives: To reinforce present continuous tense; to contrast a/an; to learn idiomatic structures; to practice reading

Materials needed: For each set of players, 48 cards made up of 12 sets or books

Preparation: Photocopy the four pages that follow (pages 125-128) onto oaktag. (You can make three or four sets, depending on the number of students in your classes.) Cut them carefully and secure each set with a rubber band.

Play: Distribute five cards to each player. The object of the game is to complete "books" of cards, consisting of the four cards in a set. The remainder of the cards go face down in a draw pile in the center of the table.

The first student selects a card with which he wishes to complete a book. He states the name of any other player in the group and asks the question: "What (or where) are you (verb)ing?"

If that player has a card with the same question, she answers the question with the complete sentence: "I am (verb)ing_____," using the picture on her card. If she has more than one card in the set, she must read the sentence for each card and hand them over to the first player. The first player may then go again, asking the same player another question or asking another player any question.

If the player asked does not have any card of the set, she says, "Go get it," and the asker must pick up a card from the draw pile. If he draws an answer to his question, he may go again. If not, play goes to the player on the left of the first player. If a player makes books and runs out of cards, he may pick up a card from the deck. If the draw pile is exhausted before all books are made, players with cards continue to ask for cards until all cards are matched in books.

Presentation: Play this version of the game after students are familiar with the simpler version. Circulate the room to be sure players are reading complete sentences and pronouncing carefully.

What are you riding?	What are you riding?	What are you riding?	What are you riding?
I am riding a horse.	I am riding a bike.	I am riding a motorcycle.	I am riding an elephant.
What are you drinking?	What are you drinking?	What are you drinking?	What are you drinking?
I am drinking milk.	I am drinking juice.	I am drinking tea.	I am drinking water.
What are you washing?	What are you washing?	What are you washing?	What are you washing?
I am washing my feet.	I am washing the floor.	I am washing my face.	I am washing my socks.

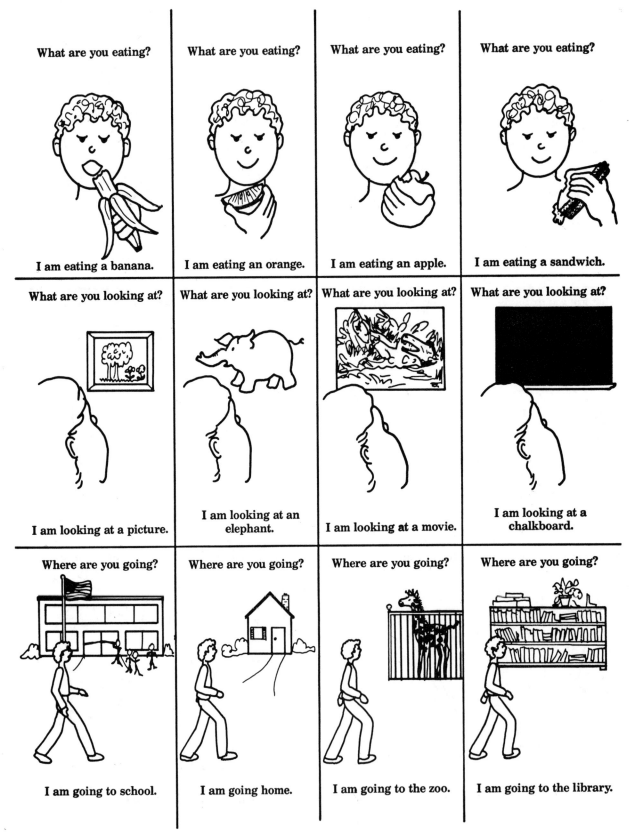

What are you eating?

I am eating a banana.

What are you eating?

I am eating an orange.

What are you eating?

I am eating an apple.

What are you eating?

I am eating a sandwich.

What are you looking at?

I am looking at a picture.

What are you looking at?

I am looking at an elephant.

What are you looking at?

I am looking at a movie.

What are you looking at?

I am looking at a chalkboard.

Where are you going?

I am going to school.

Where are you going?

I am going home.

Where are you going?

I am going to the zoo.

Where are you going?

I am going to the library.

What are you playing?

I am playing hopscotch.

What are you playing?

I am playing baseball.

What are you playing?

I am playing tag.

What are you playing?

I am playing checkers.

What are you making?

I am making a house.

What are you making?

I am making a sweater.

What are you making?

I am making a kite.

What are you making?

I am making a doll.

What are you reading?

I am reading a book.

What are you reading?

I am reading a magazine.

What are you reading?

I am reading a newspaper.

What are you reading?

I am reading a dictionary.

What are you wearing?	What are you wearing?	What are you wearing?	What are you wearing?
I am wearing new shoes.	I am wearing a new hat.	I am wearing a new coat.	I am wearing a new jacket.

What are you fixing?	What are you fixing?	What are you fixing?	What are you fixing?
I am fixing my bicycle.	I am fixing a toy.	I am fixing the telephone.	I am fixing a doll.

What are you writing?	What are you writing?	What are you writing?	What are you writing?
ABCDEFG HIJKLM	JANE		1234 5
I am writing the alphabet.	I am writing my name.	I am writing a letter.	I am writing numbers.

100. STAY AWAKE

Grades: K to 6

English level: Beginner

Objectives: To learn a fast-moving card game; to match similar cards; to learn the English needed to play and talk about the game

Materials needed: Ordinary deck of playing cards (one deck per thirteen students)

Preparation: For each child playing, one set of four matching cards is needed. The game is best for four to seven players, so you may have two or three games going on simultaneously if you have a large class. Up to thirteen may play in one group if you have a large enough table, or players may sit in a circle on the floor.

Play: The object of the game is to avoid being the "sleeper." The sleeper is the player who is the last to notice that play has stopped. Children sit around a table. Four cards are dealt to each player. Players look at their cards. They must try to get all four cards of the same number or face. They select one card to discard, lay it face down on the table to their right, and on the signal "pass" from the dealer, everyone simultaneously passes their discard to the player on their right and picks up the card given to them by the player on their left. Each player looks at the cards and either keeps it or uses it as the new discard.

When a player has four matching cards, she quietly lays the cards down in front of herself and puts her finger to her nose. Other players who notice this also quietly put their cards down and place their fingers on their nose. The last player to notice the fingers on the noses is the sleeper.

Score may be kept for a series of rounds. The first time the player is last, he gets the letter *s* after his name. The second time it happens, the letter *l* is written, and so forth. The first person to have the word *sleeper* spelled out is the sleeper and must perform some consequence that can be decided in advance (sing a song, put the cards away, or some other *mild,* good-natured consequence; avoid having the consequence humiliate the loser).

This may also be played as "Three Strikes—You're Out," taking a shorter time to determine the loser.

Presentation and sample conversation:

> We are going to play a card game called Stay Awake.
> Everyone will get four cards.
> You must get all four cards the same.
> Four aces, four queens, four jacks, four tens, or four of anything.
> Take a card that you don't want and pass it to the next person.
> Pick up the card that the other person gave to you.
> If you have four cards the same, quietly put your cards down and put your finger on your nose.

Don't say anything.

If you see someone with his finger on his nose, quietly put your cards down and put your finger on your nose.

The last person is the sleeper.

We will write all the names down.

If you are the last person, first we will write the letter *s* after your name.

The next time, you will get a letter *l*.

(etc.)

Follow up: Write about the game.

Draw a picture of the class playing the game.

Explain the game to others.

101. BINGO

What do you do when some of the students in your class can read and others are still at the bare letter-recognition stage? Play Bingo. When some kids know most of the new vocabulary and some have just arrived? Play Bingo. It's the day before a holiday and the students want a party but you want instruction going on? It's Bingo time. You'd like a painless way to introduce or reinforce important vocabulary? Bingo!

Bingo has long been a useful device of elementary and language teachers. Take advantage of the high enthusiasm and attention to reading that this fast-moving game stimulates.

Use Bingo to practice: alphabet, numbers, vocabulary, spelling words, holiday and seasonal words, map words, past tense forms of verbs, superlative forms of adjectives, synonyms, antonyms, questions and answers. (See examples at end.)

Grades: 1 through adult

English level: Beginning through advanced

Objectives: To introduce or reinforce any of the following: match symbol with symbol and sound with symbol; to recognize words; to familiarize vocabulary and spelling; to practice noun, verb, and adjective inflections; to sharpen listening and thinking skills

Materials needed: Bingo "card" for each student; markers to cover the squares; large bag to store the markers in; 24 blank flashcards (or cut oaktag into 2 × 8 strips); rubber band (optional: Funtak® or thumb tacks); prizes: stickers, small erasers, pencils, candy, balloons, stars, privileges, recycled garage-sale items, etc.

Preparation: Make enough copies of the blank Bingo card for each child in your class. Photocopy it or trace onto a spirit duplicating master. You'll find that you'll use Bingo blanks several times during the year, so you might as well make a whole bunch while you're at it.

Prepare a list of twenty-four items that you want to reinforce. With magic markers, print each word on a flashcard large enough to be seen from the back of the room.

Cut colored construction paper into small squares until you have more than enough for your students for the year, allowing for loss. Ten 9 × 12 sheets cut in roughly one-inch squares will yield more than 1000 markers, enough for forty players. Use a paper cutter if available or have your students cut papers first into strips, then into squares.

Store markers in a large plastic bag or box. Prepare a folder to store Bingo cards in. Keep sets of flashcards together with a rubber band.

Write the words or items to be used on the chalkboard. Distribute the blank Bingo cards. Demonstrate how to copy the words, one in each square, in a random fashion so everyone's card will be different. Check as they do this. When all have completed entering their words on their cards, erase the board.

For first graders, you might prepare their Bingo cards for them. Or have older, more advanced students or American student volunteers prepare cards for them.

Play: Distribute the markers. Shuffle the flashcards and place them face down in front of the caller. Students place a marker over the free space in the center. You or the caller pick up the first card, show it to the class, and read it. Tack the card to the bulletin board or Funtak® it to the chalkboard for reference.

When a student covers five words in a straight line—horizontally, vertically, or diagonally—he calls out "Bingo!" and wins whatever prize is given.

The winner reads back the words that were covered, and the class checks them against the flashcards posted on the board or bulletin board.

You may decide to continue calling words until there are two, three, or four winners, especially for younger children who will enjoy the game more if there are more chances to win.

Increasing progressions of difficulty: With the same set of words, each game may be played with more and more challenge:

1. Show the word, read it, and post it, allowing students to match letter for letter. Abler students may assist beginners.
2. Show the word; students read it.

B I N G O

		FREE ☺		

3. Read the word, give the spelling of it, but don't show it.
4. Read the word but don't show or spell it.
5. Point to the real object or show a picture; students must think of the word and cover it.
6. Describe the object without saying it. Students must guess what it is and cover it. Make descriptions complete and unambiguous, so there will be only one possible answer.

Vocabulary variations:

1. Prepare flashcards with the basic forms of verbs; students' cards contain the past tense forms.
2. Call the basic forms of adjectives; students' cards contain the superlatives.
3. Call the singular forms of nouns; students' cards contain the plural forms.
4. Call words; students' cards contain synonyms.
5. Call words; students' cards contain antonyms.
6. Call states; students' cards contain capitals.
7. Call words; students' cards contain abbreviations for the words.
8. Students must cover a word that rhymes with the word called.
9. Questions are on the flashcards; students must cover answers on their cards.

Bingo word categories suggestions

alphabet

numbers

parts of the body

objects in school

names of school personnel

food

animals

money amounts

content area vocabulary

solar system

states

occupations

furniture

weather words

clothing

school places and subjects

times

weather words

holiday words

Synonyms

small, tiny, little

good, nice

bad, awful

large, big, huge

old, ancient

see, observe

see, observe

slender, thin, lean, skinny

try, attempt

male, man

curtain, drape

scent, smell

weary, tired

sad, unhappy

glad, happy, content, joyful

strong, healthy, well

ill, sick

false, untrue

chubby, fat

wide, broad

rush, hurry

female, woman, lady

correct, right

wrong, incorrect

delicious, tasty

messy, sloppy

evening, twilight, sunset

dawn, morning, daybreak

cup, mug

make-believe, fiction

Antonyms

big, little

small, large

old, young

old, new

good, bad

yes, no

up, down

day, night

yesterday, tomorrow

brother, sister

white, black

far, near

close, open

give, take

high, low

cheap, expensive

interesting, boring

fast, slow

smart, stupid

beautiful, ugly

happy, sad

healthy, sick

come, go

arrive, leave

in, out

rain, sunshine

fresh, stale

raw, cooked

clean, dirty

neat, messy

work, play

hungry, full

hot, cold

winter, summer

solid, liquid

Abbreviations

Sunday, Sun.; Monday, Mon.; etc.

January, Jan.; February, Feb.; etc.

Street, St.

Road, Rd.

yard, yd.

tablespoon, Tbs.

teaspoon, tsp.

Mister, Mr.

Avenue, Ave.

New Jersey, NJ; New York, NY; etc.

first, 1st; second, 2nd; etc.

quart, qt.

pint, pt.

gallon, gal.

pound, lb.

ounce, oz.

gram, gm.

milligram, mg.

kilogram, kg.

centimeter, c.

cubic centimeter, cc.

kilometer, km.

inch, in.

foot, ft.

Doctor, Dr.

Reverend, Rev.

Director, Dir.

Professor, Prof.

Number, No., #

Post Office, P.O.

Attention, Attn.

telephone, tel.

Fahrenheit, F.

Centigrade, C.

college, coll., C.

university, U.

English as a Second Language, E.S.L.

English, Eng.

United States of America, U.S.A.

Holidays

New Year's Day

Christmas

Hanukkah

St. Valentine's Day

Martin Luther King's Birthday

Easter

Passover

Independence Day

Mother's Day

Father's Day

St. Patrick's Day

Flag Day

Columbus Day

Veteran's Day

Thanksgiving

Halloween

Election Day

Groundhog Day

George Washington's Birthday

Abraham Lincoln's Birthday

Definitions

A day of the week

A month of the year

A girl's name

A boy's name

A subject in school

A color

an animal

a number

Friday

January

Sally

Brian

science

blue

tiger

seven

something to eat	apple
something to write with	pen
something to read	book
something to wash with	soap
a part of the face	eye
something to wear	jacket
something to sit on	chair
something to play baseball with	ball
something green	grass
something hot	fire
something in a living room	sofa
something on your feet	toes
something fast	jet
something in the sky	moon

Follow up: Write the words in a sentence. (If you have been putting the words into sentences each time they are called, students will have ready structures.)

> A spelling test.
>
> Vocabulary use test.
>
> Write a story using as many of the words as you can.
>
> Students make up other Bingo card lists.

Presentation and sample conversation: Write the vocabulary words you will be using on the chalkboard. Help students read the words and review the meanings.

We are going to play a game called Bingo.	*(Show card and spell B-I-N-G-O.)*
Can you say that?	*(Bingo.)*
This is the Bingo card.	*(Hold up blank card.)*
And these are markers.	*(Show squares of colored paper.)*
What is this?	*(Show card then stick with Funtak® to the chalkboard so you can refer to it again. [Bingo card])*
And what are these?	*(Markers.)*
Now copy the words on the chalkboard onto the Bingo card.	*(Demonstrate by writing the first three words in random places on the card.)*
Everyone's card must be different. You can write (book) here or here or here or anywhere.	*(Watch to see that students are not merely copying the words in a straight line or copying your model.)*

Begin at the side of the square, print, and write small like this. Do not write like this.

(Demonstrate on chalkboard.)

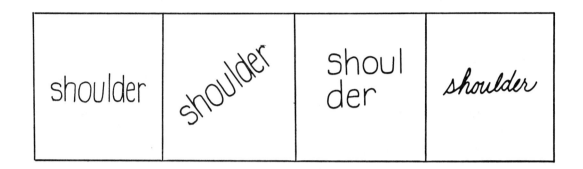

Circulate the room to check for careful copying. Those who finish early may be called upon to complete a second card for some of the beginners or for a student who is absent.

Subsequent games requiring new Bingo cards may be prepared later as homework assignments, but the first card should be supervised by you to assure proper understanding of the procedure.

When students' cards are ready, set the flashcards face down on the table in front of you.

Now we're ready to play.

Take a marker.

Cover the word *FREE* in the center of the card.

(Funtak® a marker on FREE on the card you have posted on the chalkboard.)

I will pick a word.

(Pick up the top flashcard. Let's assume it is the word BOOK. Show it to the class. Read it or allow a student to read it aloud to the class.)

Book.

(Demonstrate the meaning of the word by holding up a book. Use the word in a sentence, "This is a book," or "I have a book." Post the flashcard with Funtak® on the chalkboard so students who need to match letter for letter will have a reference to do that.)

Take a marker. Cover the word *book.*

(Demonstrate; circulate to assist; repeat the directions and demonstrate each time, as many times as necessary.)

Take a second word and repeat the procedure. Repeat with two more words. Then continue the presentation:

When you have five (*show fingers*) markers in a row—like this, like this, or like this—you are the winner.	(*Demonstrate on posted card—across, down, and diagonal.*)
Say "Bingo!" and you win a prize!	(*Show the prize.*)

Continue calling the words until someone has Bingo. Have the Bingo winner read (help if necessary) the Bingo words. Check them against the posted words.

The game is less stressful and more enjoyable when there are more winners. Continue calling words until there are at least two more winners. After the winners have read their words, let them come up to get their prizes. Teach the vocabulary of the prize items if necessary.

Take off all the markers.   (*demonstrate*)

I will put all the cards back and shuffle them. We will play again.

Other useful phrases:

I need two (*one*) more.

I don't have it.

I can't find it.

Can you help me, please?

I have four in a row.

I/he/she won once.   (*two times, three times*)

Who has Bingo?   (*I do, he does, she does*)

What's the prize?

Thank you.

6

Speaking and Guessing Games

102. JUST-A-MINUTE!©*

Grades: 2 to adult

English level: Low intermediate and up

Objectives: To improve oral language fluency; to improve pronunciation; to stress careful listening; to practice quick, logical thinking; to practice speaking in front of a group

Materials needed: Just-A-Minute! cards, paper and pencil for scorekeeping, a clock or watch with a second hand

Preparation: Make copies of the sheets of cards and cut them apart (see pages 141-146). Each student is given one card and is instructed not to show it to the others. You may photocopy them on oaktag for longer wear.

Students should be given time to examine their words before the round begins. If there are questions about the pronunciation, reading, or meaning of a word, students may consult a dictionary or the teacher.

Play: Each player is given a limited time (for example, one minute) to try to get the other students to guess as many words as possible from the list on his card.

Player One announces the title or category on his card. The player may tell about each word but may not say the word itself, may not point to objects in the room, and may not use his hands. He may describe it, tell what it is used for, where it is found, who uses it, what its opposite is, use a sentence that needs the word for completion, or any other verbal hints he can think of.

*Used with permission of Eardley Publications, © 1984.

139

Other students are to listen and guess when they think they know what the word is. They need not raise their hands, since this is a game of speed. As soon as the player hears a correct answer, he calls out "Right!" and goes on to the next word. He may skip a word and come back to it later.

At the end of one minute, the timekeeper calls "Time." The number of words guessed correctly is the player's score. The players who guessed correctly do not score points.

(Demonstrate several cards yourself and have students play a practice round without the time pressure.)

The next person (go around to the left or by volunteers) announces the new category and continues. The winner is the person who has the highest number of points at the end of the last round.

Variation: Divide the class into two, three, or four teams. Alternate play among the teams, with only team members guessing when their team is "up."

Other applications: After students are familiar with the rules of the game and have confidence and skill in speaking under time pressure, you can take written notes of student strategies, successes, difficulties, errors, and omissions. At the end of each round, a brief lesson may be taught, with additional sentence patterns, strategies, and vocabulary items presented.

Play around a table with a tape recorder in the center or near the player giving the clues. (Have students sit on their hands to decrease table noise interference.) Record a round of play and then replay the tape with students listening. Give positive comments on clues that are clear, well pronounced, and fluent. Ask the group for suggestions where clues are fuzzy or "don't work."

Useful patterns for playing Just-A-Minute!:

This is (a) _____.   (adjective, color, noun)

This is the opposite of _____.

This is like a _____.

This is part of a _____.

This can _____.

16 PICTURES GAMES

Drill, drill, drill. What student wants to drill? Few that I've met. But what if students don't know they're drilling? The following games manage to sneak in drill on essential grammatical structures and make students beg for it.

The 16 Pictures games are all played in the same manner, although each teaches a different set of structures and vocabulary. Introduce each game at the point when appropriate in the students' advancement. Stop playing while they are still begging for more, so you may return to them another time for reinforcement.

16 Pictures starts off with whole-class instruction and play, while you monitor for grammatical correctness and care in pronunciation. The game can continue in

Words That Begin With **_R_**	Words That Begin With **_S_**	Words That Begin With **_SH_**	Words That Begin With **_O_**
1. run	1. sad	1. shop	1. orange
2. road	2. sink	2. ship	2. old
3. ring	3. soda	3. shout	3. okay
4. ride	4. sleep	4. show	4. onion
5. rope	5. stove	5. shower	5. one
6. rain	6. stairs	6. shirt	6. open
7. roller skates	7. sun	7. shine	7. oil
8. restaurant	8. sandwich	8. shoot	8. out

Words That Begin With **_CH_**	Words That Begin With **_T_**	Words That Begin With **_W_**	Words That Begin With **_TH_**
1. chicken	1. toy	1. water	1. this
2. cheese	2. train	2. wagon	2. three
3. chocolate	3. tree	3. white	3. thing
4. child	4. ten	4. wonderful	4. throw
5. champion	5. toast	5. west	5. thousand
6. chest	6. telephone	6. witch	6. thank
7. chair	7. test	7. world	7. thin
8. cheap	8. time	8. whistle	8. thirsty

Body Words	Body Words	Body Words	Things in a House
1. ears	1. knee	1. mouth	1. kitchen
2. teeth	2. face	2. chin	2. closet
3. toes	3. arm	3. chest	3. window
4. hair	4. cheeks	4. hips	4. rug
5. nose	5. elbow	5. ankle	5. door
6. neck	6. stomach	6. lips	6. bedroom
7. eyes	7. shoulder	7. fingers	7. light
8. hand	8. tongue	8. forehead	8. mirror

Animals	Animals	Animals	Things in a City
1. horse	1. pig	1. goat	1. building
2. dog	2. cat	2. rooster	2. street
3. kitten	3. duck	3. fox	3. stores
4. tiger	4. donkey	4. elephant	4. people
5. alligator	5. dinosaur	5. gorilla	5. bus
6. chicken	6. butterfly	6. cow	6. taxi
7. bird	7. turtle	7. fish	7. sidewalk
8. monkey	8. snake	8. grasshopper	8. traffic light

Things to Eat	Things to Eat	Things to Eat	Things at a Party
1. hamburger	1. hot dog	1. spaghetti	1. cake
2. potato	2. rice	2. ice cream	2. games
3. cookie	3. candy	3. peach	3. soda
4. apple	4. banana	4. carrot	4. music
5. bread	5. cake	5. pie	5. food
6. egg	6. butter	6. jelly	6. laughing
7. chicken	7. fish	7. cheese	7. people
8. corn	8. popcorn	8. steak	8. dancing

Words That Rhyme With *YOU*	Words That Rhyme With *LIGHT*	Words That Rhyme With *MAT*	Words With *OO*
1. blue	1. night	1. cat	1. look
2. two	2. fight	2. fat	2. school
3. zoo	3. right	3. bat	3. pool
4. true	4. sight	4. hat	4. book
5. new	5. tight	5. sat	5. zoo
6. glue	6. bright	6. that	6. boo
7. shoe	7. kite	7. at	7. good
8. drew	8. polite	8. rat	8. moon

Words That Rhyme With *JANE*	Words That Rhyme With *GATE*	Words That Rhyme With *ME*	Words That End With *NG*
1. cane	1. wait	1. she	1. ring
2. brain	2. late	2. we	2. wrong
3. chain	3. date	3. free	3. sing
4. pain	4. great	4. knee	4. hang
5. rain	5. plate	5. see	5. long
6. plane	6. skate	6. key	6. thing
7. Spain	7. state	7. ski	7. bang
8. train	8. ate	8. tea	8. lung

Words That Rhyme With *BREEZE*	Words That Rhyme With *SPRING*	Words That Rhyme With *CRIES*	Words That Have Long *O*
1. freeze	1. king	1. eyes	1. home
2. cheese	2. sing	2. flies	2. road
3. please	3. thing	3. tries	3. cone
4. bees	4. bring	4. skies	4. bone
5. sneeze	5. spring	5. ties	5. go
6. these	6. ring	6. pies	6. most
7. squeeze	7. wing	7. prize	7. no
8. Chinese	8. swing	8. size	8. snow

Things to Wear	Things to Wear	Things to Wear	Things in a Park
1. hat	1. coat	1. jacket	1. grass
2. dress	2. blouse	2. suit	2. swing
3. shoes	3. socks	3. stockings	3. birds
4. pants	4. jeans	4. mittens	4. trees
5. shirt	5. belt	5. eyeglasses	5. flowers
6. tie	6. watch	6. necklace	6. people
7. ring	7. boots	7. skirt	7. dogs
8. pajamas	8. scarf	8. shorts	8. bench

Things in School	Things in School	Things in a Book	Things in a Handbag
1. paper	1. pen	1. word	1. keys
2. pencil	2. book	2. page	2. money
3. English	3. homework	3. chapter	3. wallet
4. desk	4. chair	4. story	4. lipstick
5. teacher	5. student	5. sentence	5. tissue
6. chalk	6. chalkboard	6. picture	6. comb
7. dictionary	7. closet	7. cover	7. pen
8. lesson	8. paste	8. title	8. change purse

Workers	Workers	Workers	Christmas Words
1. teacher	1. artist	1. beautician	1. Santa Claus
2. mailman	2. dentist	2. salesperson	2. snow
3. doctor	3. mechanic	3. president	3. bell
4. bus driver	4. truck driver	4. banker	4. reindeer
5. typist	5. secretary	5. doorman	5. church
6. barber	6. clown	6. writer	6. tree
7. policewoman	7. carpenter	7. lawyer	7. Christmas card
8. pilot	8. mother	8. waitress	8. decorations

People in a Family	People in a Family	In the Living Room	In the Bedroom
1. father	1. mother	1. sofa	1. bed
2. sister	2. brother	2. armchair	2. sheet
3. grandmother	3. grandfather	3. lamp	3. pillow
4. child	4. uncle	4. stereo	4. lamp
5. aunt	5. nephew	5. rug	5. curtains
6. son	6. daughter	6. pictures	6. closet
7. cousin	7. teenager	7. bookcase	7. clock
8. baby	8. niece	8. television	8. blanket

Weather Words	Places	Games	Football Words
1. hot	1. school	1. baseball	1. referee
2. fall	2. supermarket	2. tennis	2. ball
3. cloud	3. library	3. checkers	3. pass
4. rain	4. airport	4. Just-a-Minute!	4. kick
5. ice	5. police station	5. hide and seek	5. field
6. umbrella	6. park	6. golf	6. touchdown
7. summer	7. museum	7. basketball	7. cheerleader
8. snow	8. department store	8. bowling	8. quarterback

Kitchen Words	Kitchen Words	Holiday Words	Things to Put on Food
1. table	1. knife	1. Santa Claus	1. salt
2. spoon	2. bowl	2. jack o'lantern	2. sugar
3. stove	3. food	3. Thanksgiving	3. milk
4. dinner	4. fork	4. songs	4. butter
5. pot	5. oven	5. birthday	5. ketchup
6. sink	6. milk	6. Easter	6. gravy
7. refrigerator	7. garbage	7. Valentine	7. pickles
8. window	8. soap	8. New Year's Day	8. mustard

Things That Fly	Round Things	Map Words	Things You Can Do With Your Mouth
1. bird	1. ball	1. ocean	1. smile
2. airplane	2. penny	2. mountain	2. eat
3. kite	3. wheel	3. north	3. talk
4. bee	4. hamburger	4. river	4. sing
5. helicopter	5. ring	5. mile	5. shout
6. butterfly	6. dish	6. city	6. whistle
7. mosquito	7. circle	7. country	7. laugh
8. Superman	8. bracelet	8. lake	8. kiss

Things on Trees	Things With Wheels	Circus Words	Things You Can Do With Your Feet
1. nest	1. car	1. clown	1. run
2. apples	2. taxi	2. elephant	2. kick
3. branch	3. bicycle	3. popcorn	3. dance
4. leaves	4. roller skates	4. ticket	4. walk
5. cherries	5. airplane	5. tiger	5. jump
6. bugs	6. fire truck	6. cage	6. ski
7. seeds	7. train	7. music	7. skate
8. birds	8. bus	8. monkey	8. skip

Things on a Wall

1. map
2. paint
3. nail
4. calendar
5. picture
6. thermometer
7. clock
8. mirror

Things That Go Fast

1. jet
2. horse
3. train
4. cheetah
5. UFO
6. rocket
7. bullet
8. motorcycle

Things That Are Hot

1. sun
2. stove
3. fire
4. hot dog
5. July
6. fever
7. desert
8. soup

Things You Can Do With Your Hands

1. write
2. draw
3. type
4. pull
5. punch
6. cook
7. wave
8. wash

Words That Rhyme With *CHOP*

1. stop
2. drop
3. cop
4. hop
5. shop
6. top
7. mop
8. pop

Words That Rhyme With *SNORE*

1. store
2. more
3. four
4. door
5. score
6. war
7. pour
8. floor

Words That Rhyme With *HOT*

1. pot
2. lot
3. got
4. not
5. spot
6. forgot
7. dot
8. shot

Words With *X*

1. six
2. fox
3. box
4. ax
5. X-ray
6. extra
7. mix
8. tax

Liquids

1. water
2. milk
3. soda
4. gasoline
5. soup
6. coffee
7. oil
8. juice

Electrical Things

1. television
2. toaster
3. lamp
4. radio
5. washing machine
6. vacuum cleaner
7. fan
8. clock

Baseball Words

1. catcher
2. bat
3. coach
4. team
5. umpire
6. mitt
7. pitcher
8. score

Small Things

1. penny
2. dot
3. baby
4. eye
5. ant
6. whisker
7. pea
8. letter

Time Words

1. minute
2. year
3. clock
4. calendar
5. Tuesday
6. tomorrow
7. week
8. April

Things in the Water

1. boat
2. fish
3. duck
4. stones
5. frog
6. shark
7. crabs
8. whale

Things at the Beach

1. sand
2. bathing suit
3. pail
4. ocean
5. lunch
6. shells
7. lifeguard
8. blanket

Big Things

1. building
2. cloud
3. sun
4. airplane
5. tree
6. giant
7. mountain
8. ocean

Scary Things
1. ghosts
2. monsters
3. snake
4. fire
5. witch
6. bear
7. tiger
8. hurricane

Things on a Farm
1. barn
2. corn
3. cow
4. tractor
5. fence
6. farmer
7. grass
8. chickens

Toys
1. doll
2. ball
3. truck
4. blocks
5. doll house
6. bat
7. wagon
8. drum

Red Things
1. stop sign
2. cherry
3. apple
4. crayon
5. lipstick
6. fire engine
7. Santa's suit
8. Rudolph's nose

Words That Begin With *B*
1. baby
2. ball
3. boy
4. book
5. bottle
6. basket
7. bicycle
8. boot

Words That Begin With *C*
1. cow
2. candy
3. car
4. color
5. carrot
6. cake
7. cup
8. coffee

Words That Begin With *D*
1. dog
2. dinner
3. December
4. dance
5. doctor
6. door
7. Daddy
8. dime

Things That Are Green
1. grass
2. leaves
3. "GO" sign
4. lime
5. spinach
6. lettuce
7. dollar
8. plant

Words That Begin With *A*
1. airplane
2. alligator
3. apple
4. answer
5. artist
6. arm
7. add
8. again

Words That Begin With *F*
1. fish
2. friend
3. farm
4. February
5. food
6. finger
7. face
8. fly

Words That Begin With *H*
1. hat
2. horse
3. hamburger
4. hand
5. hair
6. house
7. happy
8. he

Words That Begin With *E*
1. elephant
2. ear
3. egg
4. eye
5. end
6. East
7. error
8. eleven

Words That Begin With *L*
1. lake
2. love
3. letter
4. light
5. lesson
6. large
7. lost
8. lip

Words That Begin With *M*
1. mother
2. mouse
3. mask
4. mop
5. meat
6. monster
7. maybe
8. mister

Words That Begin With *P*
1. potato
2. popcorn
3. pajamas
4. pot
5. party
6. pie
7. puzzle
8. park

Words That Begin With *G*
1. goat
2. gas
3. garage
4. guess
5. game
6. good
7. girl
8. gum

small groups of two or three to ensure maximum participation and practice. 16 Pictures may be played for homework when mastery is sufficient, and it may be played in a reading/writing form.

103. 16 CATS

Grades: 2 to adult

English level: Beginners

Objectives: To develop logical thinking; to motivate careful listening and pronunciation; to practice correct grammatical structures

Session one:
The cat is_____. *(adjective)*
It is_____. *(adjective)*
It's_____. *(adjective)*
It is not/isn't_____. *(adjective)*

Session two: Review Session one.

Session three:
Is the cat_____? *(adjective)*
Yes, it is.
No, it isn't. No, it's not.

Vocabulary:
same, different, cat, big, small, American, Japanese, hungry, happy, sad

Materials needed: 16 Cats game sheet

Preparation: Make enough copies of the game sheet for each student in the class

Play:

(1) Practicing declarative statements
Summary: The leader stands before the room and announces that she is thinking about a particular cat. She says four sentences about the cat as the others listen carefully. Each of the sentences will eliminate one half of the remaining cats. Students who have listened carefully will be able to identify the correct cat by the fourth sentence. The first to guess correctly then takes a turn at being the leader.

(2) Practicing questions and short answers
Summary: The leader announces that he is thinking about a particular cat. The other students raise their hands to ask questions about the cat. Four questions will pin down the exact cat.

16 CATS

Presentation and sample conversation:

We are going to play a game called Sixteen Cats.	
Look at the picture.	
How many cats do you see?	*(Sixteen)*
Are they all the same or are they different?	*(Different)*
How many cats are big?	*(Draw a large cat face on the board or gesture with your hands. [Eight])*
How many cats are small?	*(Demonstrate [Eight])*
How many cats are happy?	*(Eight)*
How many cats are sad?	*(Eight)*
How many cats are hungry?	*(Eight)*
How many cats are not hungry?	*(Eight)*
How many cats are American?	*(Point to the American Flag. [Eight])*
How many cats are Japanese?	*(Draw a Japanese flag or point to Japan on a map. [Eight])*
Listen: I am thinking of a cat. Can you guess which cat it is?	
This cat is big. It's happy. It's hungry. It's Japanese.	
Which cat is it?	*(Number 8)*

If no students were able to guess after the previous procedure, hold up the paper showing 16 Cats and repeat each sentence, showing which of the cats are ruled out and which are left in by the statement, so they can see the logic needed to determine the correct cat.

Now let's try another one: This cat is small. It's American. It's sad. It's not hungry.	*(Number 14)*
This cat is not big. It is not American. It is not hungry. It is not sad.	*(Number 6)*

On the chalkboard: After the students have had several opportunities for listening to the clue sentences, you might write the structures needed at the left and the varying vocabulary needed on the right. Help students read the words if necessary or draw a quick sketch to indicate meaning.

This cat is _____.	big	small
It is _____.	American	Japanese
It is not _____.	happy	sad
	hungry	

Choose another cat and give four clues. Let the student who guesses correctly be the teller. (You will need to know which cat the student is referring to in case correction or assistance is necessary, so have him write the number of the chosen cat for you to see or whisper the number to you before beginning to give the clues.)

Since the purpose of this game is to provide intensive drill in simple, very common structures, immediate correction of errors is appropriate before the errors are repeated and internalized.

After playing the game several times using the full form *is not,* teach the contraction, *isn't.* (On the chalkboard write: is not = isn't.) Let the group practice pronunciation of: It isn't big. It isn't small. It isn't American. It isn't Japanese. It isn't happy. It isn't sad.

If your class is large, allow several students to have a turn as leader and continue to correct errors as they occur, until the performance is relatively error-free. Then allow students to play the game at their seats in groups of three or four, so all may have several turns to practice. Circulate among the groups to assist and spot-check for errors. Leave the written clues on the chalkboard until they are not needed. Then erase them and allow students to continue without this support.

Follow up: Students play the game with a classmate, parent, or friend.

Written form of 16 Cats: Write the vocabulary words on the chalkboard if necessary.

Each student secretly chooses one of the cats and writes four sentences about the cat. They write their own name at the bottom of the paper.

On a separate piece of paper, which she keeps, the student writes the number of the cat chosen. Students work in groups of four or five and write the names of the classmates in their group. They read each other's clues, writing down their answers on their own "test paper." They exchange clues until each has read all of the others' papers. They then check their answers with each other.

Follow up: Review the game after a week. This time, focus on questions and short-answer forms.

I am thinking of a cat.

Can you guess which one it is?

On the chalkboard: Supply the appropriate question and short-answer forms:

Is the cat hungry?   *(Yes, it is./No, it isn't.)*

Is it Japanese?

To call attention to the shift of the word *is* to the beginning of the sentence, demonstrate with arrows, finger play, or flashcards that *is* shifts position, and that this is significant.

104. 16 WOMEN

Grades: 2 to adult

English level: Beginners

Objectives: To develop logical thinking; to motivate careful listening and pronunciation; to practice the following sentence structures:

Session one:

She is (*VERB*) + ing (+ *direct object*) or (*on_____*).
She is not (*VERB*) + ing (+ *direct object*) or (+ *on_____*).
She isn't (*VERB*) + ing.

Session two:

Is she (*VERB*) + ing (+ *direct object*) or (+ *on _____*)?
Yes, she is. No, she's not. No, she isn't.

Vocabulary:

standing, holding, wearing, box, flower, hat, dress, black, white

Materials needed: 16 Women game sheet

Preparation: Make enough copies of the game sheet for each student in the class

Presentation: As in the previous game, call attention to the variations in the pictures by such questions as:

Here are sixteen women. Are they all the same?	*(No)*
How many women are standing on a box?	*(Eight)*
How many women are holding a flower?	*(Eight)*
How many women are wearing black dresses?	*(Eight)*
How many women are wearing white dresses?	*(Eight)*
How many women are wearing hats?	*(Eight)*

Then introduce the patterns for the game:

Can you guess which woman this is?	
This woman is standing on a box.	
She is holding a flower.	
She is wearing a black dress.	
She is wearing a hat.	*(Number 7)*

16 WOMEN

Now guess this one:

> This woman is not standing on a box.
>
> She's wearing a white dress.
>
> She isn't wearing a hat.
>
> She isn't holding a flower.   *(Number 13)*

The person who guesses correctly becomes the leader, and play continues as in the previous game. You may write the sentence patterns on the chalkboard for reading practice or as cues to help the game along:

This woman is _____ing _____.	a hat
She is _____ing _____.	a white (*black*) dress
She isn't _____ing _____.	a flower on a box

Have the class play as a group, with corrections and drills. Divide the class into groups of two, three, or four for more extensive practice, using the chalkboard as necessary. Continue monitoring small groups. To provide more challenge, erase the chalkboard; students continue playing.

Have students play the game with others for homework.

Follow up: Review the game, playing as a class. Write patterns on the chalkboard.

Have students write clues and exchange papers, guessing the answers.

A week later, you may introduce question forms and short answers and play the game with these structures.

105. 16 MONSTERS

Grades: 2 to adult

English level: Low intermediate

Objectives: To develop logical thinking; to motivate careful listening and pronunciation; to practice the following sentence structures:

Session one:

He has _____ (*adjective*)_____ (*noun*).
He has _____ (*adjective*)_____ (*noun*).

Session two:

Does he have_____ _____?
Yes, he does.
No, he doesn't.

Vocabulary:

large, small, sharp, nose, teeth, eyes, hair

Materials needed: 16 Monsters game sheet

Preparation: Make enough copies of the game sheet for each student in the class

Presentation:

How many monsters do you see?	*(Sixteen)*
Are they all the same?	*(No)*
How many monsters have hair?	*(Eight)*
How many monsters have three eyes?	*(Eight)*
How many monsters have big noses?	*(Eight)*
How many monsters have sharp teeth?	*(Eight)*

I am thinking of a monster. Can you guess which one he is?

This monster has sharp teeth.

He has a big nose.

He has three eyes.

He has hair. *(Number 5)*

Let's try another:

This monster doesn't have sharp teeth.

He has a small nose.

He has two eyes.

He doesn't have hair. *(Number 15)*

On the chalkboard:

This monster has _____ _____.	hair
He has _____ _____.	two (*three*) eyes
He doesn't have _____ _____.	a big (*small*) nose
Does not = doesn't	sharp teeth

Follow up: Review the game orally; have students read and write sentence clues to exchange with others.

At a later session, introduce the question and short-answer forms.

16 MONSTERS

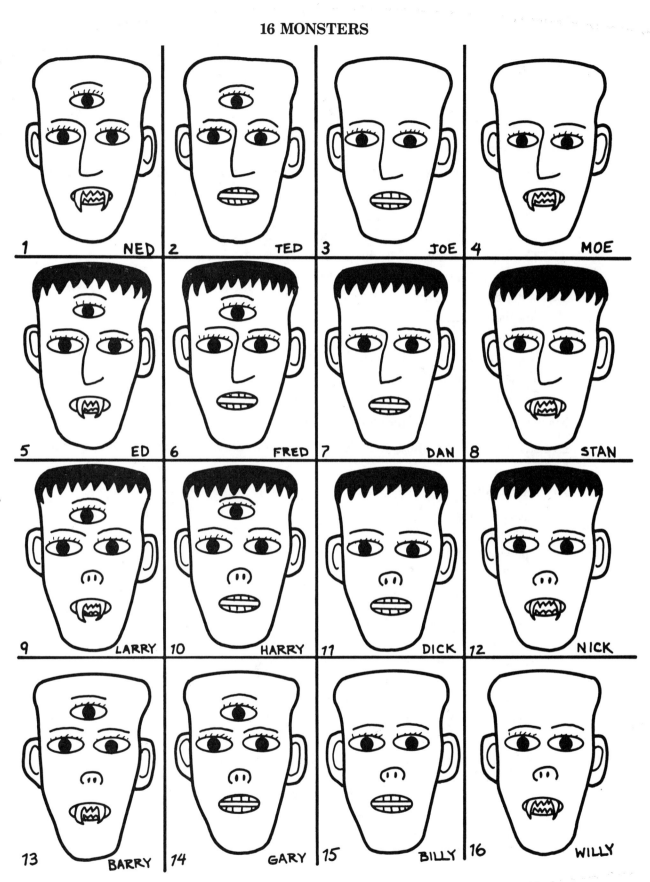

106. 16 PICTURES

Grades: 2 to adult

English level: Low intermediate

Objectives: To develop logical thinking; to motivate careful listening and pronunciation; to practice the following sentence structures:

There is a _____ in the picture.

There are _____s (and _____s) in the picture.

There isn't any _____ in the picture. There is no _____.

There aren't any _____s in the picture. There are no _____s.

Is there a _____?

Are there _____?

Yes, there is. Yes, there are.

No, there isn't. No, there aren't.

There is nothing in the picture.

There isn't anything in the picture.

Materials needed: 16 Pictures game sheet

Preparation: Make enough copies of the game sheet for each student in the class

Presentation:

Here are sixteen pictures. Are they the same?	*(No)*
There are trees in some pictures. In how many pictures are there trees?	*(Eight)*
There is a flower in some pictures. In how many pictures is there a flower?	*(Eight)*
There is a bird in some pictures. In how many pictures is there a bird?	*(Eight)*
There are houses in some pictures. In how many pictures are there houses?	*(Eight)*

Follow the same procedure as in the previous games:

1. The teacher or leader states four clues.

2. The student who guesses correctly then gives four clues. Correct her production.

16 PICTURES

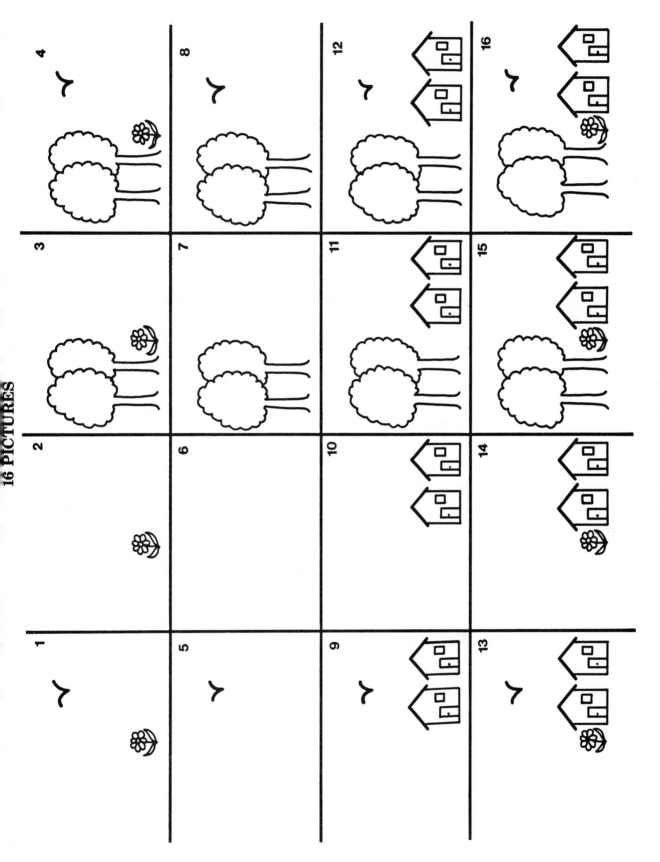

3. Write the structures on the chalkboard:

There are trees and a flower in this   *(Number 16)*
   picture. There are houses and a
   bird.

There is a flower, but there aren't   *(Number 14)*
   any trees in this picture. There are
   houses, but there isn't a bird.

107. 16 ROBBERS

Grades: 2 to adult

English level: Intermediate and up

Objectives: To develop logical thinking; to motivate careful listening and pronunciation; to practice the past tense forms of the word *be* and the past continuous tense; to practice he/she distinction

It was a _____ (man/woman).
He/She was carrying a _____.
He/She was wearing a _____.
Was it a man or a woman?
Was he/she (VERB + ing) a _____?
Yes, he/she was.

Materials needed: 16 Robbers game sheet

Preparation: Make enough copies of the game sheet for each student in the class

Presentation: "Last night I was taking a walk on Main Street. I saw a robber running out of the bank with a bag of money. The robber got into a car and drove away. The police asked me many questions and I described the robber. Can you tell which robber I saw?

The robber was a man.
He was wearing a mask.
He was carrying a knife.
He wasn't wearing a hat.   *(Number 6)*

Let's try another one:

This robber was a woman.
She was carrying a gun.
She wasn't wearing a mask.
She was wearing a hat.   *(Number 16)*

16 ROBBERS

Extensions: When students have become very familiar with the format of the games, some may want to invent their own 16 Pictures games to play with classmates. Here are some suggestions for them:

Fold an 8½ × 11 paper four times to get sixteen equal squares. Plan a set of pictures that have simple shapes. In order to draw shapes that are uniform in all sixteen squares, students may draw the shape on a small piece of index card or oaktag and cut it out. They can then trace it in each of the sixteen squares and add the differentiating characteristics.

There should be no more than four differences:

The top two rows should differ from the bottom two rows in one way.

The two right columns should differ from the two left columns.

The top and bottom row should differ from the two center rows.

The far right and far left columns should differ from the two center columns.

Four and only four clues should enable players to track down the answer. Some suggestions for simple patterns:

16 cars: differences might include wheels, windows, antennae, tail fins, doors, etc.

16 hats: bands, feathers, flowers, color, etc.

16 houses: windows, doors, chimney, flowers, roof shape, etc.

16 cups: size, handle, color, decoration, etc.

16 fish: size, color, number of fins, size of tail, eye, etc.

Students may need help in establishing the structures needed for the clues. Their ideas may require practicing several kinds of structures—have them check their sentences with you before playing their game wth classmates.

108. TWENTY QUESTIONS

Grades: 4 to adult

English level: Advanced

Objectives: To practice logical thinking; to reinforce question forms; to integrate knowledge

Materials needed: None

Preparation: None

Presentation: "We are going to play a game called Twenty Questions. But first you need to know that everything in the world is either animal, vegetable, or mineral. (Write the three categories on the chalkboard.) Tell me what these things are:

frog   *(animal)*

boy   *(animal)*

carrot   *(vegetable)*

tree   *(vegetable)*

rock   *(mineral)*

sun   *(mineral)*

water   *(mineral)*

ham sandwich   *(animal and vegetable)*

George Washington   *(animal)*

New York City   *(animal, vegetable, and mineral)*

car   *(mineral and vegetable)*

Continue to give examples until students understand the categories.

> I will think of something, and I will give you only one clue. You must guess what it is with just twenty questions. I can answer only yes or no.

Think of something everyone knows, such as the principal of the school or the President of the United States. "I am thinking of something 'animal.'" Assess the students' ability to formulate appropriate questions. Assist with the structure of the questions.

After the answer has been guessed or the twenty questions are spent, give samples of the most useful kinds of questions, working from very general to more specific as more is known.

Is this a person?

Is this person alive today?

Is this a woman?

Is/Was this person famous?

Is/Was he/she in entertainment?   *(movies, TV, etc.)*
  sports? politics? *(a president, governor, congressman, etc.)*

Is he/she a real person?

Do we know this person?

Does this person live in our town?

Does this person go to our school?

Is this person over twenty-one?

Does this person have a mustache?   *(wear glasses, teach English, etc.)*

For a nonperson animal, useful questions have these forms:

Is this alive?

Is it a special kind of animal?

Is this animal real?

Is it a mammal?   *(bird, reptile, fish, invertebrate, insect)*

Is it dangerous?

Does it live in this area?

Do people eat this animal?

In the beginning, write a synopsis of the information gotten from the questions on the chalkboard so students can build on what they already know. After each round of the game, give coaching on the kinds of questions that make a difference, helping students to avoid asking questions that are too specific too soon or that have already been covered in previous questions.

109.   I'M GOING TO MY GRANDMOTHER'S HOUSE

Grades: 2 and up

English level: High beginners and up

Objectives: To learn a common party game; to increase listening and memory skills; to utilize alphabetical order skills; to reinforce vocabulary

Materials needed: None

Play: Students sit in a circle and go in order. The first person says, "I'm going to my grandmother's house, and I'm going to take an (apple)." (The item chosen must begin with the letter *a*.) The second person says the entire sentence and adds an item beginning with the letter *b*. The third person must repeat everything and add an item that begins with the letter *c*, and so forth. Example: The fourth person may say, "I'm going to my grandmother's house, and I'm going to take an apple, a book, a canary, and some doughnuts."

In the party version of the game, a student who leaves out an item is out of the game. In the classroom, however, coaching is allowed. At some point, you may make the game competitive by dividing the class into teams and awarding points to successful completions of the sentence rather than eliminating students from play. You may permit students to coach their own team members if you wish.

Options: For beginning students, write the complete sentence on the chalkboard so they may read it rather than try to remember it. Illustrate each addition, if possible, so the task is to practice vocabulary and pronunciation rather than sheer memory.

For advanced students, you might insist on precise pronunciation and the accurate use of *a, an,* or *some.*

Several students might keep a record of the additions to the sentence. For written practice focusing on *a, an,* and *some,* students can write their own sentences with items from *a* to *z.*

The game can be played with other tenses. Examples:

I go to my grandmother's house every Sunday, and I always take _____.

I went to my grandmother's house, and I took _____.

Harry goes to his grandmother's house every week, and he always takes

_____.

7

Let's Make Something!

Preparing and sharing food with your students is an excellent way to teach English while simultaneously drawing on many other skills and concepts: health and nutrition, following directions, reading a recipe, safety, measurement and mathematics, table setting and table manners, responsibility to the group.

110. INSTANT OATMEAL

Grades: K to 3

English level: Beginner and up

Objectives: To make and serve oatmeal; to learn the English needed to talk about the activity; to lead into or follow up on the story of "The Three Bears"

Materials needed: Stove or electric burner or hot water maker, instant oatmeal, measuring cup, large bowl, small paper bowls, mixing spoon, plastic spoons, plastic knives, brown sugar, butter, milk, paper cups (unless you distribute milk in ½ pint cartons), paper towels (place mats), napkins

Presentation: You might schedule the activity for the children's snack time, if that is convenient.

Teach the names of the items used in preparing the oatmeal (porridge). Assign tasks to children, demonstrating the meanings through gestures and keeping a running conversation and commentary on the students' actions.

Here are the place mats.
What are these?   *(place mats)*
Here are the spoons.
Here are the napkins.
Who will give out the place mats?
Good, (*Carlos*), will you please give everyone a place mat?
Who will give out the spoons?

(*Joon*), will you please give everyone a spoon?

(*Maya*), will you please give everyone a napkin?

Here is the brown sugar. Here is the butter. Put a small bowl of brown sugar and a plate of butter on each table. Jin, will you put a bowl of sugar on your table? Jin is carrying the sugar.   *(etc.)*

Open the box of oatmeal.

Pour the oatmeal in the measuring cup.   *(you handle the boiling water)*

Stir the oatmeal.

Line up with your bowls.

Are you hungry?

(Pass out the milk containers or serve milk in the paper cups.)

Put sugar on your oatmeal.

Put butter on your oatmeal.

Put milk on your oatmeal.

Eat the oatmeal.

Do you like oatmeal?

Mmmm, I like oatmeal. It's good.

Clean up.

Throw the garbage in the wastebasket.

As children are serving and eating, continue a running commentary on the activity:

(*Sara*) is putting sugar on her oatmeal. She doesn't want any butter. Do you like butter, Sara? Is your oatmeal too hot? Blow on it.

Midori's oatmeal is hot. She is blowing on it. Mika likes her oatmeal with butter and milk. The oatmeal is hot and the milk is cold. The milk makes the oatmeal cool.

Who has milk on their oatmeal?

(*Nida*) has milk.

(*Carlos*) has milk.

Everyone is eating oatmeal now.

Who likes oatmeal?

Jan likes oatmeal.

Ben likes oatmeal.

But Kata doesn't like oatmeal.

Dino doesn't like oatmeal.

Is the oatmeal too sweet? Did you put too much sugar on it?

Is the oatmeal just right? Is it delicious? My oatmeal is delicious.

Are you finished?

Ami is finished. Tammy is finished.

Who wants more oatmeal? Bena wants more oatmeal.

It's time to clean up now.

Put your garbage in the wastebasket.

Follow up: Draw a picture of a bowl of oatmeal with a spoon in it. Students can copy the words *oatmeal, bowl, spoon, milk, sugar, butter.*

Write (corrected) students' sentences on a language experience chart. Read it with the children and have them read it. Example:

We made oatmeal.

We put hot water and oatmeal in a big bowl.

Then we stirred it.

We put in butter and sugar.

We ate the oatmeal.

111. MAKING BUTTER FROM CREAM

Grades: 2 and up

English level: Beginner and up

Objectives: To make butter; to discover how butter is made from cream; to learn the English needed to talk about the activity

Materials needed: Half pint of heavy sweet cream for each group of four students; clean glass quart jar with a tight-fitting screw-on cap for each group; several butter knives; fresh rye or whole wheat bread; paper plates or napkins

Preparation: The cream should be quite cold, so leave it in the refrigerator until ready to do the activity. The glass jars can be kept in the refrigerator, too.

Summary: Pour a half pint of cream into the jar. Screw the cover on tight. Shake the jar with a rhythmic back-and-forth motion until the fat in the cream solidifies, separating from the milk. This will take between ten and twenty minutes of shaking, so students should pass the jar on to others as they tire. When the butter solidifies, pour off the buttermilk, allowing students to taste it. Cut the bread into quarter slices and serve with butter. Students may deliver samples of the class-made butter to the principal, custodians, teachers, and so on.

Presentation: "We are going to make butter. Where does butter come from? (cream) Where does cream come from? (cows) We need cream and jars. We will shake the cream until it turns into butter. Then we will eat the butter on our bread."

Sample conversation and structures:

Open the container of cream.

Pour the cream into the jar.

Screw the cover on tight.

Shake the jar. Keep shaking it.
Give the jar to the next person.
Take turns shaking the cream.
Are you tired?
This is hard work, isn't it?
The butter is forming.
Butter is solid. The buttermilk is liquid.
Is it butter yet?
The butter is ready.
Pour the buttermilk into the cups.
Who wants to taste the buttermilk?
Cut the bread. Spread the butter on the bread.
Line up to get your taste of butter on bread.
Do you want whole wheat or rye bread?
Taste the fresh butter. Isn't it good?
Is it different from butter from the supermarket?
It's sweeter and fresher. It isn't salty. It's white, not yellow.

112. FRUIT SALAD

Grades: K and up

English level: Beginner and up

Objectives: To prepare fruit salad and to learn the English needed to talk about the activity

Materials needed: Bowl, large serving spoon, paper bowls, plastic spoons or forks, vegetable knives, cutting board, napkins, paper towels, bananas, apples, peaches, strawberries, blueberries, grapes, oranges, papaya, mangoes, etc., as season and availability dictate

Preparation: Set up a working area for washing, peeling, and cutting fruit. Determine the various jobs to be assigned to students.

Summary: Students wash, peel, prepare (if old enough, cut) the fruit. Talk about the different shapes, colors, peels, pits, and so on. Students serve the fruit. Discuss the taste and texture of the fruits. Clean up. Possibly plant the seeds and pits.

Presentation: Teach the names of fruits using pictures or plastic replicas. Assign something for each child to bring in—one or two pieces of fruit, or some of the utensils or paper supplies. Or bring in the fruit yourself.
  Talk about the activity as students listen. Demonstrate each step.
  "First we will wash our hands. Then we will wash the (apples, grapes, pears, peaches, strawberries, etc.). We will peel the (bananas, oranges). We will

cut off any rotten parts. We will throw away the peels and the rotten parts. We will cut the fruit into pieces and put it into this big bowl. Then we will mix the fruit with the big spoon. We will give everyone some fruit salad in the paper bowls. Then we will eat our fruit salad."

Assign students to the different jobs. Make a running commentary and conversation with students as they work or observe the workers.

> What are they doing?   *(They're washing their hands)*
> (*Pam*) is washing the *(apples).*
> (*Niki*) is peeling the *(bananas).* She's throwing the peel in the garbage.
> (*Gilda*) is cutting the peaches.
> What is (*Hyun*) doing? *(He's taking the grapes off the stems)*
> (*Kathe*) is putting the strawberries in the big bowl. She is mixing the fruit very gently.
> (*Jung Joo*), please pass out the napkins and spoons.
> Give everyone a bowlful of fruit salad.
> Let's sit down and eat.
> Mmmmm, it's delicious.
> Now let's clean up.
> (*Paula*), take your garbage to the wastebasket.
> Wipe off the desks.
> Wash the bowl, spoon, knives, and cutting board.

Follow up: Distribute plain white paper that has been prefolded to create six sections. Elicit what was done first, what next, and so on. Sketch the following steps (or steps that tell what you did in your class) on the board for the children to copy or to elaborate on. They will use their pictures as cues to retell the story of preparing and eating fruit salad. Older students can copy sentences from the board.

> Fruit salad
> We washed the fruit.
> We peeled and cut the fruit.
> We threw the peels, rotten parts, pits, and cores into the garbage.
> We put the fruit into a big bowl and mixed it with a big spoon.
> We gave everyone a little bowl and spoon.
> We ate the fruit salad. It was delicious.

Stories to read as the students eat are *The Very Hungry Caterpillar* by Eric Carle (New York: Putnam, 1981) and *Who Has the Apple?* by Jan Lööf, translated and adapted by Ole Risom and Linda Hayward (New York: Random House, 1975).

Variations: Vegetable salad (choose from lettuce, alfalfa, spinach, green pepper, carrots, tomatoes, string beans, radishes, cucumber, zucchini, etc.); salad dressing

Students may clean and cut the vegetables at school or at home under parents' supervision and bring the precut pieces to school in plastic bags to add to the large bowl of salad. A healthy lunch may be eaten in the classroom instead of the regular school lunch or going home. Add a variety of cheeses, whole wheat crackers, milk or juice.

OTHER SIMPLE FOOD PROJECTS

These additional food-making activities can be done in a similar way to the above illustrations if you have the necessary equipment.

113. POPCORN

Materials needed: Popcorn kernels, popcorn popper, butter, salt, napkins, large bowls, large paper cups (or bags) to serve the popcorn in

Summary: Follow directions on the popper. Talk about each step of the process. Melt the butter, pour it over the finished popcorn. Add salt and serve. (Goes great with a video movie in your classroom.)

114. APPLESAUCE

Materials needed: Stove, apples, knives, large serving spoon, large pot, strainer, bowls, cinnamon, plastic spoons, paper bowls, napkins

Summary: Cut the apples into quarters and cut out the cores and seeds. Peels may be left on and will be removed later when the cooked applesauce is put through the strainer. Put apples into a large pot with a small amount of water (just cover the bottom of the pot about one quarter inch). Bring water to a boil and turn down the heat. Stir apples every five or ten minutes, until they are all mushy. Strain. Add cinnamon and serve warm or cool. Talk about each step in the process.

115. PEANUT BUTTER

Materials needed: Food processor, pound of roasted peanuts, few tablespoons of peanut oil or other vegetable oil, salt crackers (optional), bread (optional), honey (optional), jam (optional)

Summary: Place a portion of the peanuts in the food processor. Teach safety rules for using a processor. (Handle the assembly and cleaning of the blades yourself.) Process until peanuts are totally mushed. Add enough oil to make the peanut butter spreadable. Add salt to taste. Serve on crackers or whole wheat bread with honey or jam. Talk and write about the activity.

116. TASTING PARTY

Grades: 2 and up

English level: Intermediate to advanced

Objectives: To describe the taste and textures of food; to conduct "research"

Preparation: Motivate, discuss, and plan for the tasting party; students bring in simple items to taste

Materials needed: Serving bowls, paper plates, smallest size paper cups, toothpicks, plastic forks and spoons, napkins, 1½ × 5 paper or index card strips to write food labels on

Students may bring in samples of their ethnic foods or, more simply, items such as these, which require minimal or no preparation:

peanut butter	jelly	honey	crackers
bread	pudding	applesauce	pepperoni
cheese	pieces of fruit	raw vegetables	lemon
sardines	popcorn	olives	pasta
nuts	juices	seltzer	pickles

Presentation: Teach the names of the foods brought in and words for qualities of tastes and textures. Add any flavors, such as chocolate or vanilla, as needed:

sweet	mushy	salty	fresh
sour	crunchy	burnt	rotten
bitter	crispy	raw	stale
hot	delicate	tangy	delicious
spicy	smooth	hard	tasty
sticky	lumpy	soft	tasteless
dry	chewy	fishy	bland
juicy	bubbly	pungent	creamy

Cut large items into small bite-size pieces. Spoon out tiny portions of soft foods into small paper cups. Pour drinks into small paper cups. Arrange and label the foods on a center table. Supply toothpicks, serving forks, spoons, as necessary.

Write the names of the food items on the board. Divide students into groups of three or four. One student in each group is blindfolded, while the others prepare a paper plate with a selection of four or five items to taste and drink. The others serve the blindfolded student one item at a time. The blindfolded student pinches her nose and tastes the food, guessing what it is. Then she smells it and tastes it again, changing the guess if needed. She must describe the texture and how it smells and tastes. The others write down the item and the guess, and let her know what it really is. When all five items have been presented, the blindfold is taken off and another student wears the blindfold. When the blindfold tests are done, students may fill their paper plate with bite-size portions of the other foods to taste.

Follow up: (Discussion)

What foods were easy to identify? Hard to identify?

Did smell help in identifying the food you were eating?

Did the texture help in identifying the food?

Which of the foods do you like?

Which were foods that you had never tasted before?

Which of the foods are healthy?

Which are called junk foods?

Why is it junk food?

Select one adjective from the list and write the name of one food that illustrates that adjective. Examples:

sweet—ice cream

bubbly—soda

soft—bread

crispy—cracker

crunchy—raw carrot

chewy—oatmeal cookie

Or select ten different foods and write as many adjectives about each as you can think of. Examples:

potato chips—salty, crispy, crunchy

pudding—smooth, creamy, sweet

Pick two items and compare them. Example:

The vanilla pudding is sweeter and smoother than the tofu. The tofu is healthier than the pudding. Both are white. (etc.)

Write a paragraph about the tasting party.

Have a tasting party at home.

Compare different brands of foods for taste and value.

117. WHOLE WHEAT MUFFINS

Grades: 3 to adult (skip any reading steps for younger students)

English level: Intermediate

Time required: Three or four 45-minute class sessions over three days

Objectives: To make a healthy snack; to learn the English necessary to talk about following a recipe

Materials needed: 2 large bowls, mixing spoons, measuring cups and spoons, muffin tins, potholder, napkins, whole wheat flour, wheat germ, raisins, baking powder, salt, butter, jam, milk, eggs, honey, vegetable oil, paper cups (optional), plus see options following; access to an oven

Options: You can cut down on the number of ingredients needed, and steps required, by buying packaged mixes for cup cakes or muffins, but you lose out on the discovery of how food is really made from raw ingredients, and the nutritional content of the snack is not as high.

Preparation: Make enough copies of the items needed and the recipe for each student in the class. Make one copy of the list of tasks. Gather ingredients. (Students may bring in the ingredients or you might take a shopping trip to get them. See Activity 150.)

Presentation: "We are going to make muffins. We will need these ingredients: muffin tin, paper cups, butter, jam, milk, eggs, flour, honey, baking powder, salt, vegetable oil, raisins, and wheat germ. And we will need these utensils: bowls, spoons, forks, measuring cups, measuring spoons, potholder, paper cups, and napkins."

Assign volunteers to bring in various items. Stress responsibility for bringing the items, but at the same time, allow for absences, forgetfulness, misunderstandings, difficulties. Allow two days if necessary to accumulate ingredients. Store perishables in the refrigerator.

Teach the names of the ingredients and names of the utensils. Distribute the recipe. Read it. Ask questions about the recipe:

How hot will the oven be?

What are the *dry* ingredients?

What liquids are needed?

How many bowls do we need?

How many muffins should we make?

(The number of muffins to be made should be determined by the number of students in class as well as the size oven available and the time available. Four tins of twelve muffins each can be baked in a standard-size oven with two baking racks. You should figure on extra muffins to offer the principal, secretary, and so on if your class is small.)

DIRECTIONS FOR MAKING WHOLE WHEAT MUFFINS

1. Turn on the oven. Set the temperature at 400 degrees.

2. Take some butter. Grease the muffin tins. (or use paper muffin cups)

3. Measure one cup of flour. Put it in the big bowl.

4. Measure one cup of wheat germ. Put it in the big bowl.

5. Measure one tablespoon of baking powder. Put it in the big bowl.

6. Measure one teaspoon of salt. Put it in the big bowl.

7. Take the big spoon and mix everything together.

8. Break an egg on the side of the second bowl. Drop the egg in the bowl. Put the shell in the garbage.

9. Break another egg on the side of the second bowl. Drop the egg in the bowl. Put the shell in the garbage.

10. Beat the eggs.

11. Measure a half cup of honey. Pour it in the second bowl.

12. Measure two tablespoons of oil. Pour it in the second bowl.

13. Measure one cup of milk. Pour it in the second bowl.

14. Beat everything in the second bowl together.

15. Pour the mixture from the small bowl into the big bowl. Mix everything together. This is called batter. Add raisins or nuts, etc.

16. Put the batter in the muffin tins.

17. Put the tins into the oven. Set the timer for fifteen minutes.

18. Wash the bowls and spoons.

19. Clean the table.

20. Use a potholder. Take out the muffins when they are done. Let them cool for several minutes.

RECIPE FOR WHOLE WHEAT MUFFINS

Preheat oven to 400°.

For 12 medium-size muffins: (multiply as needed)

1 cup whole wheat flour	
1 cup wheat germ	dry ingredients
1 tablespoon double-acting baking powder	
1 teaspoon salt	

Sift or mix the above ingredients together.

1/2 cup honey	
2 eggs, lightly beaten	liquids
1 cup milk	
2 tablespoons vegetable oil	

Mix the dry ingredients together thoroughly in a large bowl. Mix the liquids in another bowl. Add the liquids to the dry ingredients. Mix only until totally moistened.

Add any one of these optional ingredients:

  1/2 cup raisins, dates, or chopped walnuts
  1 mashed banana
  1 cup blueberries

You may substitute orange juice for milk and add:

  1/2 cup shredded carrot
  1 chopped apple

Grease muffin tins or use paper muffin tin liners.

Divide the batter among the 12 cups.

Bake at 400° for 15–20 minutes.

Cool slightly. Serve with butter or jam and milk or orange juice.

If we make twenty-four muffins, how much of each item do we need?

Read the step-by-step directions. Mime the actions with the ingredients. Cut the page and distribute different tasks to students.

Call the students to the front, one at a time, according to the number of the task. Give the direction and mime the action. As the student performs the action, say "(Name) is_____ing the _____. What is he/she doing? Right,_____ing the _____." (The actions could be measuring the flour, cracking the eggs, mixing the batter, etc.)

Additional vocabulary: hot, not hot enough, burn, burnt, ready

Distribute muffins, plastic knives, butter or honey, milk or orange juice. Have students deliver extra muffins to the students' other teachers, principal, and so on. Teach, "Would you like to have a muffin? We made them today." Enjoy!

Follow up:

What is the difference between white flour and whole wheat flour? Which is healthier?

Copy the recipe. Draw pictures of each step in the recipe. Tell the steps taken.

Write about making muffins.

Write a story about a giant muffin.

Suggest making muffins at home with a parent, trying some other variation.

Learn additional recipe terms, measurements, and equivalents: cup, pint, quart, half, quarter, three quarters, two cups equal one pint, three teaspoons equal one tablespoon, four tablespoons equal one quarter of a cup.

HANDICRAFTS AND ENGLISH

The following simple craft projects were selected because of their appeal to various ages. An activity that might seem too childish to an American will not necessarily seem so to a newcomer. In any case, the grade ranges are flexible. Look to your own experiences with your own students.

To take full advantage of the opportunity to present and practice English, follow as many of these suggested steps as apply:

1. Choose activities that will be meaningful to your particular students. Gather all materials and familiarize yourself with the instructions before attempting the activity with a class.

2. Motivate the activity, connecting it to your students' immediate needs, family and friendships, a school event, or a seasonal or holiday occurrence.

3. Read the class a story that is in some way related to the activity.

4. Build some vocabulary connected with the activity, leaving other vocabulary to be acquired while doing the activity.

5. Engage in the activity, talking about the actions and objects involved in it as you are doing it. With some activities, demonstrate the entire project first and then have students complete it as you comment on their actions. Other projects work better if students follow step by step and do not forge ahead on their own. Ask questions that require only pointing, one word, or yes/no for answers. Answer your own questions if necessary. Be enthusiastic about their language contributions and their craft work. Encourage communication in English among the students as they work.

6. Give value to the finished product—use it in a larger project, decorate with it, drink from it, sail it, make a gift of it, send it, display it, and so on.

7. Orally review how it was made or accomplished.

8. Have students tell about it.

9. Draw a picture of the object made or the process for making it.

10. Write a paragraph about it.

11. Write a creative story connected with the activity.

Once you see the potential and the practicality of teaching English through arts and crafts, with some preparation you can adapt any simple craft project into an English lesson.

118A. MAKING PLAY DOUGH

Grades: K and up

English level: Beginner and up

Objectives: To make play dough; to make objects from the dough; to learn the English needed for the activity

Materials needed: Large bowls, mixing spoons, flour, salt, water, cooking oil, and food coloring

Play Dough Recipe: (yields dough for 4–6 children)

2 cups flour
1 cup salt
2/3 cup water
(optional) food coloring

Summary: Mix the flour and salt together thoroughly. Add the food coloring to the water. Add the water a small amount at a time. Dough should hold together well but not stick to your hands when you handle it. This dough will keep for months in a plastic bag, without refrigeration. Play dough items may be baked in a 250 degree oven for two hours, or on a tray in the sun for two days.

Presentation: Show the ingredients and the utensils. Teach the names of the items.

> We're going to make play dough.
> Measure (*two*) cups of flour.
> What's this? It's flour.
> Put it in the bowl.
> Measure (*one*) cup of salt.
> Put it in the bowl.
> What's in the bowl now?   (*flour and salt*)
> Mix the flour and the salt together.
> Measure (*two thirds of a*) cup of water.
> Put food coloring into the water. What color shall we make our play dough?
> Put the colored water in the bowl.
> What's in the bowl now?   (*flour, salt, and water*)
> Mix everything together.
> This is dough. Can you eat this dough?
> Give everyone some of this dough.
> Taste it. It's salty, isn't it?
> No, you can't eat this dough. But you can play with it.
> So it's play dough.
> Let's make some things.
> Can you make a ball? Roll the play dough in your hands. Around and around. What's this?   (*it's a ball*)
> Can you make a snake? Roll the play dough on the table. Roll it and roll it. Here is a snake. (*Jenni*) made a snake too.
> What else can you make?
> Look what (*Chung*) made. (*Chung*) made a dish. (*Wilda*) made a cat.   (*etc.*)
> Look what I made. I made a turtle.
> Roll the dough flat. Draw on it. Cut out the shape. Make a hole for a ribbon.

(Make several items to give practice working with the material.)

> We will make (*Christmas ornaments, dreidles, valentines, animals, presents for Mother's or Father's Day, etc.*) to bake and get hard.

(If you want to hang the item on a ribbon or string, make the holes with a pencil point before you bake or dry it.)

Follow up: See suggestions at the beginning of the chapter. Write an experience chart:

We made play dough.

First we mixed flour, water, and salt together.

We made_____ and_____.

(Etc.)

118B. ORIGAMI

The magic of creating a three-dimensional object from a few folds of a square of paper will keep interest high during this activity. Practice each item yourself first before doing it with the class. Make something specific for a specific purpose (examples: drink from the cup; sail the boat; wear the hat; "catch bugs" with the bug catcher; decorate the room, walls, greeting cards, holiday tree with birds, flowers, etc.).

Grades: 1 and up (varying levels of difficulty)

English level: Beginners and up

Objectives: To follow directions; to learn how to fold items from paper; to learn the English needed to talk about the activity

Materials needed: Plain, unlined white or colored 8½ × 11 paper; scissors (*Note:* Construction paper is too heavy for most origami projects.)

119. THE CUP

Grades: 1 and up

Optional: Peanuts or raisins to serve in the cups when finished

Presentation: Distribute three sheets of paper to each student.

We are going to make a cup.

First we have to have a square. What is a square? Who can draw a square on the board?

Yes, that's a square.

A square has four sides. Are they all the same?   (Yes.)

1. Is this (*hold up 8½ × 11 paper*) a square?   (No.)

    Are the sides the same?   (No, they are different.)

    What is this?   (A rectangle.)

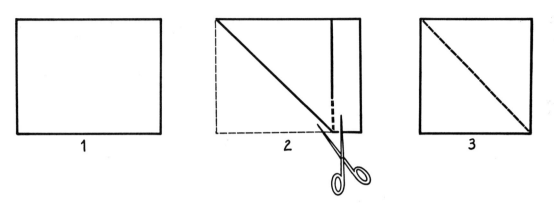

We can make a square from a
  rectangle.

2. Fold the bottom corner up to the
    top, like this.

   These sides must touch. Now you
     have a triangle here and some
     left over.

   Fold this paper over the edge, like
     this.

   Now take your scissors and cut off
     this piece.

3. Open the paper.

   Now you have a square.

4. Fold the square again.

   What do you have?   *(A triangle.)*

   Put the triangle flat on the table
     with the point up.

   Look at one side.

5. Put your finger on the middle of
    the side.

   Bring the opposite point up to the
     middle of the side.

   Now find the middle of the other
     side.

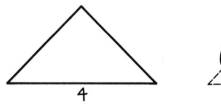

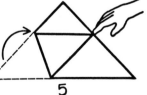

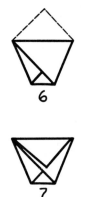

6. Bring the other corner up to this place.

7. Fold the front of the top point down, like this.

   Turn the paper over.

   Fold the other top point down, like this.

   Put your hand inside the cup and open it up.

   You can now get a drink of water in your cup.

Let's try another cup. Look at your paper. What shape is it?   *(A rectangle.)*

Can you make a cup with the rectangle? No, you need a square. What do we do first to make a square? Right, fold the bottom corner up to the top.   *(And so on.)*

Who can do it without directions now? Who can make the cup again? Let's see.

What else can you do with your cup?   *(Put in peanuts, raisins, etc.)*

Right, you can put things in your cup.   *(Distribute the peanuts or raisins into each student's cup.)*

Follow up: See additional ideas at beginning of the chapter.

   Make a cup at home. Teach another child how to make a cup.

   Decorate the cup.

   Write about making a cup:

   First we took a piece of paper.

      It was a rectangle.

      We made a square.

      Then we folded the paper until we had a cup.

      We drank water from our cup.

120. THE HAT

Grades: 1 and up

Materials needed: Newspapers or 18 × 24 construction paper

Presentation: "We are going to make a hat. We need some newspaper or big sheets of paper."

1. Fold the newspaper
   Put the newspaper on the desk, like this, with the open side down.

2. Fold one corner down to the middle, like this.

3. Fold the other corner of the paper down to the middle, like this.

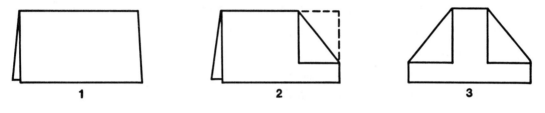

4. Fold this side of the bottom up, like this.

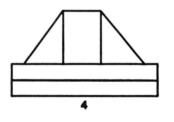

5. Turn the paper over.
   Fold this side up, like this.

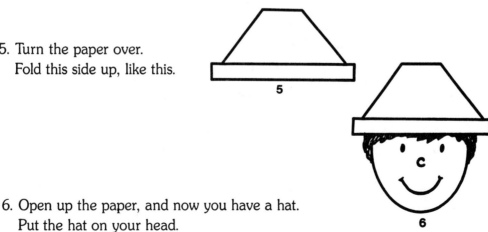

6. Open up the paper, and now you have a hat.
   Put the hat on your head.
   Decorate the hat with crayons, paste on cutout feathers, flowers (*etc.*).

121. THE BOAT

This activity goes well with the story *Curious George Rides a Bike* by H.A. Rey (Boston: Houghton Mifflin, 1973).

Grades: 2 and up

Materials needed: Newspaper or unlined white paper or construction paper

Presentation:

Let's make some boats.

Put the newspaper down like this, with the open side down.

1. Fold one corner to the middle, like this.
   (*Refer to the illustrations for the hat up to step 5.*)

2. Fold the other corner to the middle, like this.

3. Fold the bottom up, like this.

4. Turn the paper over. Fold the bottom up, like this.
   Now you have a hat. Do not put it on your head.

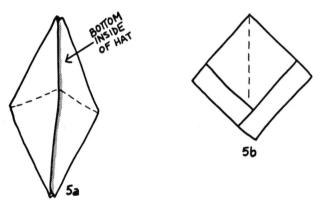
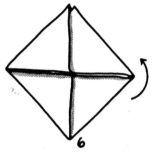

5. Open the hat up, like this, and press it down flat.
   Put it on the table with the open points down.

6. Fold one bottom corner up to the top corner.

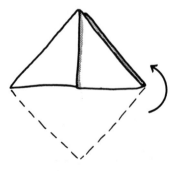

7. Turn the paper over.
   Fold the other side up to the top corner.
   Crease it carefully.

8. Open up the boat, like this: (*bottom view*)

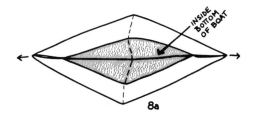

Put the boat in the sink (*tub*) or take your boat home and see if it floats.
Does it float?

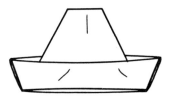

122.   THE "BUG CATCHER"

Grades: 3 and up

English level: Beginner and up

Objectives: To fold a paper "Bug Catcher"; to learn the English needed to talk about the activity

Presentation: Practice making the Bug Catcher until you are familiar with the steps. Show students how the Bug Catcher works:

   I have a Bug Catcher. I can catch bugs in the air or clean my (your) books (*clothes*). Look. It's clean now. Watch. I am going to catch the bugs in this book. (*Using two hands, open and close the catcher, opening it now to reveal the "dirty" inside.*)

Oh, yukk. Look at all the bugs I caught.

Students will want to learn to make one too.

1. Make a square.

2. Fold the square in half to make a triangle.

3. Open up the square and fold it again the other way.

4. Open the square.

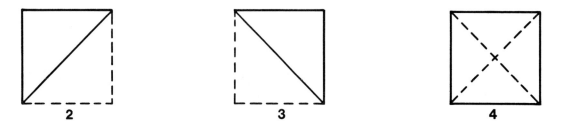

5. Fold each corner into the center.

6. Turn the square over.
   Fold each corner into the center again.

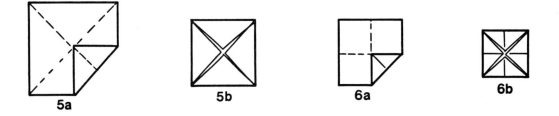

7. Fold the square in half to form a rectangle. Crease the fold.

8. Open it again and fold it the other way. Crease the fold.

9. Put your thumb and three fingers into the pockets of the square. Open and close your Bug Catcher.

10. Now you have to put in the bugs. Mark each of the four triangles in the center with a pencil.

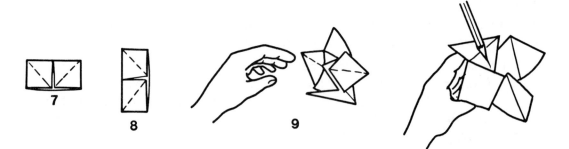

11. Open the square and on the triangles you have marked, draw tiny little bugs, spiders, worms, caterpillars, flies, and so on.

12. Using two hands, place your thumb and index finger in each pocket. You can now open the mouth from top to bottom, or from left to right.

    (*Open the "mouth" to show the clean parts.*) See, this is a Bug Catcher. Watch it work.

    (*Place the Bug Catcher on the floor, desk, one's hair, clothes, nose, etc.*) Look, I caught all these bugs. Yukk! Disgusting!

    (*Open the "mouth" to show the bugs.*)

    Where should I put these bugs? Maybe in my pocket (*hair, garbage, desk, etc.*).

Shake the Bug Catcher over the desired area. Open the mouth the other way and show that it is clean again.

To make a hand puppet: Fold paper up to step #9. Draw eyes and a nose on the top, and draw a tongue on the bottom of the inside. Talk to your puppet.

123. TISSUE FLOWERS

Grades: 1 and up

English level: Beginner and up

Objectives: To make tissue flowers for some larger decorative project; to learn the English necessary to follow instructions and talk about the activity

Materials needed: Box of tissues; heavy thread or wire ("twistie ties" are ideal); straws (optional: lipstick)

Preparation: Make several flowers in advance to show students

Presentation: Teach the word *flower* and the words for the materials

1. Fold the tissue in half, like this.

2. Fold the tissue like an accordian.

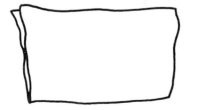

Fold the tissue this way and turn it over and fold it that way.

Turn it again and fold it and turn it again and fold it.

Make the folds very tiny.

3. When it is all folded, wrap a twistie tie around the middle (*or tie a thread around the middle*).

4. Tear a tiny bit off the top of the tissue.

5. Separate the tissue and gently pull it away. Be careful. Don't tear the tissue.

6. Bring the tissue up like this. These are the petals of the flower.

7. You can color the tops of the petals with lipstick, like this. (*Gently brush the tops of the tissue against the lipstick to give a red color to the tips of the petals.*)

The flowers may be used to decorate a doorway, bulletin board, or Mother's Day card. A bobby pin can be inserted in the thread so the flower may be worn in the hair. The flowers may also be worn as boutonnieres.

124. BANANA TREE

Grades: K and up (K to 4 will enjoy watching a demonstration and making the tree "grow" but won't have the strength to handle the cutting involved without frustration)

English level: Beginner and up

Materials needed: For a 3-foot-tall banana tree, 2 sheets of large newspaper and scissors (optional—a yardstick)

Presentation:

1. Spread the two sheets of newspaper on a long table or the floor and cut in half lengthwise. You now have four long sheets of newspaper.

2. Lay the newspaper out, one sheet at a time, overlapping by three inches.

3. Gently roll it up. The finished roll should be between one and one and a

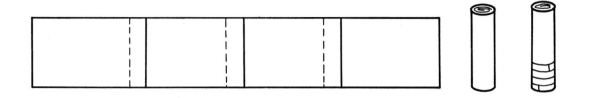

half inches in diameter. If it is too tight, it will be difficult to cut. If too loose, the finished tree will not stand up straight.

4. Tape the bottom half of the roll with transparent or masking tape.

5. With large scissors, make four or five cuts to about halfway down the "tree trunk." (You might have to do each cut several layers at a time because of the difficulty of cutting through the twelve or so layers of newspaper.)

6. Reach into the center of the banana tree and gently pull. The banana tree will grow right before the students' eyes. Students are then ready to make their own banana trees.

Sample conversation: Show a picture of a banana.

What's this?	*(Banana)*
Do you like bananas?	*(Yes; no)*
(Jorge) likes bananas. *(Jenna)* doesn't like bananas.	
Watch this. I will make a banana tree from newspapers!	
What's this?	*(Newspaper)*
How many sheets of newspaper do I have?	*(Two)*
We have to do this on the floor. Our desks are too small.	
First I cut the newspaper up the long way, like this.	
What am I cutting with?	*(Scissors)*
Now how many papers do I have?	*(Four)*
I put them down and overlap them. See, they are overlapping this much.	
I'm rolling up the newspapers.	

Roll very carefully. What am I doing?   *(Rolling the papers)*

This part will be the trunk. I'm going
   to put some tape to hold the trunk
   of the tree. What part is this?   *(The trunk)*

Now I'm going to make the leaves.

I have to cut the leaves with the
   scissors. What am I cutting?   *(The leaves)*

Right, I'm cutting the leaves.

Here's one cut. All the way down to
   the trunk.

And cut again.

And cut again.

And cut again.

Are you ready to see the tree grow?

(Optional—include a lesson on measurement and comparisons):

Before it grows, let's measure our
   banana tree with the yardstick.

How tall is it?   *(Twelve inches; one foot)*

Now I reach into the middle of the
   tree and pull.

I'm pulling the tree. Watch the tree
   grow!

Let's measure it with the yardstick.

How tall is it now?   *(Twenty-four to thirty-six inches)*

Yes, it's thirty inches tall!

Do you want to make banana trees?
   We can have a whole banana tree
   woods growing in our classroom.

Follow up: Arrange the students' finished banana trees in one corner of the
room (maybe the story corner) as a woods.

Write about the activity, practicing the past tense forms:

We made banana trees.

First we cut long sheets of newspaper.

We overlapped the papers.

We rolled the papers into a tube.

We taped the trunk.

We cut the leaves.

Then we pulled the middle up.

The banana tree grew tall.

My banana tree was_____ inches tall.

Now we have a woods in the classroom.

125. A CLOCK

Grades: K to 3

English level: Beginner and up

Objectives: To make a clock; to reinforce numbers; to practice telling time; to learn the English needed to talk about the activity

Materials needed: 7- or 9-inch paper plate for each student; crayons; black construction paper; brass fasteners; scissors

Preparation: Find the center of the paper plate and place a dot there. (You can do this by folding one plate in half, opening it, and folding it in half in a different direction. Where the two creases meet is the center.) Put a pin through the center and line up other paper plates to make pin holes in the center. Mark these pin holes with a pencil or a marker.

Summary: Have students observe a clock and note that the number 12 is at the top, 6 at the bottom, 3 and 9 at the right and left, respectively.

Students lightly write in the numbers 12, 6, 3, and 9. Check the positions. Then students fill in the other numbers, and after being checked, darken them in with crayon or magic markers.

Cut the long hand and short hand of the clock out of black paper (for a 9-inch paper plate, the long hand can be 4 inches; the short hand, 3 inches).

Place the ends of the two hands and secure them to the plate with a paper fastener. The hands of the clock can now be moved to show the time.

Presentation and sample conversation:

What's this? (Point to wall clock.)

What time is it?

We are going to make our own clocks.

Look at the clock. (Draw large circle.)

(Refer students to the wall clock.)

Where is number 12—at the top (demonstrate) or at the bottom? (At the top.)

(Student), come to the chalkboard and write number 12 at the top.

Where is number 6—at the top or at the bottom? (At the bottom.)

(Student), write number 6 at the bottom.

(Continue with 3 and 9.)

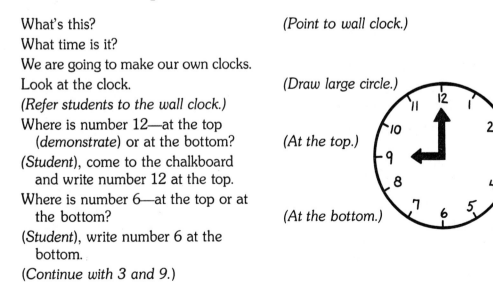

Who can write numbers 1 and 2 in
the right place on this clock?

*(Continue with 4 and 5, 7 and 8, 10
and 11.)*

The clock has two hands.   *(Hold up your hands.)*

One hand is long.   *(Extend your right hand as far in
                                                  front of you as it will go.)*

One hand is short.   *(Your left hand should extend to the
                                                  wrist of your right hand.)*

How many hands does the clock
have?   *(Two.)*

A long hand and a...?   *(Short hand.)*

Here is the center of the clock.   *(Draw a dot.)*

Who can draw a long hand pointing
to number 12?

Very good.

Who can draw a short hand pointing
to number 3?

Great. The long hand is on 12. The
short hand is on 3.

What time is it?   *(3 o'clock.)*

Great. Now we will make our own
clocks.

Take out your crayons.   *(Or distribute crayons.)*

Here are some paper plates.

What are they?   *(Paper plates.)*

(Keren), will you give everyone a
paper plate, please?

(Keren) is giving out the paper
plates.

What shape is a plate?   *(Circle.)*

Take your pencil and lightly draw the
number 12 at the top of the clock.   *(Check their work.)*

Now, where will you draw number
6?   *(At the bottom; check their work.)*

And where will you draw number 3?   *(Here.)*

(Etc.)

Follow up: Use the clocks to practice telling time. Glue or staple the clocks to
construction paper and write sentences below the clocks:

I get up at 7 o'clock.

It's 9 o'clock. It's time for school.
(Etc.)

126. THE CRAZY ONE-SIDED CIRCLE

Grades: 2 and up

English level: Intermediate and up

Objectives: To create a "Mobius strip" and to talk about the curiosity of a one-sided circle. This will give students a very simple "trick" to talk about with their English-speaking classmates.

Materials needed: 18-inch-long construction paper; tape; magic markers or felt-tipped pens

Preparation: Cut two 2-inch-wide strips from 18-inch construction paper. The ends of the first strip are taped together to form a circle. The second strip is given a single twist before the ends are taped.

Summary: The circle formed by the strip that is twisted has several curious properties about it. The *inside* and *outside* are the same (as you can demonstrate by drawing a long continuous line down the middle of the strip)! When the strip is cut on that line, it forms one large circle. When that circle is cut down the center, it forms two interlocking circles!

Presentation:

We are going to make crazy, mixed-up circles. First, I will make a normal circle from this strip of paper. Take this end and tape it to this end.

Hold up the first circle.

Here is the *outside* of the circle.

And here is the *inside*.

(Student), would you please put the marker here *(some point on the outside of the circle)*. Don't pick up your marker and draw all the way around until you get back to the start.

Now, let's look. The line is on the outside of the circle. Is it all the way around the circle?   *(Yes)*

Is there a line on the inside of the circle?   *(No)*

Very good.

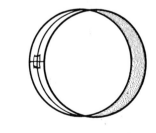

What are the two sides of this circle?

(Inside and outside.)

Now I'll make the crazy, mixed-up circle. Take this end and twist it and then tape it to the other end. This other circle is very funny. Maybe it's magic.

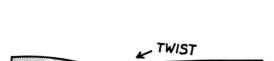

(*Student*), please put the marker here (*at a point on the circle*). Don't pick up your marker and draw all the way around the circle until you get back to the start.

Do you see anything funny?

(Yes)

(Students will be surprised to see that the marked line is on both sides of the strip!)

Did (*Student*) pick up the marker?

(No)

Did the line get on both the inside and the outside of the circle?

(Yes)

Let's try this again.

(Distribute the long strips of paper.)

You can make your own crazy circle.

Lay the strip of paper on the desk. Pick up one end and give it one twist.

Now tape it to the other end to make a circle.

Take your pen or pencil and draw one line on the circle all the way around until you get back to the start.

It really is a crazy circle.

You can do other funny things with this crazy circle.

First watch what happens when we cut this regular circle. (*Student #2*), will you cut on the line that (*Student #1*) drew?

What do you think will happen?

(You'll have two circles.)

(*Herri*) is cutting the circle.

Yes, now we have two circles. You were right.

Now let's cut this crazy circle.

(*Jee Yun*), will you cut this circle on the line that (*Student #1*) drew?

What do you think will happen? (Students guess.)

(Jee Yun) is cutting the crazy circle.

Look what's happening.

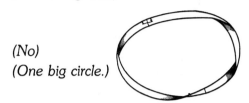

Do we have two circles? (No)

What do we have? (One big circle.)

Now you try that with your crazy circle.

One big circle! Did everybody get one big circle?

How come? (I don't know, it's just a crazy circle!)

Let's see what else our crazy circle can do.

What do you think will happen if we cut down the middle of this big circle? (Students guess.)

Let's all cut and see.

(Students cut and create two circles that are interlocked—a truly mystifying feat!)

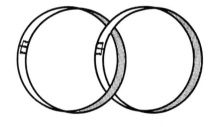

Two circles joined together! How did it happen?

I don't know, it's just a crazy circle.

Follow up: Write what was done:

We made crazy circles.

The circle had only one side.

When we cut it, it made one big circle.

When we cut the big circle, it made two circles joined together.

Encourage students to demonstrate the crazy circle to others.

127. PAPER CUP TELEPHONES

Grades: K to 6

English level: Beginners and up

Objectives: To make paper cup telephones; to learn the English needed to talk about the activity; to learn telephone-answering expressions and manners

Materials needed: Four 5-inch paper cups per pair of students; 30 feet of string per pair of students; pointed scissors or a sharp pencil

Summary: Poke a small hole in the bottom of each cup. Cut the string into two equal lengths. To make a pair of telephones, thread one end of the string through each of two cups. Pull the strings up about eight inches and tie a large knot in the end of the string. Pull the strings back so the knot is up against the bottom of the cup.

The students go to opposite ends of the room or as far as the strings will take them. Going out the door adds to the effect.

The strings should be pulled taut (but *not* touching anything), with care not to pull the string through the hole in the paper cup. One cup serves as the earpiece and the other as the mouthpiece. The voices will carry through the string as long as it is taut.

Sample phone conversation:

Hello, this is (*Tom*).
Hello, this is (*Jan*).
How are you?
Fine, thank you, how are you?
What are you doing?
I'm making a toy telephone. What are you doing?
I'm practicing English.
See you tomorrow.
Goodbye.
(*Etc.*)

128. HUMMING BUTTON

Grades: K and up

English level: Beginner and up

Objectives: To make a Humming Button; to learn the English necessary to complete the activity

Materials needed: 24-inch string; a large coat button with 2 or 4 holes

Summary: Thread the string through the buttonholes. If it is a four-hole button, thread through two diagonally opposite holes.

Tie the string. Holding the ends of the string in two hands, with the button in the center, wind the string by swinging it in a circle fifty to one hundred turns. Then slowly pull your two hands apart, and the button will hum loudly.

Presentation: Demonstrate your Humming Button to the students.

This is a Humming Button.
Listen.
First I wind it up, like this.   (*count*)
Then I pull my hands away, like this.
Now you can make one.

Here is some string.
And here is your button.
What's this?   *(string)*
What's this?   *(button)*
Put the string through one hole in the button.
Now put it through the other hole.
Tie the string in a knot.
Put the string around your fingers, like this.
Swing the string to wind up the button.
Swing it and swing it and swing it.
When it is almost all wound up, pull your hands away.
Listen.
The button is humming.

English in the Content Areas

Many teachers struggle with the problem of how to teach the content areas to students whose English is limited. Should science and social studies wait until students are more fluent and can read the text?

No waiting is needed. Science lessons—particularly science experiments, demonstrations, and hands-on activities—give the comprehensible input required for language acquisition. Social studies concepts can be gotten across through experiences, map making, and trips—all of which offer concrete and comprehensible backgrounds for vocabulary building. Much in both subjects can be imparted visually through pictures, filmstrips, movies, and video presentations. For your limited-English students, include sufficient repetition for listening comprehension. Ask frequent yes/no and one-word-answer questions to get feedback about vocabulary and actions, and allow time for students to learn the language needed to talk about the activities. Write key words and questions on the chalkboard and encourage students to use their bilingual dictionaries.

SCIENCE ACTIVITIES

Using the discovery methods of science keeps student motivation high and supplies the context for insights both into the natural world and into language.

If you are a "limited speaker of science," don't be anxious. Science is fun. Join in with your students as an observer and inquirer into the causes, interrelationships, and behavior of the things observed all around us. The content of the elementary school science curriculum is generally tangible and concrete: our bodies, senses, the weather, living things, rocks, local land formations, the sky, simple instruments and machines.

Your own sense of wonder and participation in discovery will enhance the lessons. All good science lessons should answer some questions and raise others, some open-ended.

Classroom equipment should include rulers, scales, magnets, thermometers, batteries, bulbs, and magnifying glasses. If you can manage some fish or bugs and small animals in a glass tank, you'll have lots of student-generated questions for observation and inquiry. Microscopes can add to the range of exploration.

The following unit on plants will give you a foundation for creating or executing similar units on weather, animals, machines, magnets. Flip through a good modern science textbook for a grade level suitable to your students (or perhaps one or two years below the grade level of the students) and select the activities within the chapters that are within your time/materials/abilities scope.

PLANTS

129. PLANTING SEEDS

Seeds will grow indoors anytime, but I like the first day of spring for this activity. If you select dwarf marigolds as your seeds, you will have tiny flowers for the students to take home on Mother's Day. You may also plant a variety of seeds so you will be able to note and discuss the differences in the sizes of the seeds, germination times, growth rates, appearances of young plants and leaves, and so on.

Grades: K and up

English level: Beginners and up

Objectives: To observe growth of seeds and plants; to notice and meet the needs of plants; to learn the English needed to talk about the project; to follow directions in sequence; to tell steps in sequence. (Younger students will benefit both from the science and the language learned. Older students will have an enjoyable activity, review science concepts learned in their native language, and be able to demonstrate their knowledge as they acquire the English to talk about it.)

Materials needed: Newspapers to cover the table; large spoon; sharp pencils; permanent colored markers; watering can; potting soil (10 pounds will fill 40 10-ounce cups); foam cups, one for each child, with extras; large (14 × 18) aluminum baking pans or other waterproof pans to hold the cups; 2–3 packets of seeds (dwarf marigolds just fit in this size cup—other seeds may need transplanting later)

Beans germinate and grow delightfully fast but soon are weighed down by their own stems unless staked up (pencils and rulers will serve for a time, but a large pot and a yardstick will be necessary eventually). If each student brings seeds from some fruit or vegetable that they have eaten at home, a great variety of plants may be grown. Another option is grass seeds. In this case, decorate the foam cup with the face of "Hairy Herman." The grass will grow and be the hair. Students can trim Herman's "hair" with scissors when it gets too long.

Preparation: Sketch the steps for planting on chart paper. Decorate several foam cups to suggest a variety of items that might be drawn by the students on their cups (if this is to be a Mother's Day project), such as flowers, animals, birds, butterflies, abstract geometric designs, or a face—if this is to be a "Hairy Herman."

Presentation: Have all materials ready. Demonstrate all the steps students will follow *before* distributing any materials. *Illustrate each vocabulary item and demonstrate each step as you speak about it.*

Sample conversation:

Today we are going to plant seeds.

These are *(marigold seeds)*.

First we will cover our table with newspapers. These are cups. I will give you each a cup.

This is the top of the cup, and this is the bottom.

You will take your pencil and make a hole in the bottom of the cup, like this.

Water can come out of this hole. The hole should be about this size (O). Use a colored marker. Write your name on the side of the cup. Do not write your name on the bottom of the cup.

Decorate your cup. That means, draw pictures on your cup. You can draw flowers, birds, or butterflies. You can draw anything you want. You can write "Happy Spring!" or "Happy Mother's Day!"

Mother's Day is the second Sunday in May *(show on calendar)*. The plants will be six inches tall then. You can give them to your mother for Mother's Day.

This is soil. After you decorate your cup, come up to the table to get some soil. Put the soil in the cup

with the big spoon. Fill the cup almost to the top. Pat the soil gently.

Take your pencil. Make four holes in the soil, like this.

These are seeds. Take four seeds. Put one seed in each hole. Cover the seeds with soil.

This is a pan. Put your cup in the pan.

This is a watering can. Put water on your soil.

When you finish, copy the pictures to show what you did.

Review the basic vocabulary, holding up each item as you elicit (or supply) its name: newspapers, cup, soil, pencil, seeds, spoon, colored marker, decorations, water, watering can, pan.

Distribute the cups and again give directions, demonstrating each step as the students follow. This time, encourage students to tell what you are doing, or what they are doing, as they do it.

What am I doing now?	*(Writing; you're writing your name on the cup.)*
What is *(Carmen)* doing?	*(She's drawing a butterfly on the cup, etc.)*

Have students who finish their planting ahead of the others decorate additional cups and plant additional seeds, without writing their names on the cups. These will be extras for experiments, in case of "crop failure," or for students who enter your program between planting time and the time to take home the plants.

When students finish planting their seeds, they may copy the sequence chart from the chalkboard.

Follow up: If feasible, have each student water his or her own plant daily, after you show them the proper amount. (Soil should be damp but not soaked.) Or students take turns watering all the plants. Caution about over-watering.

Using the pictures, students can review the steps for planting seeds and write directions for others to follow, or they can tell the process in the past tense.

For beginning students, build up comprehension and sentence pattern recognition by stating at random, the following sentences about the pictures. Students volunteer the number of the picture (see previous illustrations):

We poked a hole in the bottom of the cup. (1)

We wrote our name on the cup. (2)

We drew pictures on the cup. (3)

We filled the cup with soil. (4)

We made four holes in the soil. (5)

We put one seed in each hole. (6)

We covered the seeds with soil.

We watered the soil. (7)

Next week we can see the plant grow. (8)

Writing/Reading: Write the sentences in the correct order for students to read and copy.

At a later time, write sentences in mixed order for students to copy in correct order.

For further practice in reading comprehension, write the sentences leaving blanks to fill in. (Supply answers at the bottom of the page.)

For practice in word order, scramble the words in each sentence, to be written in correct order.

When plants are ready to be taken home, place each cup in a plastic bag and secure with a twist tie. Poke several holes in the bag to allow air to enter.

Extensions: Read stories such as *Jack & the Beanstalk; The Carrot Seed* by Ruth Krauss (New York: Harper & Row, 1945); and *A Garden for Miss Mouse* by Michaela Muntean (New York: Parents Magazine Press, 1982).

Have students keep a chart recording their observations on the growth of the plants.

Week #1:

What day did we plant the seeds? We planted the seeds on _____.

How many seeds did we plant? We planted _____ seeds.

What color were the seeds? _____

When did the first plant start to grow? The first plant started to grow _____ days later.

How many leaves does your plant have? The plant has _____ leaves.

What color are the leaves? The leaves are _____.

Week #2:

How many plants are growing now? _____ plants are growing.

Why do you think all the seeds didn't grow?

_____

_____

(seed was no good, dead, planted too deep, overwatered, not watered enough)

Look at the plants. Are they all growing to one side? _____

Which side do they grow on? _____

(towards the window; towards the sun)

(Turn the cups around so the plant leans into the room. Check the plants the next day.) What happened?_____

_____

(the plants grew so the leaves face the sun again—heliotropism)

Week #3:

How many plants are growing now?_____

Who has the tallest plant? _____ has the tallest plant.

How tall is it? The tallest plant is _____inches tall.

How many leaves does the tallest plant have?_____

We are going to do some experiments with the extra plants. What will happen if we put some plants under a box? *(or in the closet?)* _____

What will happen if we don't water some plants? _____

What will happen if we put a plastic bag around some plants? _____

_____

Place some of the extra plantings out of the light. Either cover them with a box or put them in a closet. Continue to water these daily. Choose some other plants and set them aside. Do not water them for one week. Choose a third set and wrap the cup in a plastic bag and seal it tight. Talk about what you are doing.

Week #4

How many plants are growing now? _____

The tallest plant is _____ inches tall.

What happened to the plants that did not have any light? The plants that did not have any light _____.

What happened to the plants that did not have any water? The plants that did not have any water _____.

What do plants need? Plants need _____.

(water, sunshine, soil, air)

Week #5

Separate the plants into two groups. Add some plant food to the water for one group. Water the other group as usual. After one week, compare the plants.

What happened to the plants that got plant food? _____

130. DISSECTING SEEDS

Grades: 3 to 6

English level: Intermediate

Objectives: To discover and observe the contents of a seed; to learn the English needed to talk about the activity

Materials needed: Kidney beans or other large beans; knives (butter knives will be safest, and if beans are softened, will do just fine; magnifying glasses, 1 per student, or at least 1 per 3 students; paper towels

Preparation: Soak seeds overnight

Presentation:

> What makes seeds grow? We are going to look inside a seed. First I soaked the seeds in water to make them soft. Now we can cut the seeds open with a knife. We will look inside the seeds with a magnifying glass.
>
> (Distribute paper towels, beans, magnifying glasses, butter knives.)
>
> What do you see? (*tiny plant and tiny root*) This is called an embryo.
>
> When the seed gets wet, the baby plant starts to grow. Where does it get its food?   (*the seed has food for the plant*)
>
> What color is the inside of the seed? What color are the baby roots and the baby leaves?
>
> Draw a picture of the inside of the seed. Label the parts: leaflet, rootlet, food.

131.   ROOTS

Grades: 3 and up

English level: Intermediate

Objectives: To observe the growth of roots in the absence of light or soil and to learn the English necessary to speak about it

Materials needed: 5 or 6 dried beans or other large seeds per student; paper towels, water, plastic bags, permanent markers

Preparation: Wet the paper towels, one per student (or students may work in teams of two, three, or four)

Presentation: "Can seeds grow with no soil? Can seeds grow with no sunshine? Let's find out." (You may write these questions on the chalkboard and accept students' guesses.)

Distribute the paper towels, seeds, and plastic bags. Teach vocabulary.

Sample listening comprehension:

> The paper towel is wet.
>
> Put your seeds on the paper towel,
>   like this.
>
> Roll up the paper towel. Put it in the
>   plastic bag.

Write your name on the outside of the plastic bag with a marker.	*(Or write your name on a paper, tape it to the bag.)*
We will look at our *seeds* every day.	

(Observe the seeds daily and have students record their observations. You may plant some of the seeds. Keep the towel damp and observe the rest of the seeds at daily or two-day intervals until they die.)

Are the seeds bigger now?	*(Yes)*
What do you think made them get bigger?	*(Water)*
Can seeds germinate (*sprout, grow*) without soil?	*(Yes)*
Can roots grow without light?	*(Yes)*
What makes the roots grow?	*(Food in the seed.)*
What do roots look like under a magnifying glass?	*(Have little hairs on them.)*
Do leaves grow without light?	
Does the plant turn green without light?	*(No)*

(Place some of the paper towels with germinated seeds in the light. Keep them moist. Observe them.)

What happened to the seeds now?	*(Leaves grow.)*
What color are the leaves?	*(Green)*
What do you think made the leaves turn green?	*(Sunlight + chlorophyll)*

(Plant some of the seeds. Dig them up after two weeks.)

What happened to the seed?	*(Got smaller; the food was used up.)*
How big is the plant now? Did it all come out of the seed?	*(No, the plant makes its own food.)*

132. THE PARTS OF A PLANT

Grades: 2 and up

English level: Intermediate

Objectives: To observe the parts of the plant and learn their names and functions; to learn the English needed to talk about the parts and their functions

Materials needed: Small plant (with roots) for each group of students; flower for each group of students; magnifying glasses; pictures of many fruits and vegetables

Presentation: Draw a plant on the chalkboard.

What are the parts of the plant?

(Roots, stem, leaves, flower)

Why does a plant have roots?

(The roots hold the plant in the soil; they take water and minerals from the soil; they can store food for the plant.)

Why does a plant have a stem?

(The stem holds the leaves up to get sunlight.)

Why does a plant have leaves?

(The leaves make food for the plant.)

What are the parts of a flower?

(Petals, pistil, stamen, anther)

Draw a flower on the chalkboard.

What is at the bottom of the pistil?
(*the ovary, containing seeds*)
When the ovary grows, it is called
the fruit of the plant.

Animals and people eat plants. We
eat different parts of different
plants. What part of each of these
plants do we eat?

spinach — (*leaves*)
asparagus — (*stem*)
beets — (*root*)
onions — (*root*)
corn — (*seeds*)
string beans — (*fruit and
seeds*)
cauliflower — (*flower*)
lettuce — (*leaves*)
carrots — (*roots*)
zucchini — (*fruit*)
tomato, bell pepper, eggplant,
squash — (*fruit*)
potato — (*root*)
peas — (*seeds*)
cabbage — (*leaves*)
celery — (*stem and leaves*)
soybeans — (*seeds, sprouts*)

133. HOW DO PLANTS GET WATER?

Grades: 2 and up

English level: Low intermediate and up

Objectives: To find out how water travels up the stem to the leaves; to learn the English needed to talk about the activity

Materials needed: Celery, glass, water, red food coloring, knife, paper towels, white string

Preparation: Make a fresh cut at the bottom of a celery stalk. Place the stalk in a jar of water. Put a teaspoon of red food coloring in the water. Observe the celery after several hours or the next day.

Presentation:

What happened to the leaves?   *(They became spotted with red.)*

Why did the leaves turn red?   *(The water went up the stalk.)*

We call this capillary action.

(You can also observe the tubes through which the water flows. Cut off a half-inch piece of the bottom of the stalk after the leaves have turned red. Observe.

Roll a paper towel into a long tube. Place one end in the water. Observe the towel. Do the same with a piece of thick white string.)

Capillary action causes water to
    move in all directions.

Capillary action can do "magic."
    Watch.

Here is a glass full of water. And
    here is an empty glass. I can make
    the water go from the full glass to
    the empty glass without picking up
    the glasses.

(Place the rolled up tube of paper towel in the first glass of water. Bend the tube and allow it to hang over the empty glass. Observe the glass at the end of fifteen minutes; an hour; the next day.

What happened?   *(The second glass now has water in it.)*

How did the water get there?   *(Capillary action in the paper towel.)*

(The students should not think that because there is a name to the process that this is an answer. It should leave them with a question: How does capillary action work?)

134. DO ALL PLANTS START FROM SEEDS?

Grades: 2 and up

English level: High beginners and up

Objectives: To discover the many ways plants can propagate; to learn the English needed to talk about the activity

Materials needed: Fresh carrots with greens still attached; sweet potato; leaves from a jade plant, snake plant, aloe, or other succulent; cuttings from ivy or other house plant; crocus, onion, or other bulb

Summary:

1. Wring off the carrot greens. Cut off the top half inch of the carrots. Place the carrot tops in moist soil. The same may also be done with the top of a pineapple or turnip.

2. Place three toothpicks in a sweet potato and put the root end of the potato into a glass of water, in the sunlight. Watch it grow. (Some sweet potatoes have been sprayed with a chemical to retard the growth of shoots. Check with your supermarket manager or test a potato at home first.)

3. Break off a stem with a few leaves of a succulent plant such as a jade plant or an aloe plant. Place it in moist earth and keep it damp.

4. Put some cuttings from an ivy, Swedish ivy, or other house plant in a glass of water. Observe. When roots form, plant the cuttings in soil.

5. Plant some crocus bulbs.

Ask students to tell what they observe. Write their sentences (reworded in good English if necessary) on the chalkboard for the class to copy in their notebooks.

Examples:

We planted carrot tops. Roots grew, and then the tops grew.

We put toothpicks into a sweet potato. We put the potato in a glass of water. Roots grew in the water. Stems and leaves grew on the top of the potato.

We planted a piece of a jade plant. It grew roots and started to grow into a new plant.

We cut some stems of plants and put them in water. Roots started to grow on the stems that were in the water. We planted them and new plants started to grow.

We planted a crocus bulb. It grew into a flower.

Conclusions: Plants can grow from seeds, roots, bulbs, stems, or leaves.

Additional activities: Grow bean sprouts in jars in the classroom. Most health food stores have a variety of beans for sprouting and complete directions. They can be eaten on sandwiches and in salads or plain.

DISCOVERING THINGS WITH OUR SENSES

135. LISTEN TO THAT!

Grades: K to 4

English level: High beginner and up

Objectives: To identify objects and activities by the sounds they make; to reinforce and practice the present continuous tense

Materials needed: Several blindfolds (Halloween masks with the eyes covered over work well); various things around the room: door, window, pencil sharpener, chalkboard, chalk, shade or venetian blinds, plus a ball, bell, whistle, book, toy telephone, squeaking toy, drum or tom tom, cymbals or metal pot covers, small musical instruments

Presentation: Draw a head on the chalkboard with two large ears.
Point to the chalkboard and write the word *ear* under the picture.

These are my ears. Ears.

We *hear* with our ears.

What can we hear?

We can hear: (*hold or point to each noisy item and teach the English word for it as you make the sound with it*).

Can you tell what you hear when your eyes are closed?

Blindfold three or four volunteers. Select students who already know most of the vocabulary items. Their responses will give more exposure to the less advanced students, who can have a later turn.

Raise your hand if you can tell what you hear.

Call on other students and signal them to perform actions with the various noise-making objects. (*Example: close the door*)

What is (*Sandra*) doing? (*blindfolded student: door*)

That's right, she's closing the door. (*or closed the door, as the case may be*)

Repeating the actions would make the present continuous tense appropriate, while a single performance calls for the past tense. Choose which you wish to practice, and be consistent, so the pattern can be noticed.

After five or six sounds have been identified, have another group of students wear the blindfolds and guess.

Sample sounds: Sharpening a pencil, bouncing a ball, blowing a whistle, playing a drum, writing on the chalkboard, turning pages of a book, jumping, running, singing, humming, clapping hands, stamping feet, moving chairs, tearing paper, biting an apple, crumpling paper, coughing, blowing nose, whistling, pulling shades or blinds, snapping fingers, and whatever else occurs to you and your students. You can also go around the room tapping on various items with a spoon to see if they can be identified by the resonance of the sound. This is more challenging to the ear, although the English involved is easier.

136.   OUR FUNNY TONGUES

Grades: 3 and up

English level: Intermediate and up

Objectives: To learn about the tongue as a muscle and a sense organ; to locate the areas of the tongue that react to sweet, sour, salty and bitter tastes; to learn the English needed to talk about the activity

Materials needed: Small pocket mirrors; apples and pears, cut into small pieces; brown sugar; salt; knife; spoons; lemons (one lemon can be cut into enough wedges for twelve children); bitter (baking) chocolate; small paper plates; paper cups; water

Preparation: Make copies of the diagram of the tongue for each student. Set out the brown sugar and salt in bowls with spoons. Slice the lemons into very thin wedges. Cut or shave the baking chocolate into very small pieces.

Presentation: Review the five sense organs: eyes, ears, nose, tongue, and skin.

What are the things we can do with our tongue?   *(speak, make other sounds such as whistling and clucking, taste food, move food in our mouths, clean our teeth, clean and moisten our lips, lick ice cream and lollipops, express our feelings)*

Let's look at our tongues.   *(distribute mirrors or let students work with a partner, and have the partners tell each other what they see)*

Stick out your tongue. Way out. What is happening? Can you hold your tongue still?

Look at the middle of your tongue. Is it flat or does it have a crease in the middle?

Look at the underside of your tongue. Is it the same as the top?

Move your tongue from side to side. Move it front and back. Move it up and down. How far can you stick out your tongue? Can you touch your chin? Can you touch your nose? Can you roll your tongue in a cylinder? Can you fold it in half?   *(these abilities are genetically determined)*

Where is your tongue when you make the sound /d/? /t/? /k/? /g/? /n/? /s/? /j/? /l/? /r/? /z/? /th/?   *(behind the teeth, touching the top of my mouth, etc.)*

How does your tongue taste food?

Look again. Is your tongue very smooth or is it bumpy?

Look at your partner's tongue with a magnifying glass. Do you see the little bumps? These are taste buds.

Name _____   **Date** _____

The Tongue

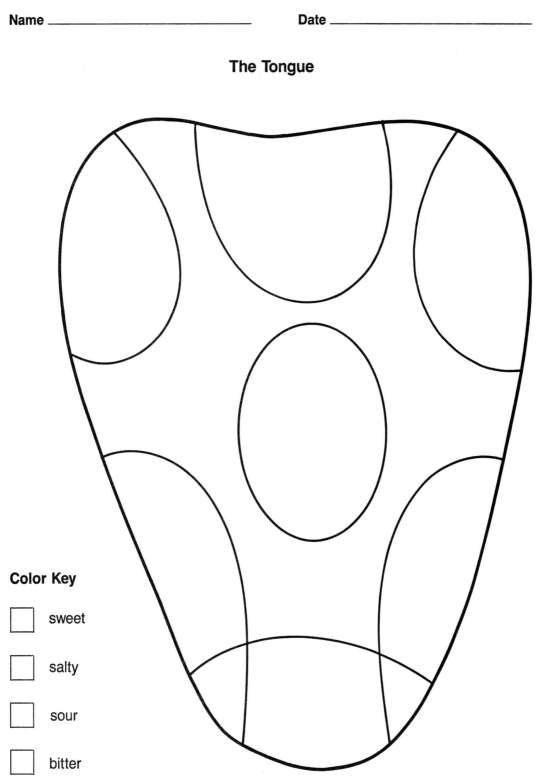

Color Key

☐ sweet

☐ salty

☐ sour

☐ bitter

Can you taste apples and pears with your tongue?

(Each pair of students needs apple and pear slices.)

One partner, hold your nose. Close your eyes. The other partner, take a piece of fruit. Don't say which one it is. Put it on your partner's tongue. Is it apple or pear?

Now let go of your nose. Can you tell if it is apple or pear now?

You need your nose to help you taste.

What can the tongue taste?

(Distribute the diagram of the tongue.)

There are four different kinds of taste buds. They are in different areas of the tongue.

We have four things to taste: sugar, salt, lemon, and bitter chocolate.   *(write the list on the chalkboard)*

Students should get a paper plate with a tiny bit of each item to taste, plus a cup of water to wash out the mouth between tastes.

Let's try sugar first.

Wet your finger and put it in the sugar and put it on your tongue. How does it taste? *(sweet)* Where on the tongue can you taste the sweet taste?

Can you taste it at the tip? On the sides near the front? On the sides near the back? In the center? In the back?

Make a key to the map of the tongue. Red will be for the part of the tongue that can taste sweet things.

Color the part of the tongue on the diagram where it tastes sweet.   *(tip)*

Now take a drink of water and wash your tongue. Swallow the water.

(Repeat the tasting and mapping with each of the three other tastes.)

Follow up:

Write about the activity.

Conduct a tasting party. (See Chapter Seven)

Trace the genetically determined abilities of the tongue in your family.

137. MAGNETS

Grades: K to 4

English level: High beginners

Objectives: To learn some of the properties of magnets; to observe which materials are attracted by magnets; to learn the English necessary to talk about the activity. (This lesson could take several days or one session, depending on the age and language competency of the students and their familiarity with magnets.)

Materials needed: Small magnet or pair of magnets for each student; assorted magnetic and nonmagnetic objects such as paper clips, scissors, thumbtacks, iron filings, salt, rubber bands, pencils, pens, nails, erasers, plastic, chalk, paper, stapler, nails, spoons, jar tops

Presentation: Distribute the magnets and ask students to take out their pencil cases. These are usually filled with a variety of magnetic and nonmagnetic items.

> These are magnets. Magnets.   *(write the word on the board if appropriate)*
>
> Magnets can pick up some things. What can your magnet pick up?
>
> The magnet can pick up paper clips. It can pick up the scissors. Can it pick up your pencil? Can a magnet pick up a crayon? Can a magnet pick up an eraser? pen? nail?   *(etc.)*

(Mix iron filings with salt.)

Can you pick up the black things from this salt?

> The black things are iron. A magnet can pick up something made of iron or steel. What things in our classroom are made of iron or steel?

(Allow a few students to go around the room experimentally tapping objects with their magnets to test for attraction. Check table and desk legs, clock, flag stand, cabinets, buttons, barrettes, etc.)

> What happens if you rub a paper clip *(or nail)* on a magnet?   *(The clip is a magnet now. It can pick up another paper clip.)*
>
> What happens when two magnets come together?   *(One side attracts and the other side repels; that is, pushes away.)*
>
> A magnet has two *poles*, a north pole and a south pole. The north pole of one goes to *(attracts)* the south pole of the other magnet, but it goes away from *(repels)* the north pole of the other magnet.   *(demonstrate)*

Allow students to work in pairs to see how this happens. Allow time for the students to experiment with what magnets will and will not pick up or magnetize.

138. MAKING A COMPASS

Grades: 3 to 6

English level: Intermediate

Objectives: To make a simple floating compass; to learn the concept of direction finding via the north magnetic pole; to learn the English necessary to talk about the activity

Materials needed: Magnet, needle, paper clip, cork, bowl of water, globe or map of the earth

Presentation:

We can make a compass. A compass helps us to find directions. We need a magnet, a needle, a cork, and a dish of water.

First we can magnetize the needle. Rub it on the magnet like this. *(Rub repeatedly on the magnet in a continuous lengthwise stroke.)*

Now the needle is a magnet. *(Demonstrate by picking up a paper clip.)*

Now push the needle through the cork like this.

Put the cork in a bowl of water. *(Be sure that it is not on a metal table or near any large iron or steel object.)*

Turn the cork. Watch where the needle points when it stops turning. Where is the needle pointing? *(Have students notice which direction in the room it is pointing.)*

Yes, the needle is pointing to the *(chalkboard, closet, etc.)*. Turn the cork again. *(wait)* Now where is the needle pointing? Turn the cork again. Now where is the needle pointing? In the same place?

Why does the needle always point in the same direction?

(Present a globe or a world map.)

This is the earth. The earth is a giant magnet. Yes, the earth is a giant magnet. There is a lot of iron here *(Queen Elizabeth Islands, north of mainland Canada)*. This is the magnetic north pole of the earth. The compass needle is pointing to this magnetic area. Is it the North Pole? No, but it is near the North Pole.

If a compass always points to the North, how can people use a compass? Who needs a compass? *(hikers, sailors, explorers)*

Follow up: On a subsequent day, review all vocabulary items and sentence structures:

A magnet can pick up a _____. It cannot pick up a _____.

A magnet has _____poles: a _____pole and a _____pole. Two like poles will _____. *(repel each other)* Two opposite poles will _____. *(attract each other)*

139. STATIC ELECTRICITY

Grades: 2 to 4

English level: Intermediate

Objectives: To observe the nature of static electricity in common objects; to learn the English needed to talk about the activity

Materials needed: "Squeaky clean" hair, a hard rubber or plastic comb (or one for each student), paper, balloons, salt, pepper, polyfoam packing material

Presentation: While students watch, tear up scraps of paper. Comb your hair until it crackles. Use the comb to pick up the pieces of paper.

> Here is some salt and here is some pepper. I'm going to mix the salt and pepper.
> Now the salt looks all dirty. How can we clean the salt? Here is a comb. I'm combing my hair. Comb, comb, comb. Now watch.

(After combing your hair until it crackles, run the comb over the top of the pile of salt and pepper. The pepper will jump up and cling to the comb.)

> What happened? The pepper sticks to the comb. We call this *static electricity.* Now the salt is clean. All the pepper is gone.

(Blow up a balloon and tie it.)

> Here is a balloon. Can this balloon stick to the wall?

(Place the balloon next to the wall. It will fall to the floor.)

> Now we can put some static electricity in the balloon.

(Rub the balloon on your hair, a student's [not Vietnamese] hair, on a woolen garment, or a carpet.)

> Does the balloon stick now? *(yes)*
> Why does the balloon stick to the wall now? *(it has static electricity in it; static electricity makes things act like magnets)*

(Distribute balloons to groups of three or four students, to generate electricity.)

> Rub the balloon on your hair *(or sweater, skirt, etc.).* Now put it on the wall.
> How long will the balloons stay on the wall? *(write down the time they are put up)*
> What made some balloons stay up longer? *(more static electricity was generated by greater rubbing)*

Distribute the "peanut" packing material of polyfoam. This is very often highly charged and can be recharged by stirring the pieces up a bit before distributing. Have students observe what happens when they try to drop the peanuts into a cardboard box from a height of several feet. What happens when someone wearing a woolen sweater or skirt tries to drop it? Supply vocabulary so they can describe what is happening (sticks to, clings, changes direction).

140. THE BALLOON JET

Grades: K and up

English level: Intermediate

Objectives: To learn how jet propulsion works; to learn the English needed to do a simple science project

Materials needed: Long balloons, clear tape, large drinking straws, a ball of thin string that will pass easily through the straws

Procedure: Show a picture of a jet plane that shows the jet (or draw a picture of one).

What makes a jet plane go? Let's find out.

1. Fasten a string about shoulder height to the wall on one side of the room. Have a student hold the other side of the string on the other side of the room.
2. Blow up the balloon. Pinch the opening shut but do not tie it.
3. Thread the string through the straw.
4. Tape the straw to the balloon, as in the illustration.

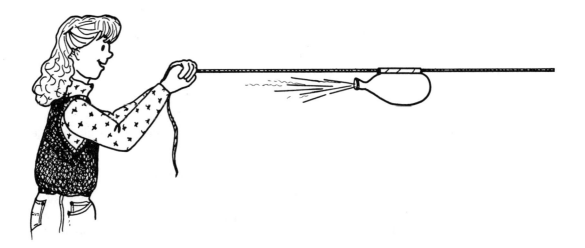

5. Hold the string taut.
6. Let go of the mouth of the balloon. The balloon will fly along the string as the air escapes.

7. Allow others to do the activity as students describe the actions.

8. Tell, then write about the activity in the past tense.

Discussion: What made the balloon move?

For every action, there is an equal and opposite reaction. Elicit other examples.

SOCIAL STUDIES ACTIVITIES

Of all the subjects in school, social studies can have the highest emotional "charge" for ESL students. In most circumstances, they have studied math and science in their own countries, and the task is to bring this background with them into English, although some students will also have to catch up a year or two. But they usually have not studied American history or geography, popular heroes, or customs and culture. A feeling of being "outside it" can pervade the subject of American culture and studies unless students are intentionally brought "inside it." They lack such elementary pieces of information as who George Washington was, where the Rocky Mountains are, how many states there are, the significance of 1492 and 1776, what happens on Halloween, Groundhog Day, or the Fourth of July. There is much of the subject of social studies that seems to depend on having "been here" all one's life. For some, there might be conscious or unconscious resistance to a sense of losing their own culture or history in the process of learning about the new one. Others will eagerly acquire all information and customs of the new culture without examining their value, and rebel against their own cultural traditions.

The ESL class can play a great role in the students' developing an appreciation of their own ethnic and national heritage, as well as preparing them for the benefits of biculturalism. Individuals who partake in and understand two cultures are uniquely equipped to have a broader view of life and to make contributions to either or both cultures based on that broader view.

The local community, its geography, economic basis, service people, and the students' opportunities and responsibilities in the community can be made comprehensible by means of class trips and guest speakers in the classroom.

Include a discussion of the students' countries' topography, governments, customs, holidays, and heroes as students learn about American topography, government, customs, holidays, and heroes. Students in your ESL class are a treasure of information about their own nations and cultures and are in a unique position to share this information with mainstream students and teachers; they need not wait until their English is proficient to do this. Pictures, music, food, dance, artifacts, and dress can all be shared nonverbally.

A social studies curriculum for the first year can be based on introductory geography of the United States and on the holidays, birthdays, and other events of the calendar. See "Before Everything Else" for a list of these.

Although ESL students are not ready for the extensive reading that social studies usually involves, visual presentations through picture books, filmstrips, movies, and video cassettes can serve to overcome this temporary handicap.

141. FILMSTRIP/MOVIE/VIDEO CASSETTE TAPE

The following general procedure can be adapted for use with any visual presentation on any topic relevent to your class.

Grades: K and up

English level: Beginner and up

Objectives: To learn key concepts and facts of American history, holidays, geography, and so on through a visual presentation; to learn some of the English necessary to talk about these facts

Materials needed: Filmstrip, movie, or video cassette tape and the equipment needed to view it

Preparation: Preview the material, listing key vocabulary items. Extract the basic ideas and rethink (or rewrite) these into short simple sentences. Prepare several questions that will be answered during the course of the presentation, to help focus students' attention. Decide if it is necessary to view the entire piece or whether some sections may be skipped over. Look for logical divisions in the material if you decide to cover it in several sessions rather than all at once; that is, eight frames of a thirty-two frame filmstrip might be suitable, or one fourth of a forty-minute movie.

Presentation: Motivate the viewing with a question or statement regarding its significance.

Examples:

Next week, February twelfth, is Abraham Lincoln's birthday. *(show picture, show date on calendar)*

We are going to see a *(movie)* about Abraham Lincoln. We are going to learn why he is a famous American.

On the chalkboard, write, "Who was Abraham Lincoln? What did he do?" Elicit already known information about the subject, if possible:

Who knows who Abraham Lincoln is? Who has a picture of Abraham Lincoln in his pocket? *(on a penny, etc.)*

Present several key vocabulary items. Write the words on the chalkboard or chart paper: slave, candidate, president, law, separate, war, union (etc.).

View the filmstrip, disregarding the accompanying text if it is (as is usually the case) too complex for the students' grasp. Rephrase the information in short simple sentences. (If a movie or video tape, you can play it without the sound and stop it frequently.) Ask students to state what they can see in the picture. Call attention to significant items.

Write additional vocabulary for students to find in their bilingual dictionaries for homework.

The following day, review the first segment, allowing students to give answers to your simple questions. Continue with the next segment of the presentation. Continue this until the presentation is complete. If desired, view the presentation with the sound track after the initial groundwork is accomplished.

142. MAP SKILLS

Grades: 2 and up

English level: Beginner and up

Objectives: To learn place names in English; to learn the English necessary to talk about puzzles, maps, land and water formations, directions

Materials needed: Wall map of the United States (the world); puzzle maps of the United States (the world)

Preparation: Assemble the puzzles

Presentation: For large groups, use the wall map; with a small group, gather around a desk that has the assembled puzzle on it.

This is a map. This is the United States. What country is this? *(The United States)*

This is north, this is south, this is east, and this is west. North, south, east, west.

As you point to each place mention:

Canada is on the north, and Mexico is on the south. Where is Canada? *(student points)*

Where is Mexico?

The Atlantic Ocean is on the east, and the Pacific Ocean is on the west. Find the Atlantic Ocean. Good. Find the Pacific Ocean. Good. Find Canada. Find Mexico. Which way is north? South? East? West?

Here is our state, _____. Here is California. Here is Texas. Here is New York. Here is Florida.

Find: *(list those places students have now seen).*

Remove several pieces from the puzzle, mix them up, and give them to different students to replace in the puzzle. Depending on students' ages, either remove several pieces at a time or disassemble the entire puzzle for reconstruction. Time the assembling of the puzzle.

Go from group to group pointing out features in the map as they assemble it and reviewing features they have already heard.

Repeat the activity frequently, introducing terms such as lake, river, bay, peninsula, and giving one or two examples of each on the map and having students discover other examples.

143. NATIONAL HERITAGE

Grades: 3 and up

English level: Intermediate and advanced

Objectives: To conduct a grade-wide or school-wide survey to determine the national origins of students in the school; to learn that the United States is a land of immigrants and descendants of immigrants, as well as Native Americans; to learn the names of various countries of the world; to begin to appreciate the many gifts brought to America from the cultures of other countries and to stimulate conversations in homes between students and parents about their cultural heritages; to understand that they are not "outsiders" in a land of "insiders" but that the United States is a "salad bowl" of different ethnic origins, each with contributions to make; to prepare a bulletin board to illustrate their findings to the rest of the school; to learn the English needed to talk about the activity

Materials needed: Wall-size world map, ribbons, yellow or white construction paper, thumb tacks or Funtak®, questionnaires

Preparation: Prepare a questionnaire on a Ditto master and make enough copies for everyone you will be surveying. A class-wide or grade-wide survey can suffice, or survey an entire school, depending on the population size. For example:

Name _____   Grade _____

Where were you born? _____

From what countries did your parents, grandparents, great grandparents, and other ancestors come?

_____   _____

_____   _____

_____   _____

_____   _____

Presentation:

Students in this class come from (an)other country (ies). What country do you come from, (*Student*)? *(repeat until each national origin is represented)*

(Optional, depending on English level.)

Were your mother and father born in that country or did they come from other countries?

We are going to do a survey. Here is a questionnaire. *(distribute)*

Let's read the questions.

(Clarify meanings; draw a "family tree" showing the meanings of parent, grandparent, great grandparent, ancestor, etc.)

A small (class-wide) survey may be conducted in person, with each ESL student assigned to ask the questions of several classmates. Or it may be done by having the ESL students distributing the questionnaires and later collecting the completed questionnaires.

Students work in groups to tally the national origins. (The total will be in excess of the number of students surveyed, as each may spring from more than one national stock.)

Write the total for each represented country on a two-inch circle of yellow or white construction paper. Post the map on a bulletin board and arrange the circles outside the map. Connect the circles to the appropriate country with colored ribbon. Title the display, "_____ _____ (Jefferson School, Grade five, or what have you) Students' National Heritage."

TRIPS

Out of the classroom for a change of scenery doesn't necessarily mean hiring a bus. An ESL social studies/language curriculum can well begin with a series of local trips, with the accompanying vocabulary, structures, map making, concept building necessary for the newcomers to anchor themselves in their new surroundings. The students may then become "scouts" for other members of their family to take advantage of the opportunities in the community.

Many ESL "survival" curricula (a mini-version of the early grades social studies curricula) begin with the self and expand the student's awareness to the people, objects, and relationships in the immediate environment, the home, the school, the community, and the world beyond. The need to build from the concrete to the abstract when teaching English-through-English suggests the effectiveness of this approach:

Begin map skills in the classroom.

Teach and practice the places and objects in the room, with Total Physical Response activities (see Chapter Two).

Prepare a handout for a map of your room, with the fixed objects unlabeled. Use the front of the room as the top of the map. A rough approximation will do. Duplicate enough for all students.

On the chalkboard, draw a rectangle representing the room. As you draw in items, have students volunteer the names of the items. Label them. When several features have been drawn and labeled (such as chalkboard, window, door), invite the students to come to the board to draw in and label additional features—as they are located in the room; that is, closets, teacher's desk, pencil sharpener, map, bulletin board, tables, desks, wastebasket, etc. Distribute the prepared maps for students to label.

Conduct "walks" through the room on the map, with students lightly penciling in the path they take.

Example: Draw a star at your own desk. Go to the chalkboard. (draw a line to the chalkboard) Go to the window. Go to the closet. Go back to your desk.

If students are ready for "right" and "left," or prepositions of place (near, next to, in front of, behind), use these structures as well.

144. THE SCHOOL

Grades: K and up

English level: Beginner

Materials needed: 9 × 12 oaktag sheets of paper, one with each important place in the school printed in large letters, with a minimal sketch of the site. You'll be able to use these for years, so the preparation is worth it. Copy the simple sketches given here:

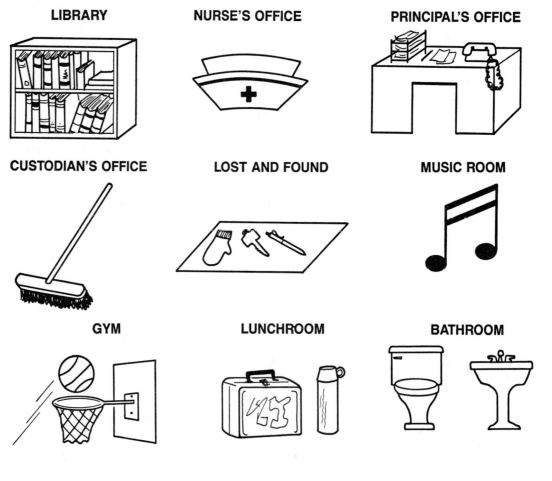

LIBRARY   NURSE'S OFFICE   PRINCIPAL'S OFFICE

CUSTODIAN'S OFFICE   LOST AND FOUND   MUSIC ROOM

GYM   LUNCHROOM   BATHROOM

WATER FOUNTAIN　　　　**STAIRS**　　　　　　**ESL CLASS**

Include sketches of other rooms around the school or a map of the school. You may be able to locate a map in the principal's or the custodian's office that will help you in getting your simplified ESL map right. If your school is multi-level, a map of the floor the ESL classroom is on will suffice.

Preparation: Take an orientation trip the first or second day of class, with an emphasis on students' knowing where the bathrooms and exits are located, and becoming familiar with the physical layout of the school. On this first trip, incorporate rules for walking quietly through the halls and on the stairs. The second trip (suggested here for incorporating language practice) may be scheduled later:

Plan your route to take in the centers of interest of the school: principal's office; nurse's office; custodian's office; lost and found; music, art, and science rooms; gym; library; classrooms for each grade; auditorium; lunchroom; kitchen; teachers' room; stairs; bathrooms; water fountains; fire alarms; fire extinguishers; etc.

Say the name of each location several times as you are on the site. On return to the room, elicit the names of the places you have just visited and write them on the chalkboard. Add any the students have forgotten. Practice reading the list of places.

Using the 9 × 12 place pictures, have students name each location. Post them in different areas of the room.

Do a Total Physical Response activity, sending students to the different "rooms" of the school. "(Jed), stand up. Go to the gym. (Mel), go to the library."

Then teach students the pattern, "May I go to the _____, please?" "Yes, you may." Allow individual students to request permission to go to the different places for as long as interest lasts. Allow students to take turns as teacher.

Work with the map handout, labeling the various rooms.

Practice questions and answers and such structures as:

Where is the ESL classroom?　*(On the second floor.)*

Where is the girls' bathroom?　*(Next to the third grade classroom.)*

Where is the music room?　*(Down the hall—the first room on the right.)*

145. THE SCHOOL GROUNDS

Grades: K and up

English level: Beginner

Objectives: To learn the names of features around the school; to develop an awareness of the school environment, rules, safety, opportunities

Vocabulary: Playground, ball field, fence, entrance, flagpole, parking lot, street, sidewalk, grass, trees, (etc.)

Preparation: Read: "Tomorrow we will go outside and walk around the school. We will see the playground, ball field, parking lot (etc.)"
   Students may copy the sentences in their notebook.

Options: Bring along American English-speaking children to work with groups of three or four students in touring the schoolyard. This serves the purpose of forming connections and bridges between the two groups and gives the Americans an investment in the language development of the newcomers. They will need to understand their role and some of the ways to communicate to LEP children (detailed in the front of this book).
   Take a camera along to snap pictures of children in various areas. These photos can be used for language stimulation, vocabulary review, structures— (Jose) is on the swing, next to the fence, near the tree, etc.
   Call attention to various features of the building—How many stories (floors) are there? How many windows do you see? What is next to the street?

Follow up: Students may draw a picture of the school, labeling the features.
   Label the features of a prepared map of the school grounds.

Writing/Reading:

Yesterday we went for a walk around our school. The school is (*big/small*). It has _____ stories. The entrance is on _____ Street. _____ students go to _____ School. We saw: (*elicit*).

146. THE SCHOOL NEIGHBORHOOD

Grades: K and up

English level: Beginner and intermediate

Objectives: To learn about the features in the immediate community around the school; to learn and reinforce safety rules for crossing streets; to learn the names of any stores, services, geographical features that present themselves

Preparation: Prepare a map of the school neighborhood. This may be copied from a school district map or from a map available through the town Chamber of Commerce. Or photocopy the appropriate section from a commercial street map of the city.

Have students locate the school on the map and mark it with a star. Find the names of the streets surrounding the school. Locate student's homes on these streets.

Writing/Reading:

Tomorrow we will go on a trip around the neighborhood. We will walk up _____ Street, turn (*left, right*) and walk on _____ Street. We will (*continue*). We will see: (*elicit*).

Vocabulary:

street	car	traffic	gas station
avenue	truck	traffic light	building
lane	taxi	stop	apartment
drive	bus	go	yard
road	van	caution	parking space
hill	baby carriage	litter	meter
sidewalk	bicycle	litter basket	fire hydrant
corner	crossing	home	gutter
garage	crossing guard	store	sewer

Include any of the following that apply:

barber shop	post office	police station	fire station
restaurant	grocery store	candy store	delicatessen

Structures: (whatever comes up) Examples:

We are walking.
Cars are going.
Cross at the corner.
The woman is pushing a baby carriage.
The buildings are tall.
That's a big store.
The streets are dirty.
Don't litter.
Throw litter in the litter basket.

Optional:

Take along English-speaking students as language sources.

Take pictures of various stores or areas to talk about later in class.

Follow the planned route, stopping to regroup and point out features as you walk. Answer questions. Give vocabulary as requested by students.

Make the trip a "treasure hunt." Students bring a list of items they must see. They check them off as they see them. They may work in teams of two, three, or four to help one another with locating the items and saying the English word.

Follow up: Prepare an experience chart:

We went on a walk around the neighborhood of the school. We saw: (elicit and list).

Students may each draw one store, street, area, or activity seen and write a sentence about it. Post these pictures where all might see them. Give time for students to talk about their picture.

Game: Concentration cards—name and pictures of items seen in the neighborhood. See Chapter Five for creating and playing this game.

Homework: Go on a walk around your own neighborhood. What do you see?

Find five things you need English words for. (Have them draw pictures or find the items in their bilingual dictionary or through an informant.)

147. THE POLICE STATION

Grades: 2 and up

English level: High beginner and up

Objectives: To learn the location of the police station, the functions and services provided by police, and how to contact the police; to build a positive relationship with police; to learn the English needed to talk about police and police matters

Preparation: Make an appointment with the police educational office for your class visit. Find out what the tour will encompass and inform them of the special language needs and limitations of your class. Suggest the use of more props, pictures, and actions when speaking to the group. Line up resource people. Plan a route to walk to the police station.

Vocabulary:

police officer	police car	uniform	badge
patrolman	beat	chief	detective
holster	gun	night stick	arrest
crook	thief	robber	suspect
murderer	jail	handcuffs	squad car
police radio	siren		

Have students locate the police station on the map. Plan a route with the class.

Writing/Reading:

> Tomorrow we will go to the police station. The police station is on _____ Street. We will learn about the jobs that police officers do. We will see: (*list*).

Options: A vocabulary "treasure hunt," as on the neighborhood trip, to be checked off as seen; a list of thought questions to keep in mind:

> How do police help people in (*this town*).
>
> What jobs do police officers do?
>
> How can I help the police?
>
> What is the police telephone number?
>
> How many police work in (*this town*)?
>
> How can someone become a police officer?
>
> Do police officers use their guns a lot in this town?
>
> The Chief of Police in our town is _____.

Follow up: Write and read about the trip to the police station:

> Yesterday we went to the police station. There are _____ policemen and _____ policewomen in our town. Police help us _____, _____, (etc.). We saw _____. We learned _____.

148. TOWN HALL

Grades: 3 and up

English level: Intermediate and up

Objectives: To learn the location and activities of the town governing body and municipal services; to become acquainted with democratic town government; to find out how the activities of the town government affect the students' lives; to inform the officials of the special language needs of your students

Vocabulary:

mayor	laws	deeds	town clerk
government	court	water department	town engineer
councilmen	judge	sanitation department	elections
meeting	clerks		

Preparation: Call Town Hall to see if there are visitors' tours for schoolchildren. Make an appointment. Line up English-speaking resource persons.

Locate the Town Hall on the map. Plan a route. Prepare an experience chart:

Tomorrow we are going to the Town Hall. We will see _____ (*list*).

Questions to bring to Town Hall:

Who is the mayor of our town?

For how long is he/she elected?

How many members of the town council are there?

How does the town government work?

How does the town government make our town a better place to live?

What can I do for my town?

Follow up: Make or read a chart of "Who's in control here?" (mayor, town council, board of education, police, fire, water, street, snow removal, etc. departments).

Writing/Reading:

We visited our Town Hall. We saw: (*list*). We learned (*list*). The mayor of _____ is _____.

149. THE FIRE DEPARTMENT

Grades: K and up

English level: High beginner and up

Objectives: To learn the location and activities of the fire department; to learn elements of fire safety; to learn how to call the fire department; to learn how to cooperate with the fire department for fire prevention

Vocabulary:

firefighter	gloves	net
fire engine	ax	hydrant
hook and ladder	siren	fire chief
hose truck	fire pole	pump
helmets	smoke	fire whistle
boots	volunteer	fire prevention

Preparation: Call the fire department for an appointment. Find out what the tour will encompass and inform them of the special language needs of your students. Suggest using more props, pictures, and actions. Locate the fire department on the map and plan a route.

Writing/Reading:

Tomorrow we will visit the fire station. We will see _____ (*list*). We will learn how firefighters work. We will learn about fire safety. We will learn what to do if there is a fire in our home.

How to report a fire: Get out of the house. Call the fire department and give your name. Tell them the address and kind of fire.

Questions to bring on the trip:

How many fires happen every day (week) in our town?

What causes most of these fires?

How do firefighters get to the fires quickly?

What things do firefighters need when they go into a burning building?

How do firefighters put out fires?

What is a false alarm?

(elicit other questions from the group)

150.   A SUPERMARKET

Grades: 2 and up

English level: Intermediate

Objectives: To learn the location and opportunities for learning English in a supermarket; to learn how to plan, select, pay for grocery needs; to learn that a supermarket has various sections and aisles; to learn the English names for the food items bought and the sections of the supermarket, and the English needed in the checkout transaction.

In connection with a unit on food, plan a lunch or a breakfast for which ingredients can be bought at a supermarket (example: salad ingredients; drinks; bread and sandwich fixings; fruit or dessert; paper plates, cups, napkins).

Preparation: Make a shopping list. Call the supermarket and inform them of the visit. Ask if it is possible to see behind-the-scenes areas such as the truck delivery areas, produce-packaging area, or the meat freezer and cutting area.

Divide your class into teams of three or four; divide the shopping list so each group is responsible for a purchase. Discuss roles and allow groups to assign tasks such as carrying money, pushing the shopping cart, selecting the item, packing the bag.

Plan the route on the map.

Vocabulary:

supermarket	bag	aisle	canned goods
shopping cart	pack	produce	junk food
checkout counter	shop	dairy	cleaning supplies
groceries	manager	shelf	freezer
money	price	bakery	hardware
cashier, checker	total	deli	toys
cash register	pay	meat	baby needs

scale	change	frozen food	cookware
spices	bunch	pound	dozen

Structures:

Where is the _____? How much is the _____? How much does this weigh?

on the shelf
in the (bakery) aisle
Push the wagon.
Weigh the fruit.
Put the groceries on the counter.
Pay the total.
Count your change.

Writing/Reading:

Tomorrow we are going to have an ESL lunch in school. We will go to the supermarket on _____ Street. We will buy _____(*list*). We will pay for the groceries at the checkout counter.

Questions to bring on the trip:

How many different kinds of food does a supermarket sell?
Where does the supermarket get all the food it sells?
What happens to the fresh food that is not sold?
What jobs are there in a supermarket?

151.   A PET SHOP

Grades: K and up

English level: Intermediate

Objectives: To buy a pet for the classroom (or only window-shop); to learn the location of, opportunities of, and animals handled in a pet shop; to learn the care and feeding and other responsibilities of a small pet; to learn the English names for animals, animal groups, animal paraphernalia

Vocabulary:

pet	hamster	litter box
mouse	fish	water bottle
mice	turtle	goldfish
dog	lizard	gerbil

puppy	chameleon	litter
cat	aquarium	
kitten	cedar shavings	

Structures:

How much is _____?

What does it eat?

What does it need?

Does it sleep in the daytime or at night?

Preparation: Decide whether you are willing to have the responsibility for a pet in the classroom. Mice, hamsters, and goldfish are classroom standbys. Check with the science teacher to get more information. You may need to check with the principal or custodian of your school, as well. The pet needs food, water, and warmth during weekends, holidays, and the summer, too, so plan for these before selecting a pet. (*Note*: It is very hard to determine the sex of young mammals, so even if you request two of the same sex, you may wind up with the additional educational experience of babies, and then a lesson in the geometric rate of population growth! To prevent this lesson, as soon as one of your pets shows signs of pregnancy, immediately find a home for the father elsewhere and find homes for the young ones singly before any reach maturity and impregnate the female again; this could be three weeks with mice, so act fast!)

Contact the pet store to inform them of your visit and the purpose. Take a preview trip so you will be aware of the opportunities for language development. See if they have someone who will be willing to devote time to show the animals to students and to answer students' questions.

Writing/Reading: We are going to a pet shop. We will buy a (mouse) for our classroom. We will buy the things a (mouse) needs. We will see other animals such as: (list).

Follow up: Set up the home for the (mouse). Have students name the animal. Assign rotating jobs of feeding, cleaning, and taming the (mouse). Teach proper handling and required gentleness, soft voices, avoiding of heights, washing of hands after touching, etc.

Elicit answers to your questions about the (mouse) and write, then read (example):

We bought a (*mouse*) at _____ pet store. We named her _____. She is (*small and soft and white*). She lives in a tank. She has _____ and _____ in her tank. We love to play with her. She eats _____.

Draw pictures of the pet and the pet shop.

Make up stories about the adventures of the (mouse) at night when no one is in the classroom.

152.   A RESTAURANT

Grades: 4 and up

English level: Intermediate and up

Objectives: To experience ordering and eating an inexpensive meal in a restaurant; to learn the English needed to talk about the activity; to learn appropriate manners when eating in a restaurant; to reinforce vocabulary for food and numbers; to reinforce arithmetic skills in figuring the check

Vocabulary:

table	order	beverage	white
waitress	price	dessert	rye
waiter	fried	check	whole wheat
manners	boiled	tax	rolls
menu	grilled	tip	butter
napkin	broiled	total	sandwich

Structures:

I would like a _____.

Do you have any _____?

This is delicious (okay, not good).

Preparation: Contact a small restaurant and plan for a lunch that will be at off-peak hours for them. Explain the purpose of the visit and your plans for it. Ask for several menus so students may plan their meal in advance.

Discuss eating in a restaurant with your class. Recommend an amount of money that students should bring with them. (You might collect this in individual envelopes to redistribute the day of the trip.) Photocopy the menu and go over the relevant vocabulary.

Help students plan their meal: sandwich or soup, drink, salad, beverage, dessert.

Line up language resource people to accompany you. Divide the class into groups of three or four to sit at separate tables.

Writing/Reading:

Tomorrow we will go to _____ restaurant to eat lunch. The restaurant is on _____ Street. I will order _____. It will cost _____. The tip will be _____.

Students select their tables, place their order with the waitress or waiter, eat with consideration for the other patrons of the restaurant, make any additional requests or complaints, handle the division of the check and the payment of the check and tip.

Follow up: Write a paragraph about the trip. Leave blanks for students to fill in.

> Yesterday we went to a restaurant. We ate lunch. I ordered _____ and _____.
> My bill was _____. I liked (*didn't like*) the _____. I sat with _____, _____,
> and _____.

153. THE PARK

Grades: K and up

English level: Beginner and up

Objectives: To become acquainted with the opportunities and activities available in a local park; to learn the English needed to talk about things observed and done in a park; to plan and enjoy an activity in the park

Preparation: Plan an activity for the park: play softball; fly kites made in class; birdwatch; feed squirrels or ducks; have a picnic. Line up English resource persons. Plan your route.

Vocabulary:

field	seesaw	temperature
grass	slide	picnic
flowers	birds	water fountain
bench	squirrels	swing
trees	wind	weather words
playground	sky	

Writing/Reading:

> Tomorrow we will go to _____ park. We will _____ and _____. We should
> wear play clothes. If it rains we will go _____.

Picture File and
Tape Recorder Activities

PICTURE FILES

In Chapter Two, the many uses of a collection of real objects were detailed. But since your physical space is limited and not everything comes in convenient garage-sale-priced miniatures, you will find a well-developed picture file to be indispensable.

There are many excellent commercial picture files on the market for use in ESL classrooms. The most useful of these have one picture per card (an actual photo in color), with the name of the object on the reverse side. There are files for vocabulary development, concept development, and phonics development. Select one that has a convenient storage container, with pictures filed by category rather than filed alphabetically or in the order in which they appear in a textbook (unless it is the text you are using in the classroom).

In addition to commercially prepared pictures, you will want to start a picture file of additional subjects, to encourage creative thinking, storytelling, emotional reactions. Students can help you with this ongoing project if there is a supply of magazines to cut during break times.

Mount pictures with staples (transparent tape ages within two years) onto 9 × 12 oaktag. Laminate those pictures that would be irreplaceable. File them in a suitable cardboard box by categories such as: adjectives, animals, clothing, faces, food, furniture, musical instruments, nature, occupations, pictures that tell a story, prepositions, sports, transportation, verbs, weather and seasons, and so on. On the back of each picture, write a word or a sentence. Also write the category it is to be filed under so students may put the pictures away without your assistance after using them.

154. VOCABULARY SOLITAIRE

Grades: 2 through adult

English level: All

Objectives: To develop vocabulary and spelling; to learn a technique for self-instruction

Materials needed: 5–25 picture cards, paper and pencil, watch or clock

Procedure:

Step One: Self-teaching. The student checks the time and counts out a number of pictures whose names are new to him. He looks at each picture and reads the word or sentence on the back. New readers of English will need help at this point from someone who can read, perhaps a classmate.

Step Two: Picture recognition. The student places the pile in front of him, picture up. He says the name or sentence for the picture and turns it over to check his answer. If correct, it goes in a "correct" pile. If wrong, it goes to the bottom of the same working pile. Step two is finished when all the cards are in the "correct" pile. He checks the clock again and notes the amount of time it has taken him to learn this number of words. That will be his target to beat on subsequent sessions with new words.

Step Three: Reading. The pile is placed face down, and the student reads the words on the back, mentally picturing the object. He turns it over to check his answer and places the card in the correct pile or the bottom of the same pile, as appropriate.

Step Four: Spelling. The student looks at the picture and writes down the name of the object. He then turns over the card and checks his spelling. Words spelled correctly are put into the correct pile, those misspelled go to the bottom of the working pile.

Instruction by an English-speaking peer, school volunteer, or tutor (small group or individual):

1. Show the flashcards one at a time, eliciting any names or sentences students can provide. Say the names of those not known.
2. Place the cards face up on a table, the floor, or tacked to the chalkboard. Have a student point to the object as you call out the name.
3. Then students give names of objects.
4. Ask questions using the objects in various structures: Which ones do you like? Which are the ones you don't like? Which ones are (green)? Which ones go together? Which are your favorite? Which ones are _____ (any appropriate adjective, etc.)?

5. Write the names of the objects on slips of paper and have students match the pictures to the names.

6. Students copy the names.

7. Test the students by removing the names and asking the students to recall the names and spell them.

This simple technique can be taught to EO (English only) students who can then take a large part in the motivation and acquisition of language by the new students.

155. CATEGORIES

1. Pictures may be sorted into categories. For example, a collection of animal pictures may be sorted into the following groups:

wild animals, farm animals, pets

animals with four legs, two legs, six legs

fish, mammals, reptiles, amphibians, birds, insects, other

animals that eat grass, that eat other animals, both, and other

animals that live in trees, water, woods, desert, underground

animals that are dangerous to people, animals that are not dangerous

fast animals, slow animals

animals I like, animals I don't like

2. The words for the various body parts and features of animals can be taught:

fur	horns	trunk	gills
skin	antlers	snout	stripes
wool	tusks	paw	spots
hair	shell	hoofs	fins
scales	feathers	flippers	tail

Adjectives describing differences among animals can be taught:

long, large, small, pointed or floppy ears

long or short neck, legs, tail, nose

soft, shaggy fur

sharp teeth or claws

Sentences describing animals can be written:

A rabbit is a small animal with long ears. If has soft fur and a small fluffy tail. It can hop very fast. It lives in a hole in the ground. Rabbits like to eat carrots and other plants.

Riddles can be made from animal descriptions:

This is a wild animal. It has four legs. It is big but it is not dangerous. It eats grass. It can run very fast. It has black and white stripes. It lives in Africa. What is it?

Students can read several riddles and soon write their own riddles.

Pictures of items in a house may be sorted into such categories as the following:

things that belong in the kitchen, living room, bathroom, bedroom

things you can sit on

things that contain other things

things with a handle

things you can eat

things you can clean with

things that make a house beautiful

things you can watch or listen to

TAPE RECORDER ACTIVITIES

The tape recorder can be the language teacher's best friend (and the language student's second best friend). Commercial tapes and teacher-made tapes can extend instructional time, provide individual practice, increase listening skills, patiently reinforce and repeat vocabulary and structures, and give a change of pace from teacher-directed instruction. (Also a boon if you ever get laryngitis, have another teacher cover your class, etc.)

Recording hints: Buy tapes of reasonable quality from an educational distributor. (Select 30-, 60-, 90-minute tapes, according to the task. Remember the recording side is one half of the designated time on the tape.) Gather all materials for your recording in a non-sound-reflecting environment with no distractions, traffic sounds, telephones, and so on. A small carpeted room is preferable to a large echoing room. Inside a cardboard refrigerator carton is good for sound control if you can manage it. Use the best available tape recorder you can borrow, rather than a cheaper kind you may be using to play the tapes back in the classroom.

Enlist a family member or friend to help in making the tape, to give a variety of voices. Aim for a cheerful delivery, with good inflection and changes of pitch. A monotone will put them to sleep! Intersperse a few moments of lively music to keep energy level and enthusiasm high. This will also make it easier to find the beginnings of new sections of material.

Check out your voice level and the clarity of producion before recording. When you finish recording, poke in the two little safety flaps that will prevent accidental erasure. If you wish to use the tapes again to record, place a small piece of masking tape or transparent tape over these holes.

One of the biggest errors in taped material is the timing. The timing should be right for the students with whom you plan to use the tape. Tape small sections of material and test them on students before you invest many hours in tape making.

Make one or more copies of your tape and save the original. Tapes have many accidents, get twisted, lost, and do soften up with repeated use, and the investment of time should not be lost when your tape is old or tangled. Having several copies of a tape available enables you to allow students to take tapes home to work on as needed.

Students need to be shown how to perform the tasks on the tape recorders. These lessons may be in English or in the native language. Demonstrate to students that they may stop the recorder to continue writing. However, rewinding and searching for the place left off will be frustrating, so they should be encouraged to play the tape in the sequence it is taped.

Label your tapes clearly so students will know the books and pages they correspond with, if any, and any other useful information for which you have room.

Store your tapes in easily accessed, labeled containers, with coded numbers to make it simple for students to return tapes to their correct location.

What Can You Record?

> your class textbook
>
> stories to read along with the tape
>
> picture dictionaries
>
> phonics books for phonics instruction
>
> a special lesson or explanation
>
> the pledge of allegiance and patriotic songs
>
> rhymes, poems, songs, chants, speeches, school cheers

156. PROGRAMMED SPELLING TEST

Grades: 3 to adult

English level: Beginner to advanced

Objectives: To provide self-checking spelling practice

Record words for students to spell in a self-checking test. After each word, the correct spelling is given, or an answer sheet may accompany the tape. About five separate ten-word spelling tests can fit on a fifteen-minute side of a tape.

Give a sample test to beginning students to get the timing right for your recording.

Sample script:

> (*music*) Learning to Spell, a tape prepared for (*Jefferson*) School ESL classes by (*your name*). You will need paper and pencil. (*pause*) Write your name on your paper (*pause*) Number your paper from one to ten. (*pause*) Are you ready? (*pause*) Great. Here is Spelling

Test A:

Number one. Boy. Boy. Jack is a boy. Boy.   (*pause*)
Number two. Book. Book. I can read a book. Book.   (*pause*)
Number three. Pen. Pen. I can write with a pencil or a pen. Pen.   (*pause*)
Number four. Go. Go. I go to school. Go.   (*pause*)
Number five. Yes. Yes. Are you in school? Yes.   (*pause*)
Number six. Girl. Girl. Janet is a girl. Girl.   (*pause*)
Number seven. Man. Man. Mr. Dane is a man. Man.   (*pause*)
Number eight. You. You. I like you. You.   (*pause*)
Number nine. I. I. I am from America. I.   (*pause*)
Number ten. Me. Me. Look at me. Me.   (*pause*)

(Continue in a similar manner with other tests.)

Test B: is, name, good, see, my no, red, the, six, run

Test C: am, in, nose, ten, cat, dog, have, he, are, day

Test D: a, she, your, on, big, what, one, this, can, do

Test E: hello, pencil, what, two, your, paper, last, open, up, door

Test F: teacher, desk, flag, map, how, fine, walk, talk, blue, three

Test G: green, four, five, class, table, face, leg, foot, hand, arm

Test H: notebook, thank you, close, down, mouth, chair, bathroom, nurse, yellow, brown

Test I: black, white, purple, seven, under, teeth, eye, ear, neck, finger

Test J: morning, please, English, crayon, put, window, chalkboard, child, clock, don't

Continue with other tests, selecting vocabulary items that will be known to the students and giving a sentence for each. This not only checks spelling but supplies useful structures and sentence patterns.

Prepare handouts for the students with the complete sentences already written, with a blank space for the spelling word. In this way, students will have reading *and* writing practice.

After some practice, you might dictate complete sentences for the students to write.

157. FOLLOWING DIRECTIONS

TPR: Make a recording of sets of Total Physical Response directions for the class to follow. Either demonstrate the actions required or allow able students to demonstrate. This is fun for everyone.

158. COUNSELING/LEARNING

This is a method of language teaching/learning that (for beginning students) works best with a bilingual teacher who is able to translate students' desired communciations into English. It can also work with a parent or other volunteer bilingual assistants. When students can communicate somewhat in English, a bilingual assist is no longer necessary, and you merely reword any nonidiomatic utterances in correct English structures.

Summary: Students sit in a circle around a table containing a tape recorder. A remote microphone with an on/off switch is important.

In their native language, explain to students that the content of the English they learn will be chosen by them. Set the scene for them and allow them to ask any questions about participating. Lower the anxiety.

Example: Scene one might be:

"You are in a new English class. You know some of the people, but you don't know other people. Begin your conversation. You may say things you already know in English. Raise your hand when you want to speak. If the English is correct, I will give you the okay and you speak it into the microphone. If it needs correction, I will tell you the correct way to say it, and you may practice it and then speak it into the microphone. If you can't say it in English, say it in your language, and I will give you the English for it. Practice it and then record it. This way, when we play back the recording, it will have only correct English on it."

Allow ten minutes for this part of the lesson. You may get between ten and twenty utterances as the group converses. Example:

Hello.
Hello, how are you?
I'm fine, thank you.
What's your name?
(*Marta*), what's yours?
(*Jose*).
Do you speak English?
No, that's why I'm in this class.
How do you like this class?
It's okay.

Are you sisters?

Yes, we are.

Where are you from?

We're from (*Costa Rica*).

It's hot today, isn't it?

Yes, I hate it.

I like the heat.

Replay the tape for listening comprehension. Clear up any questions about meaning.

Replay the tape one utterance at a time for repetition. Clear up extreme pronunciation difficulties but don't dwell on minor problems at this point. Replay the tape one utterance at a time and write the utterances on a chart paper.

Read the chart paper chorally, repeating after the teacher. Read it again individually, with each student reading the part he or she contributed. Students may copy the day's conversation.

On the following day, replay the tape. Ask students to hold the conversation again, with the same people taking the same parts they contributed the previous day.

Set an additional scene: "It is the second day of your English class. You are curious about the people in your group and want to know many things about them."

This conversation may include things incorporated from the lesson learned and new items such as "Where do you live, do you have any brothers or sisters, pets, hobbies? (etc.) Are you glad to be in America? (or anything unexpected) Since the students determine the content, it is impossible to predict the lessons in advance.

Assist and record as in Day One. Play back, repeat, write, read, and copy, as on Day One.

The material from Day One may now be reviewed, reworked, tested, played with.

Discuss the methods and content with students in their native language to get their feedback.

159. TAPE-IN-THE-BOX

Grades: 3 and up

English level: Beginner

Objectives: To follow directions; to build vocabulary and practice simple sentence structures

Materials needed: Tape, shoe box, 12–15 small items that are related in some way—examples: things to clean with, things to eat with, foods, farm animals.

(Objects are better, but a picture on a 3 × 5 card will do if you can't get all the objects in a category.)

On the bottom of each item, write a number that will correspond with the number in the directions. Label each box clearly on the top and on the end, so if they are stacked, students will know the contents. A picture might help on the label. You can photocopy this script and have it in an envelope inside the box for reading reinforcement.

159A.   BOX A (Cleanup Time)

Materials needed: Long strip of laminated paper with numbers on it from 1 to 10; soap, washcloth, comb, brush, toothpaste, toothbrush, shampoo, shoe polish, nail clipper, nail file, etc.

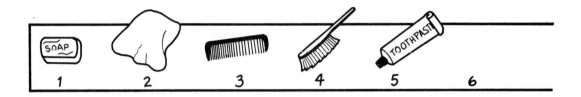

Script:

> Take everything out of the shoe box.   *(pause)*
> Take out the number line.   *(pause)*
> Put the soap on number one.   *(pause)*
> Put the washcloth on number two.   *(pause)*
> Put the comb on number three.   *(pause)*
> Put the brush on number four.   *(pause)*
> Put the toothpaste on number five.   *(pause)*
> Put the toothbrush on number six.   *(pause)*
> Put the shampoo on number seven.   *(pause)*
> Put the shoe polish on number eight.   *(pause)*
> Put the nail clippers on number nine.   *(pause)*
> Put the nail file on number ten.   *(pause)*
> Now check your answer. Look at the bottom of each thing. The number should be the same as the number on the line. Correct any mistakes.   *(pause)*
> Now listen to the names of the items as you point to them: one—soap; two—washcloth; three—comb; four—brush; five—toothpaste; six—toothbrush; seven—shampoo; eight—shoe polish; nine—nail clippers; ten—nail file.
> Say the names of the items after me: one—soap *(pause)*; two—washcloth *(pause)*; three—comb *(pause)*; four—brush *(pause)*; five—toothpaste *(pause)*; six—

toothbrush (*pause*); seven—shampoo (*pause*); eight—shoe polish (*pause*); nine—nail clippers (*pause*); ten—nail file (*pause*).

Listen to the sentences about these items.

Number one: We wash with soap.

Number two: We wash with a washcloth.

Number three: We comb our hair with a comb.

Number four: We brush our hair with a brush.

Numbers five and six: We put toothpaste on the toothbrush. Then we brush our teeth.

Number seven: We wash our hair with shampoo.

Number eight: We shine our shoes with shoe polish.

Number nine: We cut our fingernails with a nail clipper.

Number ten: We clean our fingernails with a nail file.

Now listen to these questions and point to the objects that answer them.

What can you brush your teeth with? (*pause*) Number five and number six. The toothbrush and toothpaste. We brush our teeth with toothpaste and a toothbrush.

What can you wash your hair with? (*pause*) Number seven—the shampoo. We wash our hair with shampoo.

What can you polish your shoes with? (*pause*) Number eight—shoe polish. We polish our shoes with shoe polish.

What can you wash your face with? (*pause*) Number one and number two—soap and a washcloth. We wash our face with soap and a washcloth.

What can you cut your fingernails with? (*pause*) Number nine—nail clippers. We cut our fingernails with nail clippers.

What can you comb your hair with? (*pause*) Number three—a comb. We comb our hair with a comb.

159B. BOX B (School Time)

Materials needed: Tape, shoe box, pencil, pen, eraser, chalk, ruler, marker, crayon, scissors, small book, tape, large paper clip, paper, paste, chair and table from a doll house or made from an index card

Script:

Take everything out of the box.   *(pause)*

Put the things on the number line paper.   *(pause)*

Put the pencil on number one.   *(pause)*

Put the eraser on number two.   *(pause)*

Put the pen on number three.   *(pause)*

Put the scissors on number four.   *(pause)*

Put the book on number five.   (*pause*)

Put the crayon on number six.   (*pause*)

Put the chalk on number seven.   (*pause*)

Put the chair on number eight.   (*pause*)

Put the table on number nine.   (*pause*)

Put the paper on number ten.   (*pause*)

Put the paste on number eleven.   (*pause*)

Put the tape on number twelve.   (*pause*)

Put the marker on number thirteen.   (*pause*)

Put the clip on number fourteen.   (*pause*)

Now check your answers. Look at the bottom of each thing. The number should be the same as the number on the line. Correct any mistakes.

Listen and point to the items as you hear the words: one—pencil; two—eraser; three—pen; four—scissors; five—book; six—crayon; seven—chalk; eight—chair; nine—table; ten—paper; eleven—paste; twelve—tape; thirteen—marker; fourteen—clip.

Now listen and say the names of the items: one—pencil; (remember to pause after each item) two—eraser; three—pen; four—scissors; five—book; six—crayon; seven—chalk; eight—chair; nine—table; ten—paper; eleven—paste; twelve—tape; thirteen—marker; fourteen—clip.

Listen to these sentences about the items. Point to the items as you hear them:

One: We write with a pencil.

Two: We erase with an eraser.

Three: We write with a pen.

Four: We cut paper with scissors.

Five: We read a book.

Six: We color with crayons.

Seven: We write on the chalkboard with chalk.

Eight: We sit *on* a chair.

Nine: We sit *at* a table. We can put things *on* a table. We eat *at* a table.

Ten: We write on paper.

Eleven: We paste paper together with paste.

Twelve: We can fix torn paper with tape.

Thirteen: We can draw or write with a marker.

Fourteen: We can put papers together with a clip.

Now answer these questions about the items:

What can you write with? (*pause*) Number one, number three, number six, and number thirteen—pencil, pen, crayon, chalk, and marker. We can write with a pencil, pen, crayon, chalk, or marker.

What can you read? (*pause*) Number five—book. We can read a book.

What can you put papers together with? (*pause*) Number eleven, number twelve, and number fourteen—paste, tape, or a clip. We can put papers together with paste, tape, or a clip.

What can you sit on? (*pause*) Number eight—chair. We sit on a chair.

What can you put things on? (*pause*) Number nine—a table. We put things on a table.

What can you fix torn paper with? (*pause*) Number twelve—tape. We can fix torn paper with tape.

What can you cut paper with? (*pause*) Number four—scissors. We cut paper with scissors.

What can you write on the chalkboard with? (*pause*) Number seven—chalk. You can write on the chalkboard with chalk.

What can you write *on*? (*pause*) Number ten—paper. You can write on paper.

159C. BOX C (at Home)

Materials needed: Doll house furniture: sink, refrigerator, stove, table, chairs, bed, dresser, bookcase, sofa, lamp, coffee table, armchair, etc.

Preparation: Draw (copy) a floor plan of a home with kitchen, dining room, living room, bedroom, and bathroom. Sketch in the places where the furniture would go, with numbers that correspond with the numbers you write on the bottom of the items.

Script:

This is a floor plan of a house. There are four rooms in this house, plus a bathroom. There is a kitchen, a dining room, a living room, and a bedroom.

Room number one is a kitchen. (*pause*) The sink goes in the kitchen. (*pause*) The refrigerator goes in the kitchen. (*pause*) The stove goes in the kitchen. (*pause*)

Room number two is the dining room. (*pause*) The table and chairs go in the dining room. (*pause*)

Room number three is the living room. (*pause*) The sofa goes in the living room. (*pause*) The TV goes in the living room. (*pause*) The armchair and the coffee table go in the living room. (*pause*)

Room number four is the bedroom. (*pause*) The bed goes in the bedroom. (*pause*) The dresser goes in the bedroom. (*pause*)

Room number five is the bathroom. (*pause*) The bathtub goes in the bathroom. (*pause*) The sink goes in the bathroom. (*pause*) The toilet goes in the bathroom. (*pause*)

Now check your answers. Look at the bottom of each thing. (*pause*) The number should be the same as the number of the room. Correct any mistakes.

Where is the bed? (*pause*) The bed is in the bedroom.

Where is the dresser? (*pause*) The dresser is in the bedroom.

Where are the table and chairs? (*pause*) The table and chairs are in the dining room.

Where is the refrigerator? (*pause*) The refrigerator is in the kitchen.

Where is the stove? (*pause*) The stove is in the kitchen.

Where is the bathtub? (*pause*) The bathtub is in the bathroom.

Where is the sofa? (*pause*) The sofa is in the living room.

Where is the armchair? (*pause*) The armchair is in the living room.

How many rooms are in this house? (*pause*) There are four rooms and a bathroom in this house.

What are the rooms? (*pause*) A kitchen, dining room, living room, bedroom, and bathroom.

What furniture is in the kitchen? (*pause.*) A stove, a sink, and refrigerator.

What furniture is in the dining room? (*pause*) A table and chairs are in the dining room.

What furniture is in the living room? (*pause*) A sofa, armchair, TV, coffee table, and lamp are in the living room.

What furniture is in the bedroom? (*pause*) A bed and dresser are in the bedroom.

What is in the bathroom? (*pause*) A sink, toilet, and bathtub are in the bathroom.

159D.   BOX D (Money)

Materials needed: Tape, realistic paper coins and bills; 18-inch strip with numbers

Preparation: Record the script on the tape. Glue or tape the coins and bills to the number strip. Write the money amounts in the proper place.

Script:

Number one is a penny. A penny is worth one cent.

Number two is a nickel. A nickel is worth five cents.

Number three is a dime. A dime is worth ten cents.

Number four is a quarter. A quarter is worth twenty-five cents.

Number five is a half-dollar. A half-dollar is worth fifty cents.

Number six is a dollar. A dollar is worth one hundred cents.

Number seven is a dollar bill.

Number eight is a ten-dollar bill.

Number nine is a twenty-dollar bill.

Which coin is worth five cents? (*pause*) Number two, the nickel—the nickel is worth five cents.

Which coin is worth twenty-five cents? (*pause*) Number four, the quarter—the quarter is worth twenty-five cents.

Which coin is worth one cent? (*pause*) Number one, the penny—the penny is worth one cent.

Which coin is worth ten cents? (*pause*) Number three, the dime—the dime is worth ten cents.

Which coin is worth fifty cents? (*pause*) Number five, the half-dollar—the half-dollar is worth fifty cents.

Which coin is worth one hundred cents? (*pause*) Number six, the dollar—a dollar is worth one hundred cents.

What are two dimes worth? (*pause*) Twenty cents—two dimes are worth twenty cents.

What are two nickels worth? (*pause*) Ten cents—two nickels are worth ten cents.

What are a nickel and a penny worth? (*pause*) Six cents—a nickel and a penny are worth six cents.

What are a dime and a nickel worth? (*pause*) Fifteen cents—a dime and a nickel are worth fifteen cents.

What are a quarter and a dime worth? (*pause*) Thirty-five cents—a quarter and a dime are worth thirty-five cents.

What are three quarters worth? (*pause*) Seventy-five cents—three quarters are worth seventy-five cents.

Look at the penny. The face of Abraham Lincoln is on the penny. Abraham Lincoln was the sixteenth president of the United States.

Look at the nickel. The face of Thomas Jefferson is on the nickel. Thomas Jefferson was the third president of the United States.

Look at the dime. The face of Franklin Delano Roosevelt is on the dime. Franklin Delano Roosevelt was the thirty-second president of the United States.

Look at the quarter. The face of George Washington is on the quarter. George Washington was the first president of the United States.

Look at the half-dollar. The face of John F. Kennedy is on the half-dollar. John F. Kennedy was the thirty-fifth president of the United States.

Look at the dollar. The face of Dwight Eisenhower in on the dollar. Dwight Eisenhower was the thirty-fourth president of the United States.

Look at the dollar bill. The face of George Washington is on the dollar bill.

159E. BOX E (Setting the Table)

Materials needed: Tape; items from a doll's tea set; plate, cup, napkin, plastic knife, fork, spoon, salt shaker, paper place mat (rolled up), paper cup, bowl; sketch showing the proper setting of a table, American style; number strip

Script:

Number one is a plate.

Number two is a cup.

Number three is a napkin.

Number four is a knife.

Number five is a fork.

Number six is a spoon.

Number seven is a salt shaker.

Number eight is a bowl.

Number nine is chopsticks.

Number ten is a straw.

Number eleven is a paper cup.

Number twelve is a pitcher.

Number thirteen is a place mat.

Number fourteen is a saucer.

Now check your answers. Look at the bottom of each thing. The number should be the same as the number on the line. Correct any mistakes.

Listen and point to the objects as you hear them:

    One: plate

    Two: cup

    Three: napkin

    Four: knife

    Five: fork

    Six: spoon

    Seven: salt shaker

    Eight: bowl

    Nine: chopsticks

    Ten: straw

    Eleven: paper cup

    Twelve: pitcher

    Thirteen: place mat

    Fourteen: saucer

Now we are going to set the table.

Place the plate in the center of the place mat.

The napkin goes on the left of the plate.

The fork goes on the napkin.

The knife goes to the right of the plate.

The spoon goes to the right of the knife.

The cup and saucer go above the knife.

The bowl goes on the plate.

Check your answers with the picture of the table setting.

English Bee

Is it time to review, consolidate, and let students show off what they have learned? Have an English Bee. Played like a TV quiz show, with prizes and choices of difficulty level of questions, the English Bee is an excellent oral preparation for written evaluation, or just lots of motivating fun for mastery of information, or a preholiday celebration. Invite guests if you like.

160. ENGLISH BEE

Grades: 2 to adult

English level: Beginner to advanced

Objectives: To build a sense of accomplishment of the quantity and variety of English information students have acquired

Materials needed: Questions and answers with assigned "difficulty points," appropriate to your students' abilities; score sheets or chalkboard; prizes—privileges (no homework, name on class "honors" list, early dismissal to lunch, free time, etc., or select an item from shoe box)

Preparation: You may make up your own questions from material you have covered in the classroom plus general knowledge of your school, holidays, culture, history, current events, literature, vocabulary, and grammatical items your students have been exposed to. The all-purpose questions provided here are suitable for beginning to high intermediate students in grades two to eight.

The questions may be read directly from the lists or you may copy them separately on 3 × 5 cards. If you do this, write the point value on the back of the question card and arrange the questions in piles of similar difficulty level. Decide whether students will compete individually or in teams (if there is a single brand-new student, he might receive coaching from a teammate, while others are expected to be responsible for their own answers).

If playing with teams, you should preselect the teams to balance the total English ability or select the most able (or least able, oldest, youngest) students to be team captains and pick their own teams, alternating selections. Students should sit as a team, on opposite sides of the room; they may choose a team name if they desire.

Give students a sample question from each of the difficulty levels. The "contestants" can play safe for fewer points or look for a challenge and take the risk of the higher point questions.

Decide who will be the quizmaster—this can be you, an invited guest, or a student who is not on either team. A certain amount of TV-type hype adds to the fun. Assign a timekeeper from each team to call time (for example, 15 seconds) if the question is not answered correctly.

Play: Teams shake a die to see who goes first. Highest wins.

The first person on the team states the number of points he would like to try for. A question from that pile is drawn and asked. If the student answers correctly, he earns the appropriate number of points for himself or his team.

If incorrect, no points are given. Any other student may give the correct answer, but no points are given. Points are awarded only to the player whose turn it is.

Scoring options: You may hand the question to the student who answers it correctly. At the end of the game students add up their individual totals and team totals.

Or a scorekeeper or the quizmaster may write team scores on the board. The team with the highest number of points wins.

There are seven difficulty levels. If you want to change any evaluations of difficulty for your class, do so.

One-point questions:

What's your name?

What's your last name?

Spell *no.*

Where are you from?

How are you?

Spell *book.*

Spell your name.

Do this: Stand up. Sit down.

Do this: Raise your hand. Put your hand down.

Do this: Close your eyes. Open your eyes.

Do this: Touch your nose. Put your hand down.

Count to twenty.

Say the ABC's.

What's your telephone number?

What is your ESL teacher's name?

Spell *yes.*

How many days are in one week?   *(seven)*

Say the days of the week.   *(Monday, Tuesday, Wednesday, Thursday, Friday, Saturday, Sunday)*

How old are you?

What color is your hair?

What color are your eyes?

How much are three and seven?   *(ten)*

How much are five and six?   *(eleven)*

How much are six and seven?   *(thirteen)*

What grade are you in?

Name five things in this classroom.   *(books, children, teacher, desks, chairs, pencils, chalkboard, map, etc.)*

Name three people in this classroom.

Yes or no? Today is Monday.

Yes or no? You are a girl.

Spell *go.*

Spell *boy.*

Spell *man.*

Spell *is.*

Spell *me.*

Spell *you.*

Spell *he.*

Count by twos to twenty: 2, 4, 6...   *(8, 10, 12, 14, 16, 18, 20)*

What day is today?

What color is a banana?   *(yellow)*

What color is an orange?   *(orange)*

What school is this?

Are you from Japan?

How much are seven and nine?   *(sixteen)*

Name six colors.   *(red, orange, yellow, green, blue, purple, brown, black, white, etc.)*

Two-point questions:

Where do you live?

Name the months of the year.   *(January, February, March, April, May, June, July, August, September, October, November, December)*

Spell *English.*

Do this: Go to the chalkboard and draw a circle.

Do this: Go to the window and open it.

Do this: Go to the teacher's desk and find a pencil.

Do this: Go to the chalkboard and draw a square.

How much is six times four?   *(twenty-four)*

How much is three times nine?   *(twenty-seven)*

How much is two times eleven?   *(twenty-two)*

What color is grass?   *(green)*

What color is chocolate?   *(brown)*

What color are cherries?   *(red)*

Name four things that are on your face.   *(eyes, nose, mouth, teeth, cheek, chin, eyebrows, lips, etc.)*

How many fingers do you have?   *(ten)*

How many ears do you have?   *(two)*

Spell *three.*

Spell *Sunday.*

What is today's date?

What time is it now?

Who are you sitting next to?

What number comes after thirteen?   *(fourteen)*

What number comes before twelve?   *(eleven)*

Name four things you can write with.   *(pen, pencil, chalk, marker, crayon, etc.)*

How many cents are in a dime?   *(ten)*

How many cents are in a nickel?   *(five)*

What coin is worth twenty-five cents?   *(quarter)*

How many cents are in a half-dollar?   *(fifty)*

How many cents are in a dollar?   *(one hundred)*

Two nickels are the same as one _____.   *(dime)*

A dime and a nickel are worth how many cents?   *(fifteen)*

What is a coin that is worth one cent?   *(penny)*

Name five subjects you study in school.   *(English, math, science, gym, music, social studies, reading, library, art, history, etc.)*

Spell *pencil.*

Spell *ruler.*

Spell *banana.*

Spell *yellow.*

Spell *window.*

Spell *house.*

Three-point questions:

Name five things you can wear when it is very cold outside.   *(mittens, boots, scarf, gloves, coat, hat, sweater, jacket, etc.)*

The opposite of hot is _____.   *(cold)*

The opposite of dirty is ———. *(clean)*

The opposite of north is ———. *(south)*

The opposite of good is ———. *(bad)*

What is the plural form of *man*? Spell it. *(men)*

What is the plural form of *tooth*? Spell it. *(teeth)*

What is the plural form of *foot*? Spell it. *(feet)*

This sentence has a mistake—correct it: My hands is clean. *(My hands are clean.)*

What is the weather today?

This sentence has a mistake—correct it: Give the book to she. *(Give the book to her.)*

Who was the first president of the United States? *(George Washington)*

Who is the president of the United States now?

What is the capital of the United States. *(Washington, D.C.)*

What is the capital of your country?

How many states are in the United States? *(fifty)*

What is your gym teacher's name?

What is the librarian's name?

What is the principal's name?

What is your music teacher's name?

What is the plural of mouse? *(mice)*

What is the plural of child? *(children)*

In baseball, how many strikes make an out? *(three)*

What month comes before December? *(November)*

What is the first month of the year? *(January)*

Name four vegetables. *(corn, potatoes, carrots, string beans, beets, celery, lettuce, peas, tomatoes, etc.)*

Name four fruits. *(apple, banana, orange, pear, peach, cherries, melon, etc.)*

Name four states of the United States. *(California, Texas, New York, New Jersey, Florida, etc.)*

Name ten parts of the body. *(eyes, nose, mouth, face, neck, chest, arms, legs, hands, feet, fingers, toes, etc.)*

Count by threes to thirty. *(3, 6, 9, 12, 15, 18, 21, 24, 27, 30)*

What is the last month of the year? *(December)*

What month comes between February and April? *(March)*

Name four rooms in a house. *(living room, kitchen, dining room, bedroom, bathroom, etc.)*

On what day is Halloween? *(October 31)*

How many legs do insects have? *(six)*

Whose face is on the penny and the five-dollar bill? *(Abraham Lincoln)*

What is the past tense form of *write*? Spell it. *(wrote)*

Whose face is on the quarter and the dollar? *(George Washington)*

What is the biggest animal on earth living today? *(blue whale)*

What is the capital of this state?

What is heavier, a pound of stones or a pound of feathers? *(They weigh the same, one pound.)*

What is the name of the comet that comes near the earth every seventy-four years? *(Halley's Comet)*

Whose birthday is July fourth? *(The United States of America)*

Where does the president of the United States live? *(The White House or Washington, D.C.)*

What holiday is on February fourteenth? *(Valentine's Day)*

What is the past tense form of *sleep?* Spell it. *(slept)*

Name a holiday in December. *(Hanukkah; Christmas)*

In what year did Columbus reach America? *(1492)*

What is the biggest state in the United States? *(Alaska)*

What is the past tense form of *find?* Spell it. *(found)*

What is the smallest state in the United States? *(Rhode Island)*

Who can Clark Kent change to? *(Superman)*

What two countries border the United States? *(Canada and Mexico)*

What two oceans touch the United States? *(Atlantic and Pacific)*

In what month are the birthdays of Abraham Lincoln and George Washington? *(February)*

How much is twenty-four divided by six? *(four)*

How much is twelve divided by two? *(six)*

I bought a pencil that cost twelve cents. I gave the storekeeper a dime and a nickel. How much change will I get? *(three cents)*

What is your art teacher's name?

The opposite of boring is _____. *(interesting, exciting, etc.)*

The opposite of thin is _____. *(fat, wide, broad)*

This sentence has a mistake—correct it: Jack don't like hamburgers. *(Jack doesn't like hamburgers.)*

What is the past tense form of carry? Spell it. *(carried)*

The person who flies a plane is called a _____. *(pilot)*

Name five meats. *(beef, pork, lamb, hot dog, hamburger, chicken, fish, etc.)*

What is a sentence? *(A sentence is a group of words that tells a complete thought.)*

Name five things to drink. *(milk, water, juice, soda, tea, coffee, lemonade, etc.)*

This sentence has a mistake—correct it: We wasn't happy yesterday. *(We weren't happy yesterday.)*

Name four things that are "junk foods." *(sugar, candy, soda, potato chips, gum, cake, etc.)*

What are the vowels?   *(a, e, i, o, u, and sometimes y)*

Name five farm animals.   *(pig, horse, cow, chicken, duck, donkey, goat, sheep, etc.)*

Spell *pennies.*

What is a patient?   *(A person who goes to a doctor, a hospital, or a dentist, etc.)*

Name five animals that live in the water.   *(turtle, fish, frog, shark, whale, dolphin, alligator, lobster, crab, shrimp, clam, etc.)*

Name five animals that can fly.   *(butterfly, bird, bat, duck, eagle, etc.)*

Name five animals that eat grass.   *(cow, horse, zebra, deer, sheep, donkey, elephant, goat, etc.)*

Name five animals that eat other animals.   *(tiger, lion, shark, fox, wolf, turtle, snake, alligator, etc.)*

What is a contraction? Give an example.   *(A contraction is a word made from two words: don't from do not; isn't from is not, etc.)*

Which word does not belong with the others: foot, ear, nose, mouth?   *(foot)*

Which word does not belong with the others: circle, capital, square, triangle?   *(capital)*

The person who works in a restaurant and brings food to your table is called a _____.   *(waiter or waitress)*

Which word does not belong with the others: please, thank you, you're welcome, goodbye?   *(goodbye)*

Which word does not belong with the others: nurse, dentist, mailman, doctor?   *(mailman)*

What is your zip code?

How many minutes are in one hour?   *(sixty)*

How many hours are in one day?   *(twenty-four)*

How many days are in one year?   *(three hundred sixty-five)*

Your father's wife is your _____.   *(mother or step-mother)*

Who is the governor of this state?

Who is the mayor of this city?

Say the pledge of allegiance.   *(I pledge allegiance to the flag of the United States of America and to the Republic for which it stands, one nation, under God, indivisible, with liberty and justice for all.)*

How many feet are in one yard?   *(three)*

How many inches are in one foot?   *(twelve)*

How many ounces are in one pound?   *(sixteen)*

How many cups are in one quart?   *(four)*

What animal gives us wool?   *(sheep)*

Say this correctly: Larry Lion loves lemon lollipops.

Say this correctly: This thing, that thing, and the other thing.

Say this correctly: The Chinese children shot the sheep.

Say this correctly: Clever Harvey never plays the violin.

What is the past form of *speak*?   *(spoke)*

What is the past form of *go*?   *(went)*

What is the past form of *help*?   *(helped)*

What is the past form of *sleep*?   *(slept)*

What is the past form of *see*?   *(saw)*

What is the past form of *make*?   *(made)*

What is the past form of *break*?   *(broke)*

What is the past form of *come*?   *(came)*

What is the past form of *begin*?   *(began)*

How many letters are in the alphabet?   *(twenty-six)*

How many inches are in two feet?   *(twenty-four)*

What ocean is west of California?   *(Pacific Ocean)*

How many sides does a square have?   *(four)*

Write today's date the short way.

In what room would you find a sink, a refrigerator, and a stove?   *(kitchen)*

Which word does not belong with the other three words: minutes, clock, hours, days.   *(clock)*

Spell *November.*

Spell *birthday.*

Spell *Tuesday.*

Spell *April.*

Spell *between.*

Four-point questions:

Who was John F. Kennedy?   *(A president of the United States)*

At what temperature does water boil?   *100° Centigrade or 212° Fahrenheit)*

How often do Americans hold elections for president?   *(every four years)*

Who is the vice-president of the United States?

At what temperature does water freeze?   *(0° Centigrade or 32° Fahrenheit)*

How many students go to our school?

Whose face is on the dime?   *(Franklin Roosevelt)*

Spell *knives.*

Whose face is on the nickel?   *(Thomas Jefferson)*

Whose face is on the half-dollar?   *(John F. Kennedy)*

Which planet is the largest?   *(Jupiter)*

What is a verb?   *(A verb is a word that shows action or a state of being.)*

This sentence has a mistake—correct it: Bob didn't went to the library yesterday.   *(Bob didn't go to the library yesterday.)*

What planet is the closest to the earth?   *(Venus)*

What day is the birthday of the United States?   *(July 4, 1776)*

How many teeth do adults have if they have never had any teeth pulled?   *(thirty-two)*

How many legs do spiders have?   *(eight)*

Who is King of the Apes.   *(Tarzan)*

How much does a first-class stamp cost?

If you read a story that is fiction, is it true or make-believe?   *(make-believe, not true)*

What war gave the United States independence from England?   *(The War of Independence, or the Revolutionary War)*

What season begins on June twenty-first?   *(summer)*

This sentence has a mistake—correct it: We see a movie last night.   *(We saw a movie last night.)*

What is an abbreviation? Give an example.   *(An abbreviation is a short way to write a word; for example: St. for Street.)*

This sentence has a mistake—correct it: A tree is more taller than a flower.   *(A tree is taller than a flower.)*

What do you call a person who cuts hair?   *(a barber)*

What is an adjective? Give an example.   *(An adjective is a word that describes or tells about a noun; for example: pretty, nice, long, tall, green.)*

This sentence has a mistake—correct it: Chrissy is the most tallest girl in the fifth grade.   *(Chrissy is the tallest girl in the fifth grade.)*

An instrument used to tell temperature is a _____.   *(thermometer)*

Who was Franklin Delano Roosevelt?   *(a president of the United States)*

What are the biggest living things on earth?   *(the Giant Sequoia trees in California)*

Spell *mathematics.*

This sentence has a mistake—correct it: May I have a apple, please?   *(May I have an apple, please?)*

What planet is closest to the sun?   *(Mercury)*

What do you call a person who fixes cars, airplanes, bicycles, and machines?   *(a mechanic)*

What do you call a person who makes bread, cookies, and cake?   *(a baker)*

What do you call a person who cuts meat for people to eat?   *(a butcher)*

What do you call a person who builds houses from wood?   *(a carpenter)*

What do you call a person who fixes pipes, toilets, and sinks?   *(a plumber)*

What is the biggest river in the United States?   *(The Mississippi)*

What is the biggest river in the world?   *(The Amazon)*

What is the longest river in the world?   *(The Nile)*

What is the highest mountain in the world?   *(Mount Everest)*

What is the highest mountain in the United States?   *(Mount McKinley)*

What animal does beef come from?   *(a cow)*

What animal does pork and bacon come from?   *(a pig)*

Who lived in North America before people came from Spain, France, and England?   *(Native Americans, Indians)*

Name five states and their capitals.   *(New York–Albany; New Jersey–Trenton; Florida–Tallahassee; Pennsylvania–Harrisburg; Ohio–Cleveland, etc.)*

What day is added to the calendar in a leap year?   *(February 29)*

On what day is Valentine's Day?   *(February 14)*

On what day is Halloween?   *(October 31)*

Turkey, gravy, stuffing, squash, and sweet potatoes make you think of what holiday?   *(Thanksgiving)*

What country owned the United States before it was the United States?   *(England)*

A person who fixes pipes, sinks, toilets, and bathtubs is a _____.   *(plumber)*

What do you call the space or room under the first floor of a house?   *(a cellar or basement)*

What are two words that rhyme with these two words: tack, black?   *(back, clack, Jack, lack, Mac, knack, pack, plaque, rack, sack, stack, slack, shack, snack, smack, tack, track, whack, yak)*

Bob had four apples. Sam gave him three more. How many apples did Bob have altogether?   *(seven)*

Balloons cost ten cents each. Ricky wants to buy five balloons. How much money will he need?   *(fifty cents)*

Who is Batman's partner?   *(Robin)*

On what day is Flag Day?   *(June 14)*

Spell your name backwards.

Name the states that border our state.

Five-point questions:

A Civil War was fought in America between the North and the South. When was that war, and who was president of the United States at that time?   *(1860–1865; Abraham Lincoln)*

How many feet are in one mile?   *(5280)*

Name the seven continents.   *(North America, South America, Europe, Asia, Africa, Australia, Antarctica)*

This sentence has a mistake—correct it: If I was rich, I would be happy.   *(If I were rich, I would be happy.)*

Name five oceans.   *(Atlantic, Pacific, Indian, Arctic, Antarctic)*

The daughter of an Indian chief named Powhatan saved the lives of the early English settlers in Jamestown, Virginia, led by John Smith. What was her name?   *(Pocohantas)*

What is normal human body temperature?   *(37° Centigrade or 98.6° Fahrenheit)*

Name one country the equator passes through. *(Ecuador, Columbia, Brazil, Congo, Zaire, Kenya, Sumatra, Borneo, etc.)*

Who or what sat on a wall, had a great fall, and couldn't be put together again by all the king's horses and all the king's men? *(Humpty Dumpty)*

Name five countries and their capitals. *(U.S.A.–Washington, D.C.; Canada–Ottawa; Mexico–Mexico City; England–London; France–Paris; Italy–Rome; Japan–Tokyo; Korea–Seoul; Egypt–Cairo; Israel–Tel Aviv, etc.)*

Recite a rhyme in English.

February second is a special day in America. What is it? *(Groundhog Day)*

In what state did the Pilgrims land? *(Massachusetts)*

What holiday do Americans celebrate the first Monday of September? *(Labor Day)*

A famous black man was born on January fifteenth. Who was he? *(Martin Luther King, Jr.)*

Name two words that begin with *x*. *(xylophone, X-ray)*

Six-point questions:

Name the last two presidents before this one.

Finish this sentence: The grass is always greener on _____. *(the other side of the fence)*

Name all the planets in the solar system, in order. *(Mercury, Venus, Earth, Mars, Jupiter, Saturn, Uranus, Neptune, Pluto)*

This sentence has a mistake—correct it: The story was wrote by me. *(The story was written by me.)*

What does it mean when a person has "a green thumb"? *(grows plants well)*

What does it mean when a person has a "chip on his shoulder"? *(is looking for a fight with someone)*

What does it mean when a person has a "sweet tooth." *(loves sugar and candy)*

What are five words that begin with the letter *z*? *(zebra, zero, zipper, zigzag, zither, zest, zinc, zodiac)*

Name the five Great Lakes. *(Huron, Erie, Michigan, Superior, Ontario)*

Name six common birds. *(blue jay, owl, robin, sparrow, crow, bluebird, pigeon, cardinal, starling, wren, eagle, hawk, finch, etc.)*

11

Building Social Security

Newly arrived Limited English Proficient (LEP) children undergo social and emotional stresses stemming from their household upheaval and the strangeness of both a new environment and a new language. It should surprise no one that students from a war-torn country or those who have suffered the hardships of the refugee or the frequent movings of the migrant worker show signs of these strains in their behavior. Even those who came without such trauma may have lost much self-esteem through repeated experiences in which they feel powerless and "stupid" in types of situations they previously handled competently. The familiar props for personal self-worth are missing, and often their parents are undergoing a similar loss of security and are also floundering.

161.   FACILITATING SOCIAL CONTACTS

One of the first items on the agenda is to help these children feel safe, to achieve status in their own and others' eyes, and to facilitate social contacts. Language-isolated children may otherwise spend months before their English allows them to reach out on their own, and for some, these lonely months are agonizing.

While we can't make friends for the newcomers, we can design activities to help ensure the contacts necessary for making friends. Some things you might do:

1. Have students learn each other's names just as you must learn their names.
2. Assign buddies to show the new students around the school their first day if they arrive after you have taken a class tour of the building.
3. Give meaningful work at whatever level is possible. Following directions, copying their names in the new alphabet, drawing pictures of their families and homes in the country of origin, listening to simple tapes of numbers, alphabet, greetings. Assign another child who is more advanced in English to assist.

4. Assure that lunch time will not be chaotic or traumatic for the children by assigning a buddy to fend for them and show them where to go.

5. Provide times for the students to speak their own language and move about the room.

6. Arrange seating in a way that does not isolate students from others.

7. Assign classroom chores in pairs where applicable.

8. Pair students for peer-tutoring.

9. Provide activities for teams and group cooperation.

10. Send students on errands in twos.

11. Contact and friendship with children of the same language provide much initial support to the recently arrived child. For a child who has no such contact in your class, check the school records for other speakers of the child's language and arrange for the children to meet and be aware of each other for mutual support.

12. Let students sit near others of the same language during the first few weeks. After they are over their initial culture shock, have made an adjustment to the new school, and have some listening competency in routine situations, you might rearrange the seating to alternate language groups in order to open up the contact between language groups in your class and encourage the use of English in their commentaries to each other.

Factors in Rates of Language Learning: One significant determiner of students' rates of learning English is their desire to talk to English-speaking children. This in turn is enhanced or discouraged by the amount of anxiety-free practice they get in speaking to them.

The number of children of their own language group available for socializing is a significant factor as well. The benefits of a "safe harbor" may make venturing out of it less necessary. When there is a large number in a language group, English speakers are also less inclined to try to make friends. Members of each group need teacher assistance to bridge this barrier for their mutual benefit.

Although a minority of children are teacher-directed and will happily learn English to please the teacher and other adults, most elementary school children are progressively more peer-directed as they go up the grades. This calls for lessons that students will find immediately useful in communicating with peers as well as functioning in classrooms.

The school administrators must incorporate in their overall objectives for the district an awareness of the importance of the inter-group relations and the many gifts each group has to offer to each other and to the whole school population. It may be up to you to bring it to your administrator's attention.

Classroom teachers must be sensitized to the needs of the limited-English speakers and have input in the facilitation of good relations between groups in their classes. This can be done informally in individual conferences or raps with teachers about your mutual students and their progress. Or ask the principal to include time during a faculty meeting to bring up issues relevant to the socialization of the newcomers.

The local English-only-speaking (EO) children need to be able to express their perceptions and opinions regarding the LEP children (so you know where they are coming from) and be helped in developing values and attitudes that they will perceive as fair and reasonable, as well as enhancing their own pride in being helpful, thoughtful, and generous. A child's social consciousness—both prejudice and idealism—is developing rapidly by the third grade, and if students can be made aware of the opportunities available in the differences between groups, as well as the newcomers' needs and difficulties, many EO children will take on a more considerate and helpful role.

The newcomers need to develop the skills to reach out to the EO children. They need opportunities to do this and encouragement to overcome the fear of feeling foolish, sounding funny, or being rejected. The EOs in turn must be sensitized to the difficulties of the newcomers. Laughter at the expense of a child expressing himself can be innocently motivated; it can also be very hurtful.

A third group of children are also of key importance: previous years' newcomers. They haven't quite made it into the mainstream, but their knowledge of English grants them a higher "status" than that of the non-English speakers. Although they may be out of the formal ESL program, they still need support in social and academic areas and may choose to be either helpful— serving as translators, welcomers, explainers—or harmful to the new students. They may resent the teacher's calling on them to perform additional duties of interpreting for the newcomers when they are having trouble enough getting their own work done. Their own level of language achievement may create situations in which they are tempted to scapegoat the new students.

The activities that follow are designed with two goals: (1) getting the LE students to approach the students outside their own group and (2) showing the EO students ways to initiate approaches to the LEP children and giving the EOs recognition for their efforts.

162. SHARING WORD-SQUARE PUZZLES WITH CLASSMATES

Grades: 2 and up

English level: Beginner and up

Students will learn to solve and enjoy word-search puzzles as part of the practice they need in reviewing vocabulary and spelling. After becoming familiar with solving these puzzles, they will be taught to create their own to share with classmates.

Objectives: To build vocabulary; to reinforce spelling; to create a handout of a puzzle to distribute to classmates; to facilitate social interaction; to enhance self-esteem

Materials needed: Teacher-made or commercial word-square puzzles; graph paper (1/4 inch or 1-centimeter squares); pencils; spirit duplicator masters; fine-pointed ball point pens

Preparation:

1. Create and duplicate find-a-word puzzles to review spelling of the class's current vocabulary words. This is a valuable reinforcement exercise that's fun for the students. This can begin the first month of instruction.

2. Show the students how to solve these puzzles, matching the spelling in the puzzle to the lists of words you provide. The first puzzles should be simple, with words hidden across and down only.

3. Include puzzles from time to time as vocabulary-reinforcing exercises. Increase the difficulty by including words written backwards, from bottom to top, and words hidden diagonally. Build in "false starts" (the first three or four letters of a word), to get the students to check the spelling carefully. You can also use commercial find-a-word puzzles, which will expose the students to other vocabulary. Have them check the meanings of unknown words in their bilingual dictionaries.

4. Let the students create their own find-a-word puzzles to share with classmates:

   a. Suggest categories of words: animals, birds, flowers, baseball teams, makes of cars, countries, U.S. capital cities, and let the students suggest other categories. Write these on the chalkboard. Then let each child choose a category.

   b. Have the students write a list of words (ten to twenty) associated with the category they have chosen. Students can work in pairs, to check each other's words for correct spelling. Then you check their lists.

   c. Distribute the graph paper. Demonstrate writing in the words across, down, up, and diagonally on the graph paper. When all the words have been inserted into the puzzle, check their work for neatness and spelling. After it is checked, and any corrections made, students fill in the rest of the spaces with letters at random or with letters to produce false starts.

Suggestions:

1. A fifteen-by-fifteen-letter square is ample for ten to twenty words.
2. Children should lightly mark off the boundaries of their square before entering any letters.
3. Students write a heading on the puzzle and the title of the puzzle.
4. Have space at the bottom for the checklist of words.
5. Write capital letters only. Letters should be very neat and evenly spaced.

7. Write in pencil.

8. Start out by writing in the longest words first. The short ones are easier to fit in later.

9. If all the words won't fit, no harm done. Leave them out. The checklist should reflect only those words that have been hidden in the puzzle.

10. Make enough photocopies or spirit duplicator copies for the student to share with friends, classmates, and family. The student should circle the hidden words on one copy to make an answer key.

ANIMALS

```
K  L  P  N  T  I  G  M  S  T  U  H  O  R  H
A  E  I  G  K  A  N  G  A  R  O  O  I  S  I
N  A  G  K  R  S  M  F  L  O  M  R  C  A  T
S  L  H  A  T  U  O  I  W  M  O  S  S  M  I
E  L  E  P  H  A  N  T  H  O  V  E  M  I  G
R  I  L  L  O  S  K  U  N  K  G  L  O  T  E
O  G  E  P  L  O  E  S  M  K  C  O  W  I  R
U  A  S  N  K  H  Y  T  U  F  I  S  H  F  B
S  T  U  R  T  L  E  K  O  T  U  R  A  I  I
D  O  N  A  G  I  F  L  D  Q  S  V  L  W  L
O  R  T  B  I  R  D  E  M  O  U  S  E  D  F
P  I  I  B  H  J  R  D  B  C  X  A  D  O  G
I  C  H  I  C  K  E  N  Y  C  Z  B  E  G  I
C  A  L  T  N  P  D  I  N  O  S  A  U  R  H
H  S  K  I  L  M  O  H  F  I  W  H  D  O  M
```

ALLIGATOR	CHICKEN	DOG	HORSE	MOUSE	SKUNK
BIRD	COW	ELEPHANT	KANGAROO	PIG	TIGER
CAT	DINOSAUR	FISH	MONKEY	RABBIT	WHALE

(To make spirit duplicator copies: Staple or tape their graph paper to a duplicating master sheet. Remove the protective sheet. Demonstrate that students are now to go over each letter very firmly with a fine-pointed ball point pen. Run off as many copies as needed.)

The student keeps the original, with the answers marked, to serve as a check to the puzzle doers.

Assignment: Distribute the word-search puzzles to classmates. You may choose to facilitate this and enhance the status of the project by sending a note to the classroom teacher about the activity. She may announce that the word-search puzzles may be done as part of the seat work for the day. The ESL student can distribute the copies and is to be the source of the answers. Another possibility is that the ESL student may distribute copies of the puzzle before school, at lunch time, or at any free-play time available in the class. Discuss the results the following day.

163. INTERVIEWS

Grades: 3 and up

English level: Beginners and intermediate +

Objectives: To practice speaking and listening to classmates and native speakers; to gain information about classmates that will help initiate further conversation; to practice converting raw data into statements about the person interviewed

Materials needed: Doll, stuffed animal, or a large picture of a person; paper and pencil

Presentation:

   A. *Beginning level*

      1. Write a contrived paragraph such as the following on one section of the chalkboard and read it with the students:

> My classmate *Lorena Melendez* is from *Texas*. She is *eleven* years old, and is in the *sixth* grade. She has *two* brothers; she *doesn't* have a sister. She has been in *Fort Lee* for *three* years. She can speak *Spanish* and *English* and a little *German*.

      2. Prop the doll or stuffed animal on a chair in front of the class. Erase the underlined data from the above paragraph, leaving blanks for the information that will be inserted. You can answer for the doll or select a good student to "interpret" for it.

      3. Say, "We're going to write a paragraph about Mr. (Bear)." Elicit the questions they will need to ask the animal character to complete the paragraph.

      4. Write the questions the class dictates on an adjoining section of chalkboard.

      5. A student should write the answers in the blanks of the paragraph as they are given by the "animal."

   Questions:

      What's your name?

      What's your last name?   *(How do you spell that?)*

      Where are you from?

      How old are you?

What grade are you in?
Do you have any brothers?
Do you have any sisters?
Can you speak (*Spanish*)?
Can you speak another language?

6. The students ask additional questions.

7. The students read the new paragraph about the animal character.

8. They then *copy the questions.*

9. Say, "We interviewed Mr. (Bear). Now you are going to interview someone in this class."

10. Assign them to work in pairs. When everyone has asked all the questions and written the responses, they are to write a paragraph about the classmate, with the same sentence patterns as the one on the board. (Optional for those who finish before the others: Draw a picture of the classmate and ask other questions and write additional sentences.)

11. Several students read their paragraphs to the class.

12. Now you are going to interview another person, who is not in this class. Choose someone who is in another class and who does not speak your language."

13. Some children may feel too shy to approach another child to interview. Write a note to other classroom teachers to this effect:

    "The ESL students are practicing interviews in order to develop listening, speaking, and reaching-out skills. Could you please help by selecting several friendly students in your class who would be willing to answer some simple questions?"

14. The students conduct the interviews before school, lunch time, on the bus, and so on. In class, have students discuss their experiences and convert the raw data into paragraph form.

B. *Intermediate level*

The paragraph on the board may read as follows:

Bucky Bear was born in *Amarillo, Texas,* on *June 15, 1978.* He came to *Fort Lee* when he was *5* years old. He lives *in room 203 of the Jefferson School, at 13 Anderson Avenue,* with his *three brothers and his parents.* His favorite subjects in school are *lunch* and *recess.* He has *two* hobbies. One is *watching children learn English,* and the other is *listening to stories.* His favorite TV *shows are NOVA* and *Bugs Bunny.* He hates *fire drills and cold nights.* He wants to be *an ESL teacher* when he grows up.

As with the beginning level, elicit the questions needed to get this information. In addition, elicit other questions about their American classmates; for example, What is your favorite food? (movie star, music, singer, group, movie, teacher, etc.)

164. SURVEY

Grades: 2 and up

English level: Beginner, intermediate

Objectives: To motivate cross-language contact; to practice asking questions; to create a simple graph

This is different from the interview in that only one question is asked, but a large number of people are surveyed for their responses. The written summary is not a paragraph but a graph.

Materials: 1/4-inch graph paper (or students may use a ruler to create a graph)

Presentation:

1. Do a practice survey first—one that requires only simple observation. Discussion of the observations by class members can motivate a curiosity for more information that will come from questioning.

   Observation surveys:

   What kind of shoes are boys in 3G wearing today? (sneakers, sandals, loafers, boots, lace-ups)

   What color eyes do girls in 4H have?

   What color shirts (blouses or dresses) are students in 5T wearing today?

   How many girls in 5T are wearing dresses, skirts, jumpers, pants?

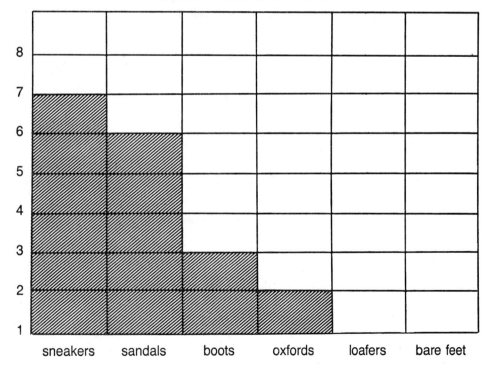

SHOES WORN IN CLASS 4G

2. Distribute the graph paper and show students how to label categories and shade in a square for each person, showing the trait being observed. After completing the graph, students show it to the class as they tell the class what they found. For example, "Six people are wearing sneakers, five are wearing sandals, two are wearing boots, one has oxfords," and so forth.

3. Suggest several survey questions, such as:

   What are the favorite foods (TV shows, colors, movie stars) of students (or boys or girls) in 6M?

   What time do children in 5T wake up in the morning? (or go to bed)

   How many brothers or sisters do children in the class have?

   How many come to school by bus, by car, by bike, or by foot?

   If the children in 3G could be animals, what animals would they be?

165. OPINION POLL

Grades: 3 and up

English level: Intermediate and up

This is a step beyond the survey. Students will not tally responses on a graph but write down the information in phrases or sentences, creating a brief news article.

Preparation:

1. Contrive an opinion poll such as the following for the students to read:

   Q: What do you think of the school lunches?

   A1: I think we should have ice cream more often.

   A2: The line is too long. I don't like to wait so long, and the food isn't that great.

   A3: I don't know. I bring my lunch because I like peanut butter and jelly sandwiches every day.

   A4: They're really good.

   A5: Yukk.

2. Suggest several other controversial topics that would produce a variety of answers. Elicit ideas from the students; for example:

   How much homework do you think teachers should give? Why?

   How much TV do you think is the right amount for a child to watch?

   What should the school do about littering, fighting, cheating, etc.?

   What is the worst punishment you ever got? For what?

3. Let each child choose a topic. Ask five (or more) people their opinions and write down what they say.

4. Post these opinion polls for all to read. You can also photocopy the polls and create a newsletter for reading material and discussion.

166. LUNCH-TIME OR AFTER-SCHOOL GAME CLUB

Grades: 1 and up

English level: All levels

Objectives: To create social bridges between English-only speakers and LEP students; to provide opportunities for LEP students to relate to EO speakers in an informal play situation; to learn rules and skills required for American games and the English needed to play and talk about the activities; to reinforce EO students for sharing and taking responsibility toward others; to teach EOs simple techniques for working with LEP children to give them a chance to learn some foreign words, phrases, and games themselves

Materials needed: Select from the following:

Picture files

Sets of concentration games (See Chapter Five)
Games such as:

pocket video games	checkers	cards	Old Maid
Spill and Spell®	hangman	Junior Scrabble©	puzzles
Just-a-Minute!©	Yahtzee©	Othello©	tangrams
Parcheesi	Chinese checkers	ring toss	etc.

All games should have simple rules in which either a minimum of English is needed to play or the point of the game is to practice English. Games that can be finished within the time constraints are preferable (that is, Monopoly is undesirable if you have only thirty-five minutes). These games can be donated, bought at garage sales, homemade, or brought in by the children.

You might consider setting up your program so that the lunch hour is a "teaching" hour, and you schedule time to eat your own lunch either before or after. It this is impossible, parent volunteers, school aides, or whoever is in charge of the children's lunch hour may be available to supervise after the program has been set up and the activities are running smoothly.

Place: A classroom where chairs and desks can be moved, and where games may be stored

Preparation:

1. Collect games and prepare a storage shelf, labeled so games can be easily located and replaced after playing. (You might code shelves and games so that games marked with a large *2* are to be put away on shelf #2, etc.)

2. Decide how often and how long the game club will run. Setting limits in advance and starting out on a small scale will ensure the program's viability. In my school, we started three days a week during the months of January and February and had six parent volunteers (two per day) to assist in the program.

3. Decide which of your LEP students will be participating. What worked for us in Fort Lee was to reserve the game club for the more advanced class (fourteen students), with each of them being allowed to invite one English-speaking person (total twenty-eight). Those too shy to invite someone were helped in this by their classroom teacher. Since the game club was an interesting alternative to other lunch-time activities, American children were eager to participate.

4. Explain the purpose and the opportunity of the game club to the class or classes who will be participating. Determine the level of interest. Have them think about whom and how to invite. If necessary, help with these invitations by explaining the program to the mainstream teachers and have them help select guests for the LEP students.

5. On the first day of the program, welcome the EO children and explain the purpose of the game club and the valuable role they are playing in it. Let them know that their contribution is to talk about the games, the names of the playing pieces, and the rules, as well as to enjoy the games. Show students the location of the games, the rules of the club (that is, English will be the "official" language of the games; games are to be properly cared for and put away at the first bell; etc.).

   Assign on a rotating basis the job of putting the games neatly away. (This may be done by the aides or parent volunteers.)

6. After eating, the students may play in groups of two, three, four, or more. Allow children to select games they are familiar with. You may work with one group teaching them rules of a new game, allow the EO children to explain the rules of others, and go around spot-checking the activities until they are running smoothly.

   Get feedback after each session to determine the level of interest and discover any problems that need your attention.

167. ROLE PLAYING

Grades: 4 and up

English level: Intermediate and advanced

Objectives: To provide opportunity to use English in familiar and stimulating situations; to develop creative use of language; to express emotions in English

Materials needed: None, except as noted

Preparation: Select the role-playing situations that would be appropriate to your class; make as many copies of the role plays as needed; cut into segments and keep segments together with a clip

Presentation: Student *A* gets her part, not knowing what student *B's* role will be, and vice versa. Everyone else in the class gets a copy of both roles in the conversation and reads it silently before the action begins. (See pages 270-271.)

The two (or three) players stand or sit in front of the class and talk through the conversation until it is resolved. Encourage the players to stick to their roles and make every effort to get the other person to go along with their point of view.

At the end of the interaction, discuss the feelings the participants had about the roles they played. Have the audience give their feedback on how effective the communication was. Other volunteers may now enact the situation with perhaps a different outcome.

ROLE PLAYS

1A You like a person in your class and want to invite him or her to your house after school to do homework together.	**1B** A person in your class has invited you to his or her home but your mother doesn't let you go to other people's houses unless she talks with their parents first.
2A You had no time in school today to write down the homework questions. It is now nine fifteen. Call your friend and ask him or her to dictate the questions to you. You have to go to bed at ten o'clock.	**2B** A classmate calls to get the homework. You would have to dictate ten questions to him or her. You are in the middle of watching an exciting TV program, and you don't want to miss any of it. The program is over at ten o'clock.
3A You love to swing on the tire swing but another child has been on it for a long time and doesn't seem to be giving it up. Ask the child to let you have a turn.	**3B** You love to swing on the tire swing and you got to it first. You don't want to give it up to anybody.
4A Your class is going on a trip to the zoo today. Last week, the teacher told everyone to bring in $4.00. Today was the deadline for bringing in your $4.00 trip money. You really want to go to the zoo, but you didn't bring your money. Try to get the teacher to let you bring the money tomorrow.	**4B** You are a teacher planning a trip with two classes. There are a lot of things to do to prepare for the trip. Your rules are to give students one week to bring in the trip money. If they don't pay by then, they can't go. You only make exceptions for very good reasons. It's too much work for you.
5A Your pocket video game is missing from your desk. You are sure none of your friends would take it. A new student sits next to you. You are sure he or she must have taken it. Accuse that student and insist that he or she give it back.	**5B** You are new in school. So far you have only one friend. You saw your friend go into the desk next to yours and take out a pocket video. You're not sure if she just played with it or kept it. The student who owns the pocket video says that you took it. You don't want to get your friend in trouble because she is the only person who has been nice to you in this new school. But you don't want people to think you are a thief either. Defend yourself.

ROLE PLAYS (continued)

6A You have a test in social studies and another one in science tomorrow. You hope that the English teacher will not give a test in ESL for tomorrow. You won't have time to study for all three tests. Try to get her to change the date.	**6B** You are the English teacher. You regularly give tests on Wednesday. Remind your class that they have a test tomorrow. You need the grade for the report cards next week. You can't give the test Thursday or Friday because you need time to correct the papers for the report card grades.
7A There are no assigned seats in the lunchroom but you always sit in a certain seat. Today there is another person in your seat. You don't see another place to sit at this table where your friends are. Tell the person that he or she is sitting in your seat and could he or she please move.	**7B** There are no assigned seats in the lunchroom, and you want to sit next to your friend. You sit in an empty seat across from him or her. Someone tells you to move but you feel you don't have to. That person can sit at another table. You were there first.
8A You hate cats. Your beautiful pet parakeet flew outside last week and a black-and-white cat caught it and ate it. You see that cat and you throw some small stones near it to scare it away. It isn't moving very fast, so you throw a few more stones.	**8B** You see a person throwing stones at a poor old cat. The cat seems lame and can't move very fast. Talk to the person to make him stop throwing stones.
9A Your mother has to go to the dentist and you have to stay with your seven-year-old brother. You were invited to your friend's house. You call to ask if you can bring your younger brother along. If you can't bring him, you can't go.	**9B** You wanted your friends to come over to talk about personal problems. Your best friend asks if his or her little brother can come along. In your opinion, he is a nosy pest and would spoil the whole afternoon for everyone. Tell your friend to do something else with her brother and come without him.
10A You have two friends you like very much, but one of the friends does not like the other one. You plan to invite both of them to your birthday party. Speak to the first friend to invite him or her.	**10B** You like your friend and want to go to his or her birthday party. However, your friend will probably invite someone else you dislike very much. You think that being in the same room with this person will ruin the party for you, so you decide not to go if that person is going. When your friend invites you, tell him or her your feelings.

Index